TTL Cookbook

By

Don Lancaster

Howard W. Sams & Co., Inc.
4300 WEST 62ND ST. INDIANAPOLIS, INDIANA 46268 USA

International Standard Book Number: 0-672-21035-5
Library of Congress Catalog Card Number: 73-90295

Printed in the United States of America.

Preface

In mid-1972, an electronic revolution took place. For the first time in electronic history, you could go out and buy a logic gate for a nickel, provided you bought four of them at once in a single 20-cent package. This made the logic gate the cheapest available electronic component—cheaper than most quality resistors and far cheaper than any capacitor, transistor, or most other solid-state devices. These gates were made of Transistor-Transistor-Logic (TTL), a very versatile, widely available, and very fast way of performing logic operations.

The extremely low cost did two things. First and foremost, it opened up a fantastic number of still expanding applications for digital circuitry. At long last, doing things digitally was not only better than using traditional analog circuits, but now it was often cheaper as well.

Secondly, as a by-product, the low cost made many hallowed design techniques obsolete. How many engineering and computer hours can you afford to spend to "minimize" a design in order to save a few 5-cent parts? With TTL, many of the traditional design methods such as state minimization, Karnaugh mapping, and Boolean equations and other textbook methods of the fifties and sixties are not only no longer needed, but they often end up as a tremendous waste of time and can even make a product more, rather than less, complicated.

Instead of the traditional design methods, the concept of *redundancy* is used instead. In this concept, a more general or more universal logic block is used and then restricted to perform the desired task. This method usually works directly with the truth table to be solved. It often is a one-package solution and gives the desired result with designs that take only a few seconds and, ironically, almost always take fewer packages and much less time than traditional "minimum" designs.

This book is about TTL. It shows you what TTL is and how to use it. It is written at a time when the TTL family is more or less mature, and a wide variety of medium and large scale functions are available from many manufacturers. While it was written with the same philosophy as the author's *RTL COOKBOOK* (20715), so much has changed in so short a time that about the only similarities you will find are the overall chapter organization and the emphasis on basics and applications. Very little material is repeated, and the two books complement each other.

In Chapters 1 and 2, we look at the basics of what TTL is, who makes it, where to get data, how to interconnect it, how to power it and work with it, and so on; in short, the basic information you need to know to intelligently hook up the circuits and get them to work.

Chapter 2 is a sort of catalog of TTL devices, with several handy features. Each device mentioned anywhere in the book is also shown here in an industry-wide coverage that presents only the essential information, along with the pitfalls that sometimes get buried in a footnote on a manufacturer's data sheet. Much of Chapter 2 is also available on a large wall chart (Cat. No. 21080). This *User's Guide to TTL* can be mounted for "all-at-a-glance" convenience. Logic is covered in Chapter 3. We start with the usual basics, and then we look at the new instant logic designs that use redundant networks, particularly the data selector and the Read-Only Memory. Designs that take seconds instead of hours and yield single-package solutions to traditionally difficult problems are emphasized. Some ASCII computer code examples are included as well.

Astable signal sources, monostable circuits, and simple bistable circuits compose most of Chapter 4, along with some other interface and simple TTL circuits for input conditioning, etc.

The clocked logic is covered in Chapter 5, where we look in detail at the JK and D-type flip-flops and consider a wide variety of their applications. Counters and counting techniques are the subject of Chapter 6, with comprehensive design information given for any modulo from 1 to 1000. This is followed in Chapter 7 by the shift-register circuits, along with several design examples. One very interesting and little known shift-register application involves the pseudo-noise or pseudo-random sequence generators. These are covered in depth. The chapter ends with a quick look at rate multipliers, a little-used and often misunderstood device with a tremendous amount of untapped applications potential.

Finally, Chapter 8 ties everything together with some whole-system applications, showing typical ways you can interconnect and synergetically use the concepts of the earlier chapters. Material here ranges from digital instruments, through electronic music and computer terminal tv typewriters, and finally ends with some very simple "project type" suggestions that are handy for learning logic or for school training aids. The projects are introduced in such a way that considerable design effort by the builder is needed, rather than a by-rote, "do it this way" type of instruction.

DON LANCASTER

This book is dedicated
to Bowseretta and
Good Old Bartholomew Dog.

Contents

CHAPTER 1

Some Basics of TTL

A *digital logic family* consists of a group of integrated circuits or other elemental, compatible blocks that can be combined in various ways to perform a series of "yes-no" decisions based on the presence or absence of "yeses" and "nos" on various inputs, and possibly taking into account the history of previous "yeses" and "nos" gone before.

Depending on how you interconnect these logic blocks, you can build a computer, a calculator, an electronic music system, a digital voltmeter or counter, a television terminal readout display, a color-tv dot-bar generator, educational demonstrators, or any of thousands of other possibilities. While a single "yes-no" decision by itself usually is not too useful, the proper combination of grouped "yes-no" decisions taken together can represent a number, a word, a command, a musical note, a test signal, or practically anything else you might like.

One digital-logic family that is extremely popular today is called *Transistor-Transistor-Logic,* otherwise known as TTL, T²L, or "Tee Squared Ell." Important advantages of TTL are its low cost (as low as 30¢ per package in single quantities on the surplus market), its high-speed capability (20 MHz typical; to 125 MHz with special devices), its moderate drive capability and noise immunity, and the industry-wide availability of hundreds of different devices. This gives you a broad selection of simple and elaborate logic blocks that may be directly interconnected to produce more unique functions with fewer packages than virtually any other present logic system.

TTL started out as many device lines by many manufacturers. Today, the bulk of the available and useful devices are in a 5400–7400 numbering system, originally pioneered by Texas Instruments, but now an industry standard. The 7400 line is lower in cost and is useful over a 0- to 70-degree C environment. The 5400 line is a premium military line good from −55 to +125 degrees C. There are a few important non-7400 TTL devices, particularly in the Motorola MC4000 MTTL, the Signetics 8200, and National Tri-State® product lines. Some of these devices offer unique advantages and are widely second-sourced, but even these are beginning to pick up 7400-type number equivalents as they become more of an industry standard (see Chart 2-1).

Chart 1-1 lists some of the major TTL manufacturers. All of these firms have extensive catalogs of TTL devices with many more details

Chart 1-1. Some of the Leading Sources of TTL

Advanced Micro Devices 901 Thompson Place Sunnyvale, CA 94086	Raytheon Semiconductor 350 Ellis Street Mountain View, CA 94040
Fairchild Semiconductor 313 Fairchild Drive Mountain View, CA 94040	Signetics 811 E. Arques Avenue Sunnyvale, CA 94086
ITT Semiconductors 3301 Electronics Way West Palm Beach, FL 33407	Sprague Electric Co. 481 Marshall Street North Adams, MA 01247
Motorola Semiconductor Box 20912 Phoenix, AZ 85036	Stewart Warner Corp. 730 East Evelyn Avenue Sunnyvale, CA 94086
National Semiconductor 2900 Semiconductor Drive Santa Clara, CA 95051	Texas Instruments Box 5012 Dallas, TX 75222

in them than we can present here. These are often bound into books selling from $2 to $4. If you are going to do anything at all with TTL, be sure to have several of these books on hand, for not every manufacturer produces all of the more popular TTL parts. A few of the better design handbooks are listed in Chart 1-2.

There is a tendency to assume that most integrated-circuit logic families are pretty much the same, particularly if they work on the same +5-volt supply. This simply is not so, and each logic family has some unique characteristics and use restrictions that are all its own. In the case of TTL, the first-time user is often surprised that the outputs of his circuits never seem to get much more than halfway up to the +5-volt supply, and that unconnected inputs pull themselves up

Chart 1-2. Some TTL Design Books

Fairchild TTL Data Book	Fairchild Semiconductor 313 Fairchild Drive Mountain View, CA 94040
MTTL Data Book	Motorola Semiconductor Box 20912 Phoenix, AZ 85036
Signetics Digital-Linear-MOS	Signetics 811 E. Arques Avenue Sunnyvale, CA 94086
The TTL Data Book	Texas Instruments Box 5012 Dallas, TX 75222

to a positive value. Further, he finds it is very difficult to get the inputs down to ground where they belong for a "low" input condition, unless whatever is pulling them down can *sink* a reasonable amount of current. It turns out there are very good reasons for these design quirks of TTL; most of these peculiarities are necessary for reliable, high-speed operation. Let us take a closer look at a typical TTL device and see what the basic input-output characteristics are.

THE TWO-INPUT, POSITIVE-LOGIC NAND GATE

Fig. 1-1 shows the internal schematic of one-quarter of a 7400 NAND gate. This is one of the most versatile building blocks in the TTL line. In fact, you could build almost any TTL circuit with nothing but this

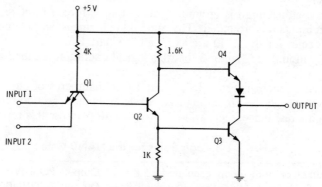

Fig. 1-1. Two-input positive NAND gate.

particular device if you had enough of them and did not mind all the extra packages. We will shortly see that this is an elemental logic block whose output is positive if either input is grounded, and whose output is grounded only if both inputs are positive.

Suppose that neither input is connected. There is no current out of either emitter of our dual-emitter input transistor, so it does not behave as a transistor. Instead, the base-collector junction is forward biased, and a current flows from the +5-volt supply through the junction diode and into the base of Q2. Q2 will turn on. This also turns on Q3. It robs Q4 of base current, so it simultaneously turns Q4 off. The output goes to within a few tenths of a volt of ground, and we say the output state is *low*. Note that in this condition, the output is capable of absorbing or sinking to ground considerable outside-world current. This is why TTL is called *current-sinking* logic.

If we connect both inputs to a voltage that is more positive than the voltage drop across a few diodes (2.4 volts to be exact), transistor Q1 still does not behave as a transistor, since the emitter-base junction remains reverse biased. While we should never leave a TTL input unconnected because of noise problems, there is no difference between an unconnected input and an input connected to a voltage greater than 2.4 volts but equal to or less than the +5-volt supply.

With both inputs positive or at a positive logic 1, the output of the gate goes to ground. What happens if we ground one input? Q1 now behaves as a transistor, and it turns on, pulling its collector near ground. This turns Q2 off, which then turns off Q3. With Q2 off, the current now can flow through the base junction of Q4. Q4 is now free to turn on. The output swings positive. Note that the output cannot reach the positive supply, for there has to be some voltage drop across the 1.6K resistor, and we get a 0.6-volt drop across the base-emitter junction of Q4 and a second 0.6-volt drop across the output diode. The output typically will only go positive by 3.3 volts or so on a +5-volt supply.

When either input is grounded, the output is forced positive. What if both inputs are grounded? The same thing happens, so the operating circuit rules for the 7400 are as stated in Chart 1-3.

We will find in Chapter 3 that this logical operation is called a positive-logic NAND or a negative-logic NOR function.

When an input is grounded, about 1.6 milliamperes of current has to flow through the grounding lead. If we attempt to ground the input through a resistance, there will be a voltage drop across this resistance,

CHART 1-3. Logic Rules for the NAND Gate

Either or both inputs grounded	Output POSITIVE
Both inputs positive	Output GROUNDED

and the emitter will not be pulled close enough to ground to let the gate operate reliably. The maximum permissible low-state input voltage is around 0.8 volt. At any input above that, the gate will either lose noise immunity or stay in its active region and possibly oscillate. Thus, any resistive connection to ground should be less than 500 ohms (with the regular 7400 TTL family), and any input-low connection must place and hold the input below 0.8 volt positive.

These input and output conditions may seem strange when compared to older logic families. There is one big benefit. When two TTL circuits are cascaded, they "look" at each other transistor-to-transistor. There are no coupling resistances or stored charges to contend with, and the logic family thus turns out to be extremely fast in operation.

A CLOSER LOOK

Circuits in the TTL logic family may be directly interconnected—the output of one to the input of one or more other packages. The drive capability of a digital logic IC is called its *fan-out*. Its input needs needs are called its *fan-in*. The voltage and current conditions needed for a medium-power TTL gate usually are normalized to a fan-in of one unit load. The average TTL gate can drive ten unit loads, and thus has a fan-out of ten. The typical TTL input has a fan-in of one, and all newer TTL devices are designed to have a unity fan-in. Logic blocks with higher fan-outs are usually called *buffers;* these typically have a fan-out of 30. Another type of logic block may be called a decoder-driver or simply a driver. Here the outputs are converted to a group of currents or voltages compatible with some outside-world device, such as a 7-segment readout or a Nixie® tube, and "fan-out" as such has no meaning as these outputs do not drive additional TTLs.

If you exceed the fan-out of a gate, the noise margin first becomes impaired, and then the voltage and current swings become too small to operate all the attached loads reliably. Fortunately, it is only rarely that you have to interconnect more than ten inputs to a single TTL output.

There are usually only two steady-state output conditions on a TTL gate. The *output-low* state is within a few tenths of a volt of ground and is called a positive logic 0. It is capable of sinking considerable current, usually 16 milliamperes. The *output-high* state is usually called a positive logic 1. When it is connected to other TTL circuits, all it has to do is hold the emitters of the various inputs reverse biased. It need only provide for leakage currents. The output-high state is above 2.4 volts and well below the positive supply; 3.3 volts is typical.

Remember that a TTL output-positive logic 0 pulls to ground and sinks a lot of current; a TTL output-positive logic 1 simply provides a positive voltage a little over half the supply voltage.

If we ever want the full power-supply voltage as an output, we can use the circuit of Fig. 1-2, where we add a 2.2K pull-up resistor. This is never needed in a TTL-only circuit, but is handy if we are interfacing some other logic family or want the full supply swing for outside-world circuits. Without the resistor, a positive logic 1 is about 3.3 volts with a +5-volt supply.

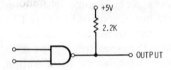

Fig. 1-2. A pull-up resistor may be added to a TTL gate if the full supply-voltage swing is wanted as an output.

Another unique feature of TTL that almost always causes trouble if it is not understood is the way in which the output switches. In the output-low state, only the bottom one of the *totem-pole* pair of transistors conducts. In the output-high state, only the top transistor in the totem-pole output conducts.

During the transition from low to high or vice-versa, both transistors conduct heavily. The instantaneous current is perhaps ten times the normal supply current. This speeds up the switching time of the output stage nicely, but at the same time, it pulls a large *current spike* out of the power-supply lines. This spike could be a fraction of an ampere or more and typically lasts 10 nanoseconds.

Unless a good bypass capacitor is provided immediately beside the IC, this current spike can raise havoc with other ICs in the system! This is an inherent feature of TTL and is one of the key sources of its speed. We will be looking at some bypassing rules soon when we talk about power supplies. Another inherent feature of the current spiking and high-speed potential taken together is that TTL can and usually will behave erratically in "rats nest" breadboarding or in traditional "perf-board" construction unless extreme care is taken with layout and conductor shapes and sizes.

The TTL output swing is from a few tenths of a volt of ground with a large current-sinking capability up to a positive voltage somewhere above half the supply voltage that needs only hold subsequent inputs positive and provide a very small leakage current.

The TTL input swing is also two-state. In the low condition, we have to sink 1.6 milliamperes to ground, and regardless of how we do it, we have to guarantee that the emitter voltage is 0.8 volt or less. In the high condition, all we have to do is hold the input positive above 2.4 volts and provide a very low leakage current. An unattended, unconnected TTL input will pull itself high to the positive logic 1 condition, but will be susceptible to noise and ringing. Good practice calls for an unused input to be tied to +5 volts or tied to a logically similar input. (The military practice of tying to +5 volts via a 1K resistor is usually not justified by the benefits and causes more problems than it solves.) As a practical matter, TTL inputs can usually be floated in a breadboard circuit if there is no lead connected to the package pin, but in final circuit versions, all inputs must be properly terminated.

A few TTL output structures differ from the totem-pole type we have just discussed. One version is called an *open collector* system. A second is called the *Tri-State®* logic system. These are in the minority and are covered in more detail in Chapter 3.

There are also some protective diodes placed on the inputs to all newer TTL gates. When these are added, the actual 7400 schematic looks like Fig. 1-3. Most TTL gates have input clamping diodes as

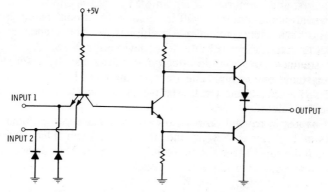

Fig. 1-3. Protective diodes connected to input gates.

shown. The purpose of these diodes is to prevent high-frequency ringing, particularly when longer leads or sharp rise inputs are applied. They improve the high-frequency noise immunity considerably. By the same token, they and the rest of the IC can be immediately destroyed if an input is brought below ground by more than 0.6 volt from a low-impedance source. This can be a problem in interface circuits. Preferably, the inputs should never be allowed to go below ground. If they must be below ground in your particular circuit, be sure to limit the reverse bias current to 10 mA or less with external series resistance. Avoid reverse biasing, if at all possible.

OTHER LOGIC BLOCKS

While the two-input NAND gate is an extremely versatile logic block, there are hundreds of others available. A one-input gate is called an *inverter* or a *noninverting buffer* or *driver,* depending on whether the output follows or complements the input. In complementary circuits, the output will be a zero when the input is a one and vice versa. Other two-input gates are available that perform different logic on the two inputs. These include the AND, OR, NOR, NAND, and EXCLUSIVE OR gates and are detailed in Chapter 3. We can have more than two logic inputs, with three-, four-, and eight-input NAND gates being common.

Gate-only circuits usually operate immediately and without regard to the history of the ones and zeros fed to the device. If history is important, we get into memory and counting devices, such as *JK Flip-Flops, D Flip-Flops, Latches,* and so on. Gates and the simple flip-flops are usually called SSI, short for *small-scale integration.*

One step beyond SSI is MSI or *medium-scale integration.* Here gates and flip-flops are suitably interconnected to produce system blocks that are called shift registers, counters, adders, decoders, data selectors, distributors, and memories. When an MSI device is aimed at one specific special-purpose task, it will have some functional name instead, such as a parity generator, a rate multiplier, a priority encoder, or a decoder-driver. The majority of TTL devices are MSI.

LSI stands for *large-scale integration* and is usually reserved for entire systems on a chip. The only common TTL LSI chip is the 74181 Arithmetic Logic Unit, used for central calculations in a computer or calculator.

In Chapter 2, we will take a closer look at the more popular TTL devices and see what they do and how to use them. One of the big benefits today in TTL is the incredible variety of MSI devices available.

PACKAGES

Some TTL is available in Mil-spec ceramic flat packages. These are expensive and very hard to use. The majority of devices are available in the common 14- and 16-pin DIP or dual in-line package, where plastic and more expensive ceramic versions are common. A very few TTL devices have too many input pins for the 16-pin package; these are reserved for the larger 24-pin DIP.

The pin conventions of the three common packages are shown in Fig. 1-4. The supply connections usually, but not always, go on diagonally opposite pins. On a 14-pin package, pin 7 is ground and 14 is +5 volts. On a 16-pin package, pin 8 is ground, and 16 is +5 volts. Pin 12 is ground and pin 24 is +5 volts on the 24-pin package. There are just enough exceptions to these supply rules, particularly with early devices, that you should double check each device before wiring it.

Usually, more than one logic block goes into a package. For instance, a quad 2-input gate contains four separate 2-input gates in a single package. A dual 4-input gate holds two separate 4-input gates in the same package. Except for the supply and ground connections, the individual blocks are completely independent. They may be used

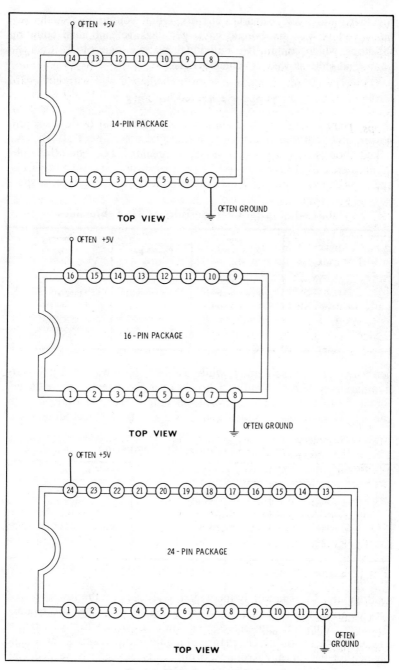

Fig. 1-4. TTL package numbering.

together or in totally separate circuits. Other common examples are hex inverters with six 1-input gates per package, and dual counting flip-flops, which contain two individual bistable logic blocks that can count and shift as well as remember data.

TYPES OF TTL AVAILABLE

There are several different *subfamilies* of TTL that trade off speed, power, and additional complexity for special uses. The TTL we have talked about so far is usually known as *regular* TTL. The other subfamilies are called *Low-Power* TTL, *High-Power* TTL, *Schottky* TTL, and *Low-Power Schottky* TTL. Table 1-1 compares the typical char-

Table 1-1. Typical Characteristics of TTL Subfamilies

Family	Gate Propagation Time	Power per Gate	Maximum Counter Frequency
Regular TTL	10 nanoseconds	10 milliwatts	35 megahertz
High-Power TTL	6 nanoseconds	22 milliwatts	50 megahertz
Low-Power TTL	33 nanoseconds	1 milliwatt	3 megahertz
Schottky TTL	3 nanoseconds	19 milliwatts	125 megahertz
Low-Power Schottky TTL	10 nanoseconds	2 milliwatts	45 megahertz

acteristics of each subfamily, while Table 1-2 shows the usual part-numbering system to identify a family of a given temperature range. Finally, Table 1-3 is a rough "rule of thumb" for the tradeoffs you can expect in terms of speed and power as you change subfamilies.

Table 1-2. TTL Subfamily Numbering

Family	−55° to +125° C	0° to +70° C
Regular	5400	7400
High-Power	54H00	74H00
Low-Power	54L00	74L00
Schottky	54S00	74S00
Low-Power Schottky	54LS00	74LS00

Regular TTL

Regular TTL is normally the widest available and the lowest-priced type of TTL, and it has far and away the greatest variety and second-sourcing. A typical gate-propagation time is 10 nanoseconds; this is the time it takes for a logic change at a gate input to appear as a logic change on the output. Around 10 milliwatts per gate is needed, and counting flip-flops go as high as 35 MHz.

Such devices as the Motorola MC4016 and MC4018 and the Signetics 8280 and 8288 counters were originally "non-7400" devices. They now have 7400 equivalents and are *essentially* identical to regular 7400 TTL. They may have a slightly different fan-in requirement and the output positive-voltage swing may be slightly different, but the

Table 1-3. A Comparison of TTL Subfamilies

Family	Speed	Power
Regular	X1	X1
High-Power	X2	X2
Low-Power	X1/10	X1/10
Schottky	X3.5	X2
Low-Power Schottky	X1	X1/5

devices can usually be freely mixed with traditional 7400 devices. Fan-out is normally ten regular TTL devices.

Low-Power TTL

Low-power TTL exchanges power consumption for speed and is identified by an L in the part number. For instance, a 74L00 is a low-power, commercial version of the 7400 regular TTL NAND gate. There is roughly a 10:1 tradeoff in the low-power version—$\frac{1}{10}$ the speed to counters at $\frac{1}{10}$ the power, although the simpler gates run $\frac{1}{4}$ the speed on $\frac{1}{10}$ the power. Flip-flops and counters have a maximum toggle frequency of 3 MHz or so. Within the low-power subfamily, the fan-out remains ten, but a low-power TTL gate can drive only one regular TTL gate. While the 54L00 and 74L00 series TTL do offer low-power consumption, many of their advantages are being preempted by the CMOS logic families, particularly the RCA 4000 series COSMOS and the Motorola MC14000 series McMOS lines.

High-Power TTL

The high-power TTL devices are designated with an H in the part number. 74H00 is the equivalent of a 7400 gate, and so on. Typically you get twice the speed for twice the power. Counters are good to 50 MHz. Within the high-power subfamily, the fan-out remains at 10, but the fan-in is typically 1.3 times regular TTL loads. Thus, a regular TTL gate can drive at most only 7 high-power TTL inputs. High-power TTL is largely being replaced by the newer Schottky TTL which is faster and draws less supply power. Quite a few high-power devices remain available. One advantage they do have over the Schottky devices is that the outputs are "quieter," a handy feature in high-speed digital-to-analog converters, but hardly useful elsewhere.

Schottky TTL

Schottky TTL is an improved version of TTL that has a better speed/power tradeoff than the older types. To do this, Schottky diodes (a fast diode with a 0.3-volt forward drop) are placed across most of the transistors in the basic TTL gate. This prevents the transistors from saturating and thus eliminates any storage-time delays inside the transistors. The part numbers have an S in them, as in a 74S00. Propagation delays of 3 nanoseconds are combined with flip-flops that can run at 125 MHz.

Where high speed is essential, Schottky TTL is a logical choice. Its competitor is MECL and other emitter-coupled logic families which in general are much faster, but considerably more difficult to use.

A high-speed, unsaturated logic family such as Schottky TTL presents serious restrictions in the type and quality of test equipment you must have to work with it intelligently. A 60-MHz triggered oscilloscope is essential and a 120-MHz one is preferable. As might be expected, Schottky devices are much more critical as to layouts and supply decoupling than ordinary TTL because of their higher speed. Nevertheless, where high speed is essential, they are often the simplest solution to system problems in the 30- to 120-MHz range.

Low-Power Schottky TTL

Devices such as the 74LS00 are emerging as a more recent variation on TTL. The low-power Schottky TTL family is slightly faster than regular TTL, but requires only $\frac{1}{5}$ the power. It does this by using the Schottky diodes to eliminate storage-time effects, but then raises the circuit impedance levels to slow things down to normal and pick up power savings. For many applications, this represents a near-optimum combination of values. Being newer and inherently more complex than regular TTL, the LS series is higher priced. As of this writing, it also does not have as extensive a variety of devices or suppliers as the regular 5400/7400 series TTL does.

Which Family?

While all these variations of TTL are available as design options, the regular-power traditional TTL remains the cheapest and usually the widest available choice. Very often, it is also the best overall design choice. 74S is essentially replacing 74H, and 74L is being challenged by CMOS. 74LS will represent a good choice when it is cost competitive with regular TTL and has enough different devices readily available.

The best rule today seems to be to choose regular TTL unless you have a specific speed problem, and then choose 74S. Remember that for all but the simplest high-speed systems, you will need a high-performance oscilloscope and high-quality circuit layouts to intelligently use the faster subfamily. If ultra-low-power operation is essential, particularly at low clocking frequencies, consider using CMOS as an alternate to the low-power TTL subfamily.

POWER SUPPLIES AND SPIKE DECOUPLING

Good power-supply design is essential with TTL. When choosing a power-supply design, there are three important considerations: assurance of a regulated supply of voltage, provision for a low-impedance supply distribution system, and effectiveness in decoupling the current spikes that happen every time a totem-pole output stage changes state in either direction.

TTL needs a single 5-volt positive supply. It should be regulated within 250 millivolts of this value, particularly if there are many ICs in the system. While some simple gate circuits can be run with batteries or wider-range unregulated supplies, a solid, tightly regulated supply is almost essential for any circuit that is more complex. You can use batteries with TTL if you place a regulator between the battery and the circuit. Allowing for the drop across the regulator, this means a supply in the 7.5- to 12-volt range.

At the TTL package, the absolute limit recommended for supply on most devices is 7 volts. There are some specific TTL devices whose output lines can withstand 15, 30, and even 60 volts, but even these packages must have their supply pins tightly held at 5 volts.

Power-Supply Circuits

Fig. 1-5 shows a 5-volt, 750-milliampere, regulated, line-operated supply, while Fig. 1-6 shows a battery and regulator circuit. In both

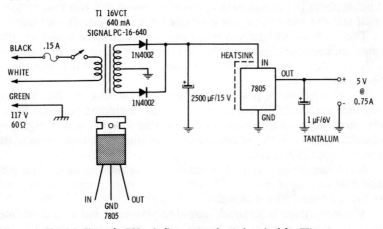

Fig. 1-5. Five-volt, 750-mA, line-operated supply suited for TTL use.

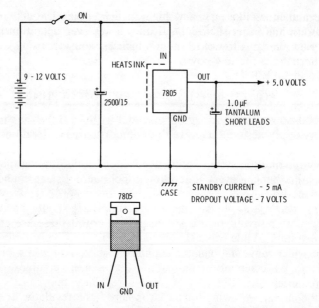

Fig. 1-6. Battery-powered TTL supply. Maximum current depends on battery chosen.

circuits, a type 7805 regulator (Fairchild, Motorola, etc.) gives a single-package, low-cost (around $2) way of precisely sensing and holding the output at 5 volts. The dropout voltage of the regulator is about 2.5 volts, so a minimum input supply of 7.5 volts must be used. If you need more than 100 mA in your circuit, the regulator should have a heatsink, either to a free-standing vertical unit intended for this regulator (IERC, Wakefield, etc.) or mounted to the case or chassis. The regulator is automatically current limiting at 750 mA and protects itself and the rest of the power supply from short-circuit damage.

The 1-μF electrolytic shown on the output must be a high-quality tantalum capacitor and must be very near the regulator as it greatly aids the stability and transient response of the sensing electronics inside the 7805.

If you need more power, fixed 5-volt regulators good to several amperes are available from several sources, including National Semiconductor, or pass transistors may be added to lower-power regulator circuits, following the manufacturer's recommendations on a data sheet or application note.

Any other power supply that can deliver the right amount of current and hold its output in the 4.75-volt and 5.25-volt range from no load to full load can be used as well.

At 5 volts, there is no shock hazard to personnel, but as you get into heavier current supplies for large systems, the supplies start looking more and more like an arc-welding circuit. Screwdrivers have been burned in half in more than one instance, so, even with current limiting, use extreme care not to short a high-current supply.

How Much Current?

There is only one accurate way to calculate supply-current needs. This is to check the data sheet for each and every component in the system and add up the totals. There is usually a difference in power consumption on a gate whose inputs are all 1's from one whose inputs are all 0's, and this should be allowed for if the circuits are predominately in one state.

TTL power needs are essentially independent of frequency, except for very high speeds where additional current must be allowed for. A TTL MSI counter that changes only twice a day to show the AM/PM position of a clock needs about the same operating current as a device running at 100 kHz.

Usually two power values are given on the data sheet. Typical values may be used rather than maximum, provided the power supply has at least an extra 25 to 50% capacity.

A quick, but much less accurate, way to calculate the supply power is to use the estimates of Chart 1-4, which has some average currents for more-or-less typical regular-power TTL. For instance, if your system has 3 counters, 2 shift registers, a dual flip-flop, 2 gates, a hex inverter, and 6 pull-up resistors, you will need around 350 mA. A supply that can handle 450 to 500 milliamperes would be recommended, and the circuit of Fig. 1-5 would be ideal.

Another way to estimate supply power is on a package dissipation basis. Very simple TTL circuits need 75 milliwatts per package. Circuits of medium complexity need about 125 milliwatts, and very large ones need about 250 milliwatts. By dividing the total milliwatts by 5, you will get the current in milliamperes. Once again, enough supply reserve should be provided to allow for worst-case operation and possible circuit expansion.

Chart 1-4. Estimating Regular TTL Currents

Each simple gate package	8 mA
Each hex inverter	12 mA
Each more complex gate	18 mA
Each dual flip-flop	25 mA
Each MSI block	60 mA
Each 2.2K pull-up resistor	3 mA

Final values should be multiplied by at least 50% and preferably should be doubled.

Supply Leads

The interconnections between supply and circuit have to be low impedance at all frequencies below 50 MHz with regular TTL, and at all frequencies below 150 MHz with Schottky TTL. Sudden changes or high-speed operation in one TTL circuit must not be subject to carryover into other circuit areas via the supply lines. Low impedance means low inductance. This is most easily achieved by short lengths and wide, thin conductors. Low impedance means that several different values of capacitors have to be used in parallel. While a 50,000-μF electrolytic might be an excellent ripple filter on a power supply, its power factor and self-resonant frequency allow it to provide little or no high-frequency bypassing. In fact, at high frequencies, an electrolytic usually looks like a large inductor. Thus a 50,000-μF electrolytic needs a 1-μF tantalum, a 0.01-μF disc, and possibly a 500-pF mica capacitor in parallel with it, with the smaller capacitors placed as near as possible to the potential sources of high-frequency noise. It is not the total capacitance, it is how the capacitance is distributed throughout the circuit that determines how quiet the supply lines will be.

The supply runs themselves should have the lowest possible impedance. Wide foil runs on pc boards are essential, with a ground at least $\frac{5}{16}''$ wide recommended as the main ground distribution run on a pc board, and $\frac{1}{4}''$ the minimum width for a master supply run. When power leaves a pc board, it should go by way of heavy terminals or through several connector pins in parallel. If the regulator circuit allows it, each board should have additional electrolytics in addition to high-frequency bypassing. Runs outside the pc board should be very heavy leads of minimum length. Flat bonding-strap material or the removed outer shield of a large shielded cable is ideal, but No. 14 or No. 16 wire may be used in smaller systems.

When several pc boards with TTL are used, it is usually better to put one smaller regulator on each board rather than to have one huge regulator at the main power supply. How much time and effort you spend on supply distribution depends on the size of the system and how far it is from the farthest IC back to the power supply. The best overall rule is to use a distribution scheme that is somewhat more than you think you will need—*and then make it heavier!* Glitches and erratic operation traced to supply problems are very hard to find, so extra effort at the beginning can eliminate a lot of headaches.

How you treat ground-return leads is equally important. Ideally, there should be only one common ground-return point for your entire system, and the location should be preferably at the point where the regulator is sensing the output voltage. In larger systems, more exotic ways of transmitting information from pc board to pc board may be needed. These include such things as *line drivers* and *receivers*—or *optical couplers* may be used to isolate both signal and ground. The rule in any system is to give the TTL a chance to operate properly. Good practice calls for buffering or gating reset lines before they leave a pc board and not running input ground-return signals through the same lead that is carrying the master current back to the supply.

One effective solution to power-supply distribution is to use miniature laminated-buss distribution systems. You can purchase these or build your own out of tape and flat metal. The object is to place wide, flat conductors close together, but insulated from each other, and use one for supply and one for ground. This minimizes and distributes the inductance and provides lots of distributed bypassing capacitance at the same time. Another benefit of the busses is that they often can reduce a multilayer pc board to a double-sided one, or a double-sided one to a single-sided one.

Despiking Capacitors

TTL is not only sensitive to supply- and ground-line noise, but it also generates a lot of its own noise when any totem-pole output structure changes state and draws a heavy current spike from the supply lines. These narrow spikes must be kept from going through the supply system, ringing the lines, and upsetting other stages. Local capacitors have to be used to momentarily provide the energy for the supply during the output transitions. These are called *despiking capacitors.* Small disc capacitors in the 0.1- to 0.01-μF range, 10 volts or higher, with the shortest possible lead lengths are recommended. Other capacitor types will self-resonate on their own lead lengths and look inductive at the frequencies where they are needed most.

Here is a list of rules for capacitor placement. But the cardinal rule is this: Use enough for your needs—*and then add some more!*

Use one 0.01- to 0.1-μF short-leaded disc capacitor for every four gate packages.

Use one 0.01- to 0.1-μF short-leaded disc capacitor for every two MSI packages.

Use a separate 0.01- to 0.1-μF short-leaded disc capacitor for every package separated more than three inches from the nearest bypass capacitor.

Use a 10-μF 6-volt tantalum electrolytic where the +5-V line leaves any printed-circuit board.

Enough despiking capacitors properly placed are absolutely essential for proper TTL operation. Note that a 1-μF capacitor at the supply is *not* equivalent to 20 capacitors of 0.05 μF each, properly spread through the system. This is, first, because the capacitors are not in parallel—they are separated by the inductance and transmission time of the interconnecting leads. Second, the larger single capacitor has a much lower resonant frequency for a given lead length and style of capacitor, so it is more likely to behave as an inductive reactance at frequencies of interest.

Remember to always use despiking capacitors; small discaps with ultra-short leads, no fewer than one for every four ICs, are essential for proper TTL operation.

If you are using Schottky or high-speed TTL subfamilies, be sure to consult the manufacturer's application notes for further recommendations. Ground-plane type of construction and terminated inputs are sometimes needed with these higher speed subfamilies, particularly in larger systems or where the timing and overlap may become critical. These families are inherently more sensitive to noise since they are faster.

BREADBOARDING AND MOUNTING TECHNIQUES

There is one very simple rule about using perf-board and "rats nest" hand-wired construction with TTL—*DON'T!* One possible exception to this is the newer perf-board techniques where foil tapes are used for lead routing. Here there is at least a chance of minimizing supply distribution problems, provided the foil runs are wide and thin. Careful use of these newer techniques can sometimes be made in simpler systems without too many problems.

There are several good ways to safely and properly mount TTL, both for breadboarding, system tests, and final circuits. One of these systems is shown in Fig. 1-7 and consists of a large plastic block with

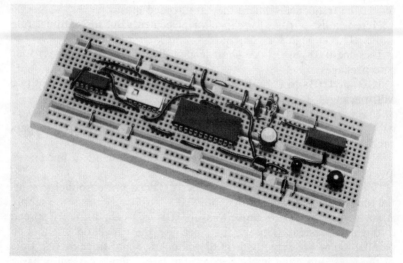

Courtesy API, Inc.

Fig. 1-7. API Super Strip.

integral multiple conductors made of flat strips. Dual in-line packages and other components simply plug in as needed. Wires and components are easily added and removed, and circuit changes are quite simple. While they are somewhat expensive (about $18 for a medium-sized version), they rapidly pay for themselves if you do much breadboarding or rework, particularly on smaller (7 ICs or less) systems. Several firms offer these test modules in complete systems that include power supplies, pulse generators, state indicators, and other support circuitry. These are obviously more expensive, but they are often a good choice where extensive breadboarding is needed.

Wire-Wrap Systems

One widely used industrial mounting technique is wire wrapping, based on socket and panel systems. The ICs push into sockets from the front. At the rear, long pins stick out (Fig. 1-8). Wires are twisted

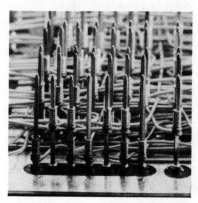

Fig. 1-8. Augat wire-wrap panel.

Courtesy Augat, Inc.

onto these pins, using special tools. The connection system is as good as soldering, possibly better, and the wires are easily changed and the panels are reuseable. The cost is high ($200 for a medium-sized panel), as are the prices of automatic tools for wrapping and unwrapping. Still, wire wrap often ends up being the most economical route for a medium- or larger-size TTL system where only a few units have to be built or where field changes or customizing are to take place. These boards are starting to turn up as surplus at bargain prices, and hand wrapping and unwrapping tools are also becoming available at reasonable cost.

Sockets

It is usually very easy to remove a TTL IC that has been soldered to a pc board, particularly if a solder syringe or other removal tool is used. Because many of the present day ICs are so inexpensive, reuse is not very practical, particularly if you have to pay someone to remove the old ICs. The obvious exceptions are expensive ICs or systems that are not fully debugged.

Sockets are available for TTL, but often they cost three to five times as much as the IC they are supporting, besides adding bulk and height to the circuit. Sockets are best used in testers and other places where you purposely want to make frequent changes of the ICs in use or under test.

A very interesting and practical solution to the reuse problem is a device that is available through most semiconductor and surplus houses. This is called the *Molex Soldercon* system and is simply a group of prespaced socket pins on a metal carrier, available in numbers of 7, 8, or 12, or as a continuous strip. As many as you need are cut off and simultaneously soldered into the pc board. The common carrier is then broken off and the IC is inserted. Cost is under 1¢ per point, and none of the bulk of a socket is present.

While the *Soldercon* pins are not intended for continuous testing or repeated insertions, they can be reused dozens of times. They do not interfere with most TTL test procedures, and the TTL leads remain solder-free.

One good possibility is to mix direct soldering with the *Soldercon* system. Low-cost ICs can be directly soldered in place, while more expensive or potentially reusable ICs can be "unsocket" mounted.

PC Boards

Printed circuitry gives the best overall control and the lowest installed price for TTL, provided the system is complete and checked, and provided there is enough volume to justify the costs of the initial pc layout.

One approach is to use "universal" pc boards. These are available from several sources and are listed in most distributor's catalogs. They consist of a pc board with several dozen DIP patterns, often with supply runs connected and despiking capacitors present or provided for. You then add ICs and wires as needed for your complete system. Changes are easy to make, and the boards are theoretically reusable, although the component removal effort often exceeds the replacement cost.

Sometimes, construction projects in technical magazines offer pc boards already etched, drilled, and marked for a particular project. As these usually have amortized several hundred or even a thousand dollars of layout, mask, and process time, they generally are a bargain. Services are also available that deliver a pc board to you in exchange for the artwork. Cost, quality, and services offered vary with the company. Unless a firm is specially set up for a rapid turn-around service, charges above $20 per board are typical.

You can also do your own pc layouts, either on a 1:1 basis or on the more accurate 2:1 or 4:1 photographic reduction systems. Pc materials are usually carried by most electronic distributors.

Newer pc processes use ammonium persulfate etchant and are generally less messy and better behaved than the older ferric chloride systems. Best results with ammonium persulfate may be obtained by supporting the board to be etched upside down and having it well-covered by the solution at a temperature of 90 to 100 degrees F. New developers such as CAE Dye-Veloper have an integral dye that lets you verify if the pattern is good before etching. The dye is powerful and should only be used while wearing old clothes and in areas where spills will not hurt anything. The mercury catalyst specified for use with ammonium persulfate is highly poisonous. It is best not to use it for short runs or home etching setups. Etching time will be somewhat longer without the catalyst.

One possible do-your-own pc process starts with a 2:1 or 4:1 replica of the desired layout, often built up by taping stock artwork and pc layout symbols on a Mylar sheet. This is then taken to a photolithographer and converted to a 1:1 litho negative at a cost of around $2. A chemically cleaned pc board is then carefully coated with spray-on light-sensitive photoresist such as Dynachem DCR-3140A. The resist is then heated and hardened. You then expose the pc board by contact printing, either in the sun or with a quartz lamp. The board is then developed, etched, and drilled.

Fancier versions of this basic process let you do double-sided and multilayer boards. If the final layout is relatively simple and is needed in quantity, silk-screen processes are available that are much faster and far cheaper than the one-at-a-time photo processes.

TESTING AND MONITORING STATES

Logic systems are tested, debugged, and serviced by sequentially operating them and comparing the results against what the circuit is supposed to do. This testing can be done *dynamically* at the intended system operating speed, or *statically* on a one-step-at-a-time basis.

Dynamic testing is usually done in conjunction with an oscilloscope. The scope MUST have a triggered sweep and its speed should be good enough to handle the particular circuit problem. A 5-MHz triggered-sweep oscilloscope can handle most routine low-frequency TTL testing, although scopes as fast as 125 MHz may be needed for critical testing of Schottky TTL systems, particularly if delays and overlap are critical.

Static or dynamic testing is greatly simplified with an IC Glomper clip such as the one shown in Fig. 1-9. These clips snap onto an IC and bring out pins for easy testing. One design rule often learned the hard way is to do your pc layouts so that Glomper clips like this will fit. This means keeping resistors and despiking capacitors far enough away from the sides and ends of the IC to let the Glomper clip fit on. End-to-end spacing should also be sufficient, particularly with 14-pin packages, so that the Glomper clip can fit over either end, even if it has 16 pins.

Fig. 1-9. API Glomper clip.

Static testing is usually much simpler than dynamic testing, and it should be done first if something obvious is wrong with the circuit operation. One essential piece of test equipment is called a *bounceless push button,* a circuit that gives you a noise-free single command on request. Several suitable circuits are covered in Chapter 4.

A second essential ingredient to static testing is a *state checker*. This is any means of verifying what the output and input pins of each IC are doing at any given time. At zero or very slow speeds, a voltmeter is an excellent state checker. The 0's should be less than 0.8 volt; the 1's more than 2.4 volts. High-frequency counting chains will give a meter indication halfway between these values if the duty cycle is 50-50 and if the frequency is fast enough that the meter averages out. Do not forget to verify ground and supply voltages when state checking.

A *logic pen* is a state checker that is easier to use. Touching the tip of the pen to the IC pin either lights or does not light one or more lamps, indicating a 1, a 0, or pulsed operation. Some of these units are quite sophisticated and include pulse detection and other elegant circuitry. They are priced accordingly. A simple state checker you can build into a test lead or ball-point pen is shown in Fig. 1-10. The clip lead is connected to the positive supply. The light emitting diode lights for a grounded-output state and remains off for a high-output state. Fan-in is about 6.

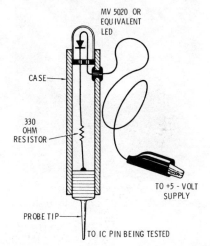

Fig. 1-10. Simple logic-state checker.

A more elaborate state checker (Fig. 1-11) is called the *Digiviewer*. It simultaneously monitors, via a modified Glomper clip, all 14 or all 16 pins of an IC under test. The states are displayed on panel lamps. A slide that shows the circuit for the IC under test fits over the panel lamps. In this way, the states are easily related to their logically similar pins.

Any of the slow or static test methods are useful for servicing, checking for good ICs, or testing circuits of proven design. They also can indicate the presence of a brief pulse, such as those generated by a counter being reset or something similar. Various techniques of checking duty cycle vs voltage or brightness will indicate whether counting chains are operating. They usually will not indicate problems caused by glitches, high-frequency pulse overlap, improper setup times, or other inherent high-speed problems, possibly caused by a poor circuit design. Two other minor limitations are that they might give a "wrong" logic indication of an unterminated, open-collector output stage, and the capacitive loading caused by the test cable can upset a very few TTL devices such as monostables and high-speed Schottky counters.

Courtesy Popular Electronics

Fig. 1-11. Digiviewer logic state checker.

INTERFACE

Getting signals into and out of TTL is called *interfacing*. There are three types of interface: TTL to TTL, TTL to other logic, and TTL to outside world.

TTL to TTL

We have already seen that most TTL circuits can be directly connected to any of the others, so long as fan-out rules are observed. Whenever you interface between TTL subfamilies, you have to be very careful about the available fan-out. For instance, most low-power TTL gates will only drive two regular TTL gates. Regular TTL will only drive 6 or 7 high-power TTL or Schottky TTL inputs. Low-power Schottky can only drive 3 regular TTL inputs or 1 high-power or Schottky TTL input. Some of these relationships are shown in Chart 1-5.

As a general rule, any given subfamily has a fan-out of 10, except for a few buffer circuits with higher fan-outs, typically 30. Some old TTL designs had fan-in requirements of 2 and sometimes even 3 loads on certain inputs, but the majority of new designs have a fan-in standardized at 1 when referred to its own subfamily.

Chart 1-5. Some TTL Subfamily Fan-out Rules

Regular TTL . . . . Will drive 10 regular TTL inputs
Will drive 40 low-power TTL inputs
Will drive 6 high-power TTL inputs
Will drive 6 Schottky TTL inputs
Will drive 20 low-power Schottky TTL inputs

Low-Power TTL . . . . . . Will drive 2 regular TTL inputs
Will drive 10 low-power TTL inputs
Will drive 1 high-power TTL input
Will drive 1 Schottky TTL input
Will drive 5 low-power Schottky TTL inputs

High-Power TTL . . . . . . Will drive 12 regular TTL inputs
Will drive 40 low-power TTL inputs
Will drive 10 high-power TTL inputs
Will drive 10 Schottky TTL inputs
Will drive 40 low-power Schottky inputs

Schottky TTL . . . . Will drive 12 regular TTL inputs
Will drive 40 low-power TTL inputs
Will drive 10 high-power TTL inputs
Will drive 10 Schottky TTL inputs
Will drive 40 low-power Schottky TTL inputs

Low-Power Schottky . . Will drive 5 regular TTL inputs
Will drive 20 low-power TTL inputs
Will drive 4 high-power TTL inputs
Will drive 4 Schottky TTL inputs
Will drive 10 low-power Schottky inputs

Usually, 7400-Series regular-power TTL can be freely intermixed with Motorola 4000-Series MTTL or Signetics 8200-Series TTL, although you should always check the individual data sheets to be sure. There are sometimes slight differences in output high voltage due to different types of totem-pole output design. These do not affect TTL-

Table 1-4. Comparison of Output Current and Input Needs

TTL Subfamily	Output Provides	Input Needs
Regular	16 mA	1.6 mA
Low-Power	3.6 mA	0.18 mA
High-Speed	20 mA	2.0 mA
Schottky	20 mA	2.0 mA
Low-Power Schottky	8 mA	0.4 mA

to-TTL interface but can make a difference in going between logic families. For instance, some 8000-Series TTL will directly interface with MOS without needing a pull-up resistor, while a 7400-Series usually needs one.

Table 1-4 compares output low-state current with input low-state needs for the various families. If you have a more complicated intermix, simply add up the input currents you need to drive it and make sure the sum is less than the available drive capability. In wide-temperature designs or where you are driving a large number of inputs, the high-state currents need also to be considered for exactness. Values in Table 1-4 have been conservatively rounded off to eliminate having to make this calculation for most circuit problems.

TTL to Other Logic

Interfacing between logic families is usually easy to do, but there are several problems. You must select the supply and ground connections between the families to optimize the logic states. You have to honor the output voltage and current swings of the one logic family and provide the minimum 1 and 0 conditions of the other. For detailed interfacing information, you have to carefully study the manufacturer's data on the IC line to be interconnected. However, Figs. 1-12 through 1-16 give some general interface guidelines that usually work.

RTL—RTL to TTL or vice versa may be directly connected (Fig. 1-12). Grounds of both systems are common, and the RTL may be driven from its usual 3.6-volt positive supply or from a 5-volt TTL supply. No RTL loads should be presented to an RTL device that is driving TTL.

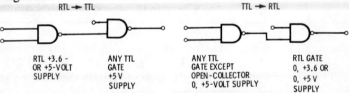

Fig. 1-12. RTL-to-TTL and TTL-to-RTL interfacing.

DTL—DTL to TTL and back again are usually directly compatible (Fig. 1-13). Consult data sheets for fan-out information.

MOS—Silicon gate or n-channel low-threshold MOS sometimes needs a pull-down resistor on its outputs to properly drive TTL (Fig. 1-14). When TTL drives MOS, a *pull-up* resistor is usually needed. TTL fan-out into MOS is very high, but MOS fan-out into TTL is usually one input and often you cannot simultaneously drive MOS and TTL. Older, high-threshold PMOS families may need open-collector outputs and pull-up resistors on the TTL drivers if the positive sup-

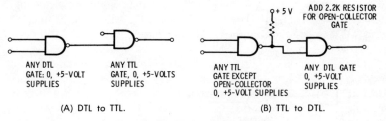

(A) DTL to TTL.

(B) TTL to DTL.

Fig. 1-13. DTL-TTL interfacing circuits.

ply voltage is +12 V. Older MOS runs on a +12-V, −12-V supply system. Newer silicon-gate MOS runs on +5 V, −12 V, and the +5-V supply should be common with the +5 V of the TTL. Newest of all is n-channel MOS. It usually works on a single +5-V supply and is directly compatible with TTL.

CMOS—CMOS (Fig. 1-15) can directly drive low-power TTL. It can drive *one* regular-powered TTL input if a device is chosen with two parallel transistors to ground, as shown in Fig. 1-15, or it can drive several TTL inputs, using a buffer, such as the CD4049 or CD4050. TTL can directly drive MOS, although noise immunity is

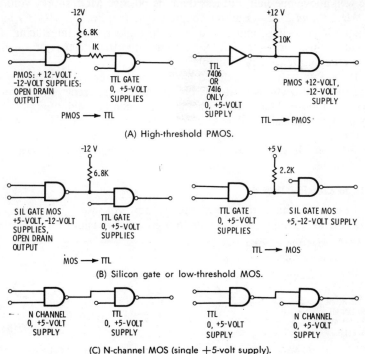

(A) High-threshold PMOS.

(B) Silicon gate or low-threshold MOS.

(C) N-channel MOS (single +5-volt supply).

Fig. 1-14. Some typical MOS-to-TTL interfacing techniques.

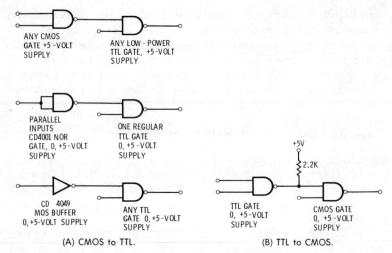

| (A) CMOS to TTL. | (B) TTL to CMOS. |

Fig. 1-15. TTL-CMOS interfacing.

improved with a pull-up resistor. The minimum TTL high state should be well above one-half, but less than the positive MOS supply voltage.

MECL and ECL—Emitter-coupled logic families (Fig. 1-16) have unique logic swings, and it is difficult to build simple interfacing. Instead of this, commercial IC logic translators that do the job quickly and reliably are readily available.

If the family to be interfaced has wildly different supply- and voltage-swing restrictions or if it is on an entirely different power-supply system, a more elaborate interfacing system can be used. One possibility is to use optical couplers that isolate both signal and ground. A second possibility is to use integrated-circuit line drivers and receivers for translation. Be sure to consult individual data sheets when intermixing IC families.

TTL to Outside World

In a sense, this entire book explains how you use TTL processing to get from outside-world signals to a group of outside-world outputs.

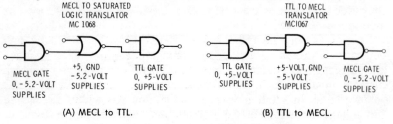

| (A) MECL to TTL. | (B) TTL to MECL. |

Fig. 1-16. TTL emitter-coupled logic interfacing.

We will pick up much more detail as we go along, but the general concepts of interfacing are as follows.

At a TTL input, you have to guarantee a current-sinking capability of at least 1.6 milliamperes at a voltage of 0.8 volt or less for a low-input condition. You also have to guarantee a minimum voltage of +2.4 volts and provide only for a leakage current as an input-high condition. The input swings cannot normally be allowed to exceed the positive supply or go below ground.

The high-to-low transitions and vice versa must be very fast, and one and only one transition can be allowed per intended input change. This means push buttons and other mechanical contacts must be suitably conditioned to make them bounceless and noise free, and that low-frequency and analog signals must have snap-action added to them to improve the rise time. These techniques are further covered in Chapter 4.

TTL will directly drive a light emitting diode, provided a suitable current-limiting resistor is placed in series, as shown in Fig. 1-17A. Incandescent lamps can be driven with a small transistor, as shown in Fig. 1-17B. Note that the output-*low* condition on TTL is more suitable to provide lots of current. Interface to the outside world should optimize this fact.

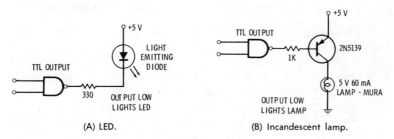

(A) LED.   (B) Incandescent lamp.

Fig. 1-17. TTL lamp drivers.

TTL-to-analog conversion may be done simply with 1K, 2K, 4K, and 8K resistors summed into an op-amp, or TTL-compatible D/A converter ICs, such as the Motorola MC1406 and MC1408, may be used.

In general, any interface system requires that you rapidly and bouncelessly provide guaranteed input-high conditions (high voltage/low current) and guaranteed input-low conditions (low voltage/high current) at all TTL inputs without exceeding the supply or going below ground. In addition, it requires that you stay within the current and voltage limitations of the TTL output stage. Chapter 6 discusses more output interface circuits, particularly those dealing with readouts.

TOOLS

All of the small hand tools used for electronics can be used for TTL work, with the "jeweler"-sized tools being preferable to the larger "electronic" ones. Traverse-cutting pliers are particularly handy for TTL lead cropping. A small soldering iron with a fine tip is a must. One good combination is an Ungar 1235 unit of 40 watts with a PL-338 tip.

Some means of removing ICs is also needed. A solder syringe and its wire cleaner is one good route to take, while solder-removing capillarity braid is another.

A miniature pin vise with a No. 68 drill is handy for cleaning pc board holes and adding components, while a carbide-tipped machinist's scriber is one easy way to open a run on a pc board, but still allow a "solder blob" to fill in later.

A good pocket magnifier, a high-intensity lamp, and a hobby knife with renewable blades are some useful items to have on hand when working with TTL.

You will almost certainly want to add a homemade bounceless push button, a Glomper clip or two, and a state checker to your basic tools. These are almost essential for any work with TTL.

"BAD" AND "BURNED OUT" INTEGRATED CIRCUITS

Occasionally you will get a faulty IC—maybe one or two out of a hundred from a quality distributor, perhaps a few more from a surplus source unless you are obviously buying seconds. TTL ICs will also withstand more than a reasonable amount of abuse, including output shorts, brief applications of reversed supply polarity, excess voltage, and so on. In short, TTL ICs are reliable and rugged.

There is a tendency to blame the poor IC for every circuit problem, including incorrect logic design, pc layout errors, shorted outputs, solder blobs, lack of pull-up resistors on open collector outputs, unconnected supply leads, layout mixups (watch the 7400 and 7402!), poor supplies and bypassing, layouts done topside and etching done backwards, floating inputs, etc.

If an experimental or breadboard circuit appears defective, the problem is almost never a bad or burned-out IC. Every other possibility should be exhausted before an IC is replaced. The rule, and this is the hardest one in this book to learn, is simply: *Always blame yourself first, the IC last.* If you follow this rule, you will find that it saves time and money 99% of the time.

By the same token, if you ever do find a genuinely bad IC, be sure to destroy it so it does not work its way back into some other circuit later on.

SOME CONVENTIONS

In the rest of this book, we have omitted the obvious connections to an integrated circuit in order to make the circuit function we are trying to show more apparent. This is very common in all digital logic circuits. Thus, every circuit in the book needs a +5-volt, regulated and properly despiked supply and a ground return connected to all ICs in use. All unused input leads must go somewhere—disabled to +5 volts or (very rarely) ground, or tied to a logically similar input. Presets, preclears, enables, inhibits, and other control pins must be properly provided for. These connections are all shown in Chapter 2 and on the data sheets. As you go from circuit to breadboard, be sure not to overlook any of them.

We also have not tried to keep track of fractional ICs. A "7400" callout usually means one-quarter of a 7400 NAND gate. A "7473" usually means one-half of a 7473 dual JK flip-flop, and so on. As you use a circuit, be sure to check back to Chapter 2 or the manufacturer's catalog to see how many of these you get per package, and what all the remaining pins on the package do. Output leads that are unused should be left unconnected; all others must go somewhere.

Some TTL Integrated Circuits

This chapter is primarily a catalog of the more popular TTL circuits. It differs in several ways from the detailed information you are likely to find in a manufacturer's catalog.

First, it covers only the essential information you might need to connect or intelligently use the integrated circuit. Second, it includes only the more popular devices, the ones you are most likely to be using.

Third, it is an industry-wide selection that favors no particular manufacturer or product line. It includes non-TTL and support devices (timers, regulators, etc.).

Finally, and most important, this chapter explains as simply as possible what the circuit does and at the same time points out use restrictions or hangups.

As an additional aid, particularly when you are working with several ICs at once, the information in this chapter is also available on a large poster (Catalog No. 21080). You can wall mount this poster for instant reference for TTL layout and servicing work.

Unless otherwise noted, all the listed parts need a +5-volt regulated and despiked supply and operate with a fan-in of one load and a fan-out of ten loads. Only the regular TTL subfamily is shown; other subfamilies usually have identical pinouts.

An *input-low* state means the input is pulled below +0.8 volt and 1.6 milliamperes is being pulled out of the input. An *input-high* state means the input is being held more positive than 2.4 volts and that a small leakage current is being provided.

Both the currents and the propagation delays are typical averages. The following list is an index and selection guide for this chapter. The devices are listed by type number and are covered in the order shown.

Type Number	Description
HD0165	*Special Circuit, Keyboard Encoder,* 4-bit output
PROM1-0512	*Memory,* read-only, sixty-four 8-bit words
555	*Timer,* astable or monostable
2513	*Support,* MOS alphanumeric character generator
CD4001	*Gate,* CMOS quad 2-input interface element
MC4016	*Counter,* decade, ripple down, presettable, unit cascadable
MC4018	*Counter,* base 16, ripple down, presettable, unit cascadable
MC4024	*Astable,* dual, voltage-controlled
7400	*Gate,* quad 2-input NAND
7401	*Gate,* quad 2-input NAND, open collector
7402	*Gate,* quad 2-input NOR
7403	*Gate,* quad 2-input NAND, normal pinouts, open collector
7404	*Inverter,* hex
7405	*Inverter,* hex, open circuit
7406	*Inverter,* hex, open circuit to 30 volts
7407	*Driver,* hex, open circuit to 30 volts, noninverting
7408	*Gate,* quad 2-input AND
7410	*Gate,* triple 3-input NAND
7414	*Schmitt Trigger,* interface, hex
7416	*Driver,* hex, inverting to 15 volts
7417	*Driver,* hex, noninverting to 15 volts
7420	*Gate,* dual 4-input NAND
7430	*Gate,* single 8-input NAND
7432	*Gate,* quad 2-input OR
7437	*Buffer,* quad 2-input NAND
7440	*Buffer,* dual 4-input NAND
7442	*Decoder,* BCD to 1 of 10, TTL output
7445	*Decoder,* BCD to 1 or 10, 30-V, 80-mA output
7447	*Decoder,* BCD to 7 segment, 40-mA, 30-volt output
7473	*Flip-Flop,* dual JK level-triggered, preclear only
7474	*Flip-Flop,* dual D, edge-triggered, preset and preclear
7475	*Memory,* quad latch, level sensitive
7476	*Flip-Flop,* dual JK level-triggered, preset and preclear
7483	*Arithmetic Unit,* 4-bit full adder
7485	*Arithmetic Unit,* 4-bit magnitude comparator
7486	*Gate,* quad EXCLUSIVE OR

Type Number	Description
7489	*Memory,* 64-bit (sixteen 4-bit words)
7490	*Counter,* decade, ripple, not presettable
7492	*Counter,* base 12, ripple, not presettable
7493	*Counter,* base 16, ripple, not presettable
7495	*Shift Register,* 4-bit, right-left, parallel in and out
7496	*Shift Register,* 5-bit, parallel in, parallel out
7497	*Special Circuit,* binary-rate multiplier (base 64)
74107	*Flip Flop,* dual JK level-triggered, preclear only
74121	*Timer,* monostable multivibrator, not retriggerable
74122	*Timer,* monostable multivibrator, retriggerable
74123	*Timer,* dual monostable multivibrator, retriggerable
74141	*Decoder,* BCD to Nixie tube
74142	*Counter,* decade with latch and Nixie driver
74148	*Special Circuit,* 8-bit priority encoder
74150	*Data Selector,* 1 of 16
74151	*Data Selector,* 1 of 8
74153	*Data Selector,* dual 1 of 4
74154	*Data Distributor,* 1 of 16
74155	*Data Distributor,* dual 1 of 4
74157	*Data Selector,* quad 1 of 2
74160	*Counter,* decade, synchronous, presettable, up only
74161	*Counter,* base 16, synchronous, presettable, up only
74164	*Shift Register,* 8 bits, serial in, parallel out
74165	*Shift Register,* 8 bits, parallel in, serial out
74167	*Special Circuit,* rate multiplier, 74167
74174	*Memory,* hex D flip-flop, edge-clocked
74175	*Memory,* quad D flip-flop, edge-clocked
74180	*Special Circuit,* parity generator checker
74181	*Arithmetic Unit,* computer central processing unit
74190	*Counter,* decade, up/down, synchronous, presettable
74191	*Counter,* base 16, up/down, synchronous, presettable
74192	*Counter,* decade, up/down, synchronous, presettable
7805	*Support,* regulator, fixed 5 volt
DM8093	*Driver,* quad, Tri State
DM8094	*Driver,* quad, Tri State
8223	*Memory,* read-only, 256 bits (thirty-two 8-bit words)
8280	*Counter,* decade, ripple, presettable
8281	*Counter,* base 16, ripple, presettable
8288	*Counter,* base 12, ripple, presettable
8290	*Counter,* base 10, high speed, ripple, presettable
8291	*Counter,* base 16, high speed, ripple, presettable.

The following paragraphs list the devices according to their function.

Arithmetic Units:

Adder, 4-bit binary 7483
Arithmetic Logic Unit, CPU 74181
Magnitude Comparator, 4-bit 7485

Counters:

Base 10 (decade):
Ripple down, presettable MC4016
Ripple up, presettable 8280
Ripple up, presettable, high speed 8290
Ripple up, not presettable 7490
Ripple up, latch, Nixie output 74142
Synchronous up 74160
Synchronous up/down 74190
Synchronous up/down, carry/borrow 74192
Base 12
Ripple up, presettable 8288
Ripple up, not presettable 7492
Base 16
Ripple down, presettable MC4018
Ripple up, presettable 8281
Ripple up, presettable, high speed 8291
Synchronous up 74161
Synchronous up/down 74191
Ripple up, not presettable 7493

Data Distributors:

1 of 16 74154
1 of 8 7442
1 of 4, dual 74155

Data Selectors:

1 of 16 74150
1 of 8 74151
1 of 4, dual 74153
1 of 2, quad 74157

Decoders and Decoder/Drivers:

BCD to 1 of 10, TTL output 7442
BCD to 1 of 10, 30-volt, 80-mA output 7445
BCD to 7 segment, 40-mA, 30-volt output 7447
BCD to Nixie, 60-volt output 74141

Flip-Flops:

Dual JK, preclear only, special pinouts 7473
Dual JK, preclear only, standard pinouts 74107
Dual JK, preset and preclear 7476
Dual D, edge-clocked 7474

Gates:

Two Input:
NAND, quad 7400
NAND, quad, open collector 7401
NAND, quad, open collector, std pins 7403
NOR, quad 7402
OR, quad 7432
AND, quad 7408
EXCLUSIVE OR, quad 7486
Three Input:
NAND, triple 7410
Four Input:
NAND, dual, ... 7420
Eight Input:
NAND, single, ... 7430

Interface and Support Circuits:

CMOS Quad 2-input NOR gate interface CD4001
Character generator, MOS alphanumeric 2513
Hex Schmitt trigger interface 7414
Regulator, fixed 5-volt, ¾ ampere 7805

Inverters, Buffers, Drivers:

Inverting:
Hex, TTL output 7404
Hex, TTL output, open circuit 7405
Hex, 15-volt, open-circuit output 7416
Hex, 30-volt, open-circuit output 7406
Multiple Input:
Quad 2-input NAND buffer 7437
Dual 4-input NAND buffer 7440
Noninverting:
Quad Tri State, low enable DM8093
Quad Tri State, high enable DM8094
Hex, 15-volt open-circuit output 7417
Hex, 30-volt open-circuit output 7407

Logic Function Generators:

See Chapter 3 for details.
Any function of *five* variables 74150
Any function of *four* variables 74151
Any two functions of *three* variables 74153
Any four functions of *two* variables 74157
Any eight functions of *six* variables PROM1-0512

Memories:

4-bit, level-clocked 7475
4-bit, edge-clocked 74175
6-bit, edge-clocked 74174
64-bit RAM, sixteen 4-bit words 7489
256-bit (Read-only) thirty-two 8-bit words 8223
512-bit (Read-only) sixty-four 8-bit words PROM1-0512

Shift Registers:

4-bit, right/left, parallel in/out 7495
5-bit, parallel in/out 7496
8-bit, series in, parallel out 74164
8-bit, parallel in, series out 74165

Special Circuits:

Keyboard Encoder, 4-bit output HD0165
Rate Multiplier, binary 7497
Rate Multiplier, decade 74167
Parity Generator/checker 74180
Priority Encoder, 8-line 74148

Timers:

Astable/Monostable 555
Voltage-Controlled Astable, dual MC4024
Monostable, not retriggerable 74121
Monostable, retriggerable 74122
Monostable, dual, retriggerable 74123

Some recently assigned 7400 numbers for popular TTL integrated circuits are given in Table 2-1 on the next page.

Table 2-1. Recently Assigned 7400 Numbers for Popular TTL Integrated Circuits

Traditional Number	TTL Assignment	Function	Original Manufacturer
PROM1-0512	74186	Read-Only Memory, 64 × 8	Harris
MC4016	74416	Decade Counter	Motorola
MC4018	74418	Base-16 Counter	Motorola
MC4024	74424	Dual Astable	Motorola
DM8093	74125	Tri-State driver	National
DM8094	74126	Tri State driver	National
8223	74188	Read-Only Memory, 32 × 8	Signetics
8280	74176	Decade Counter	Signetics
8281	74177	Base-16 Counter	Signetics
8290	74196	Decade Counter, fast	Signetics
8291	74197	Base-16 Counter, fast	Signetics

All these parts are listed and referenced by their traditional numbers.

KEYBOARD ENCODER, 16-KEY

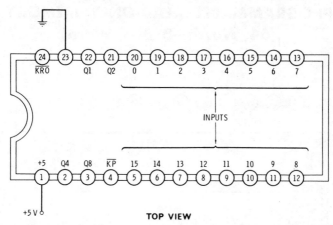

TOP VIEW

This is a keyboard encoder. When any single input is *high,* it produces a binary code corresponding to that input on outputs Q1, Q2, Q4, and Q8.

Note the unusual supply connections. The inputs are RTL-style current sourcing; the outputs are TTL compatible. An input is turned *on* if it goes above +3.5 volts. It stays *off* if grounded or left unconnected. Unconnected inputs may safely be left unconnected, unlike virtually all other logic circuits.

If no inputs are high, the $\overline{KP}$ output remains high. If any input goes high, the $\overline{KP}$ output drops, indicating a key-pressed condition. If more than one output goes high at the same time, the $\overline{KRO}$ or key rollover output also goes to ground, indicating an invalid code.

Outputs are binarily weighted 1-2-4-8. For instance, input 7 gives a 0111 output code.

Required source current is 3 milliamperes.

Current per package .... 88 milliamperes

Settling time .... 200 nanoseconds

PROM1-0512
(74186)

PROGRAMMABLE READ-ONLY MEMORY
(64 Words—8 Bits/Word)

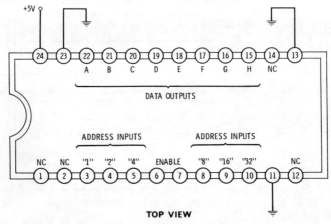

TOP VIEW

This device is a Read-Only Memory. It can be field programmed once to provide sixty-four different 8-bit words. See Chapter 3.

For a given input address, the word programmed at that address is output on the Data Output lines. Both Enable inputs must be high to get an output. The memory is expanded to other packages by connecting identical outputs together and *enabling* only one package at a time.

ROMs may be used for random logic generation, to generate complex waveforms, or to provide a microprogrammed sequence of states. Refer to original data sheet for programming information and to Chapter 3 for more application details.

Response time .... 55 nanoseconds

Current per package .... 80 milliamperes

TIMER—ASTABLE OR MONOSTABLE

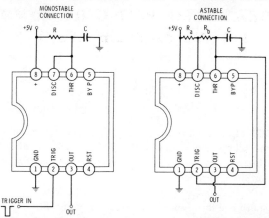

This circuit may be used for astable or monostable in timing applications from microseconds to hours. Complete details for its use appear in Chapter 4.

As a monostable, the circuit is triggered by bringing the Trigger input momentarily below 2 volts. The output pulse width is determined by R and C, and the curves are shown in Fig. 4-26. R can vary from 1K to 3.3 megohms. C can range from 500 pF up. TTL fan-out is more than ten.

As an astable, the circuit is free running. The charging time is determined by R_a and R_b in series with C. The discharging time is determined by C and R_b. Design curves appear in Fig. 4-16. The minimum value of R_a is 1K; the maximum value of $R_a + R_b$ is 3.3 megohms. TTL fan-out is more than ten.

The RST input (pin 4) will drive the output low if it is grounded. If unused, it should be tied to +5 volts. The Bypass input should be bypassed to ground with a suitable capacitor (0.1 μF upward) in critical timing applications.

The output is high during the monostable *on* time and low otherwise. The output is high during the astable charging time and low during the discharge time.

Operating current . . . . 3 milliamperes

MOS ALPHANUMERIC   2513
CHARACTER GENERATOR

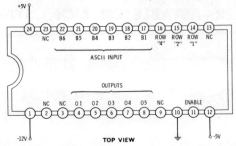

This is a MOS alphanumeric character generator. It generates all the numbers and all the alphabet in a 5 × 7 dot format suitable for display on a line-scan tv set. Output is five simultaneous dots for any given row on the character.

Note that there are three supplies: −12, −5, and +5.

The desired ASCII character is placed on inputs B1 through B6. The row of the character to be output is binarily coded onto the Row 1, Row 2, and Row 4 inputs. All these inputs are TTL compatible if a 2.2K pull-up resistor is used.

For the selected row of the selected character, a dot pattern appears on outputs O1 through O5. O1 is on the *right* side of the character. O5 is on the *left*. These outputs are usually parallel-loaded into a TTL shift register such as the 74165 and marched out as serial video. Output O5 should go to the shift register stage nearest the output; Output O1 should go to the shift register stage nearest the input.

The shift register should be loaded not earlier than 700 nanoseconds after the address or ASCII character changes on the inputs of the 2513. The output of the 2513 is directly TTL compatible without any pull-up or pull-down resistors. See Chapters 3 and 8.

The Enable must be *low* to provide an output. All outputs are *high* if the enable is high.

Maximum response speed . . . . 600 nanoseconds

Current per package . . . . 25 milliamperes

CD4001

CMOS NOR GATE

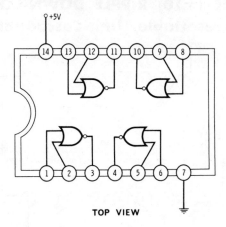

TOP VIEW

This is a CMOS Logic Block. It is useful whenever a very high input impedance is needed in a TTL system. There are four independent positive-logic NOR gates in the package.

With either input high, the output is low. With both inputs low the output is high.

The output will drive a low-power input or a low-power Schottky TTL subfamily input directly. The output will drive one regular power TTL input *if both CMOS inputs are paralleled and driven from the same source.*

More details appear in Chapter 3.

Propagation time .... 65 nanoseconds

Supply current .... negligible

MC4016
(74416)

DECADE (÷10) RIPPLE DOWN-COUNTER
(Presettable, Unit-Cascadable)

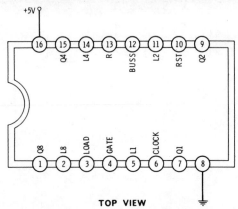

TOP VIEW

This is a single-package, decade, divide-by-10 counter. It counts backwards in the BCD code from 9 down to zero.

Outputs Q1, Q2, Q4, and Q8 are weighted 1-2-4-8. Load inputs L1, L2, L4, and L8 are weighted 1-2-4-8.

The ground-to-positive transition of the clock advances the circuit one count. For use as a conventional counter, connect RST to +5 and ground the Load input. The clock must be conditioned to be bounceless and noise free.

For use as a unit-cascadable decade counter, or to count to some modulo less than 10, refer to Chapter 6. This counter is unique in that the number loaded is the number divided by in unit-cascadable systems (see Chapter 6).

The circuit may be reset to zero by briefly bringing the RST input low. RST should be held at +5 volts, otherwise.

State 0 is decoded and appears at the Buss output. One resistor in one package should be connected to the Buss output by shorting pin 12 to pin 13.

Typical toggle frequency . . . . 8 megahertz

Package current . . . . 50 milliamperes

NOTE: This is a MTTL device; not to be confused with CMOS 4016 analog switch.

MC4018
(74418)

BINARY (÷16) RIPPLE DOWN COUNTER
(Presettable, Unit-Cascadable)

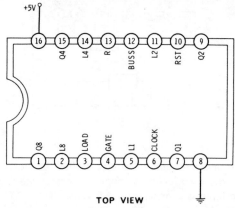

TOP VIEW

This is a single-package hexadecimal or divide-by-16 counter. It counts backward in the binary code from 15 down to zero.

Outputs Q1, Q2, Q4, and Q8 are weighted 1-2-4-8. Load inputs L1, L2, L4, and L8 are weighted 1-2-4-8.

The ground-to-positive transition of the clock advances the circuit one count. For use as a conventional counter, connect RST to +5 volts and ground the load input. The clock must be conditioned to be bounceless and noise free.

To count to some modulo less than 16 or to unit-cascade the counters, refer to Chapter 6. The number loaded is the number divided by in unit-cascade systems.

The circuit may be reset to zero by briefly bringing the RST input low. RST should be held at +5 volts otherwise.

State 0 is decoded and appears at the Buss output. For unit cascadability, one resistor in one package should be connected to the Buss output by shorting pin 12 to pin 13.

Typical toggle frequency .... 8 megahertz

Current per package .... 50 milliamperes

NOTE: This is a MTTL device; not to be confused with CMOS 4018 counter.

MC4024
(74424)

DUAL VOLTAGE-CONTROLLED ASTABLE

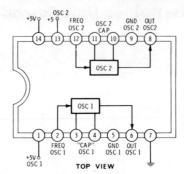

Contains two independent voltage-controlled oscillators. In fixed-frequency mode, a capacitor is connected across the Cap terminals and the Freq input is connected to +5 volts.

In variable-frequency mode, a capacitor is connected across the Cap terminals and the Freq input is connected to a bypassed variable voltage from +3 to +5 volts. A 3:1 frequency change can be obtained.

In a crystal mode, a crystal replaces the capacitor and the Freq input is connected to +5 volts. Crystals in the range of 3 to 20 megahertz work best. Lower-frequency crystals may need additional padding or phase shift.

Capacitor size (nominal) is determined by $C = 300/f$ where C is in microfarads and f is in hertz.

Output can drive ten TTL loads.

Note that there are three supply terminals and three ground terminals. All must be connected if both oscillators are used.

The separate supplies are handy to decouple oscillators to minimize interaction. The separate grounds may be used to gate the oscillators on and off. Gating via the positive supply is not possible.

Maximum operating frequency .... 25 megahertz

Package current requirements .... 37 milliamperes

NOTE: This is a MTTL device; not to be confused with CMOS 4024 counter.

QUAD 2-INPUT NAND GATE

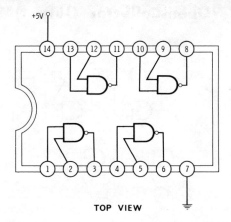

TOP VIEW

All four positive-logic NAND gates may be used independently. On any one gate, when *either* input is *low* the output is driven *high*. If *both* inputs are *high* the output is *low*.

Propagation delay .... 10 nanoseconds average

Current per package .... 12 milliamperes average

QUAD 2-INPUT NAND GATE
(Open-Collector Output)

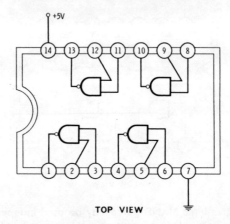

TOP VIEW

All four positive-logic NAND gates may be used independently. On any one gate, with *either* input *low* the output is driven to an *open circuit*. When both are high, the output is low. An output-high state can be obtained only by adding an external resistor, usually 2.2K, from output to +5 volts.

The pinouts on the 7401 are different from the logically similar 7400 and 7403.

Propagation delay .... 8 nanoseconds to output low, 35 nanoseconds to open circuit

Current per package .... 8 milliamperes average

QUAD 2-INPUT NOR GATE

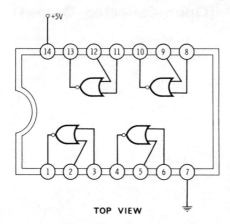

TOP VIEW

All four positive-logic NOR gates may be used independently.
On any one gate, with *either* input *high* the output is *low*.

When *both* inputs are low the output is *high*. Note that this circuit
is both logically different from the 7400 and has different pinouts.

Propagation delay .... 10 nanoseconds average

Current per package .... 12 milliamperes average

QUAD 2-INPUT NAND GATE
(Open-Collector Output)

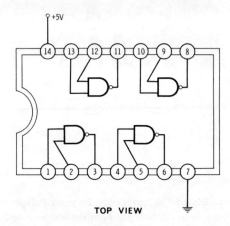

TOP VIEW

All four positive-logic NAND gates may be used independently. On any one gate, with *either* input *low,* the output is driven to an *open circuit.* When both inputs are high, the output is *low.* An output-high state can be obtained only by adding an external resistor, usually 2.2K, from output to +5 volts.

The pinouts on the 7403 are identical to the logically similar 7400. The circuitry is identical to the 7401. Note that this is a NAND gate, not a NOR gate.

Propagation delay .... 8 nanoseconds to output low,
35 nanoseconds to open circuit

Current per package .... 8 milliamperes average

HEX INVERTER

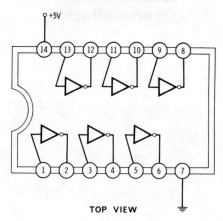

TOP VIEW

All six inverters may be used independently. On any one inverter, the *low*-input condition drives the output *high*. The *high*-input condition drives the output *low*.

Propagation delay .... 10 nanoseconds average

Current per package .... 12 milliamperes average

7405

HEX INVERTER
(Open Collector)

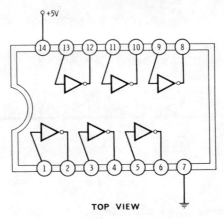

TOP VIEW

All six inverters may be used independently. On any one inverter, the *low*-input condition drives the output to an *open circuit*. The *high* input condition drives the output *low*. An output-high state can be obtained only by adding an external resistor, usually 2.2K, from output to +5 volts.

Propagation delay . . . . 8 nanoseconds to output low,
40 nanoseconds to open circuit

Current per package . . . . 12 milliamperes average

7406

HEX DRIVER, INVERTING
(Open Collector to 30 Volts)

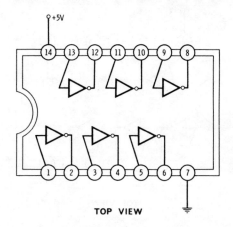

TOP VIEW

All six inverting drivers may be used independently. On any one inverter, the *low*-input condition drives the output to an open circuit. The *high*-input condition drives the output *low*. In the low state, the circuit can sink 30 milliamperes in the output-low condition and can withstand up to 30 volts on the output in the output-high condition. An output-high state can be obtained only by adding an external resistor to some positive voltage less than 30 volts. Note that the *supply* voltage remains at +5 volts.

Propagation delay .... 10 nanoseconds to output high,
15 nanoseconds to output low

Current per package .... 30 milliamperes average

HEX DRIVER, NONINVERTING
(Open Collector to 30 Volts)

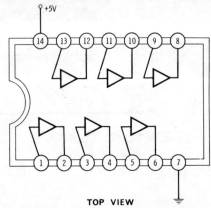

TOP VIEW

All six noninverting drivers may be used independently. On any one driver, the *low*-input condition drives the output *low*. The *high*-input condition drives the output to an *open circuit*. In the low state, the circuit can sink 30 milliamperes. In the output-high condition, the output can withstand 30 volts. An output-high state can be obtained only by adding an external resistor to some positive voltage less than 30 volts. Note that the *supply* voltage remains at +5 volts.

Propagation delay .... 6 nanoseconds to output high,
20 nanoseconds to output low

Current per package .... 25 milliamperes average

QUAD 2-INPUT AND GATE

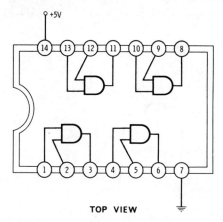

TOP VIEW

All four positive-logic AND gates may be used independently. On any one gate, when *either* input is *low,* the output is *low.* When both inputs are *high* the output is *high.*

Propagation delay .... 15 nanoseconds average

Current per package .... 16 milliamperes average

TRIPLE 3-INPUT NAND GATE

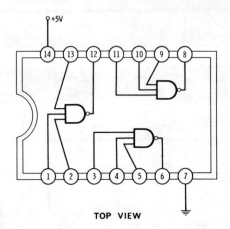

TOP VIEW

All three positive-logic NAND gates may be used independently. On any one gate, when *any* input is *low,* the output is driven to a *high* state. When *all* three inputs are *high,* the output is driven to a *low* state.

Propagation delay .... 9 nanoseconds average

Current per package .... 6 milliamperes average

HEX SCHMITT TRIGGERS (Inverting)

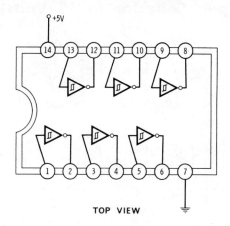

TOP VIEW

All six Schmitt triggers may be used independently. On any single trigger, a *low* input produces a *high* output. A *high* input produces a *low* output.

Unlike a normal TTL gate, the inputs possess a snap action used to condition slowly changing or noisy inputs. The input impedance of this circuit is about 6K. The trip point for a *positive-going* signal is 1.7 volts. The trip point for a *negative-going* signal is 0.9 volt. The snap action or *hysteresis* range is 0.8 volt.

Propagation delay .... 17 nanoseconds typical

Current per package .... 30 milliamperes average

HEX DRIVER, INVERTING
(Open Collector to 15 Volts)

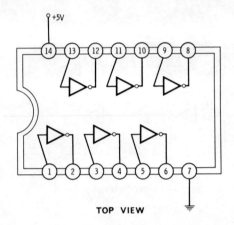

TOP VIEW

All six inverting drivers may be used independently. On any one inverter, the *low*-input condition drives the output to an *open circuit*. The *high*-input condition drives the output *low*. In the low state, the circuit can sink 40 milliamperes. In the open-circuit or high-output condition, it can withstand up to 15 volts on the output. An output high state can be obtained only by adding an external resistor to some positive voltage less than 15 volts. Note that the *supply* voltage must remain at +5 volts.

Propagation delay . . . . 10 nanoseconds to output high,
15 nanoseconds to output low

Current per package . . . . 30 milliamperes average

HEX DRIVER, NONINVERTING
(Open Collector to 15 Volts)

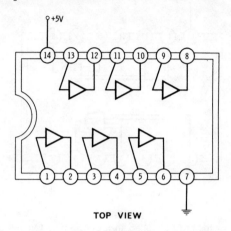

TOP VIEW

All six noninverting drivers may be used independently. On any one driver, the *low*-input condition drives the output *low*. The *high*-input condition drives the output to an *open circuit*. In the low state, the circuit can sink 40 milliamperes. In the output-high or open-circuit state, the output can withstand 15 volts. An output-high state can be obtained only by adding an external resistor to some positive voltage less than 15 volts. Note the *supply* voltage remains at +5 volts.

Propagation delay .... 6 nanoseconds to output high,
20 nanoseconds to output low

Current per package .... 25 milliamperes average

7420

DUAL 4-INPUT NAND GATE

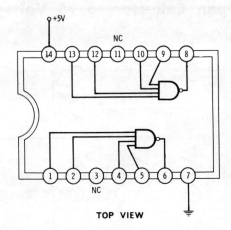

TOP VIEW

Both 4-input gates may be used independently. On either gate, *any* input-*low* condition drives the output *high*. When *all* inputs are high, the output is low.

Propagation delay .... 10 nanoseconds typical

Current per package .... 4 milliamperes average

8-INPUT NAND GATE

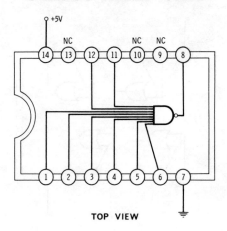

TOP VIEW

There is only a single gate per package. *Any* input-*low* condition drives the output *high*. When *all* inputs are *high* the output is *low*.

Propagation delay .... 10 nanoseconds typical

Current per package .... 2 milliamperes average

QUAD 2-INPUT OR GATE

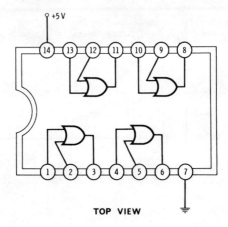

TOP VIEW

All four positive-logic OR gates may be used independently. On any one gate, when *either* input is *high,* the output is driven *high.* When *both* inputs are *low* the output is *low.*

Propagation delay .... 12 nanoseconds average

Current per package .... 19 milliamperes

QUAD 2-INPUT NAND BUFFER

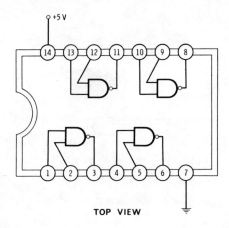

TOP VIEW

All four positive-logic NAND buffers may be used independently. On any one buffer, when either input is *low,* the output is *high.* When *both* inputs are *high* the output is *low.*

Any output can drive 30 TTL inputs. Thus the 7437 has three times the drive capability of an ordinary quad gate such as the 7400.

Propagation delay .... 11 nanoseconds average

Current per package .... 5 milliamperes, all outputs high,
34 milliamperes, all outputs low

DUAL 4-INPUT NAND BUFFER

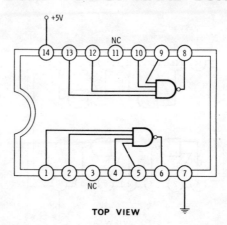

TOP VIEW

Both positive-logic NAND buffers may be used independently. On either buffer, when any input is *low,* the output is *high.* When *both* inputs are *high,* the output is *low.*

Either output can drive 30 TTL inputs. Thus, the 7440 has three times the drive capability of an ordinary dual gate such as the 7420.

Propagation delay .... 11 nanoseconds average

Current per package .... 17 milliamperes, output low,
4 milliamperes, output high

BCD TO 1-OF-10 DECODER (TTL Output)

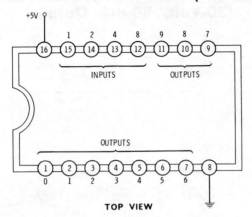

TOP VIEW

This package accepts a 1-2-4-8 Binary Coded Decimal (BCD) input code and provides a *grounded* output for the selected state. For instance, a 0111 input or "1" = 1, "2" = 1, "4" = 1, and "8" = 0 gives output line No. 7 a *low* state; all others remain high.

Outputs are TTL compatible and can sink 16 milliamperes. For higher currents, go to the 7445.

Note that the package can serve as a binary to 1-of-8 decoder simply by grounding pin 12.

Slight settling glitches and overlaps during address (input) changes are possible. Any input code over 1001 sends all outputs *high*.

Propagation delay .... 17 nanoseconds

Current per package .... 28 milliamperes

BCD TO 1-OF-10 DECODER/DRIVER
(30-Volt, 80-mA Output)

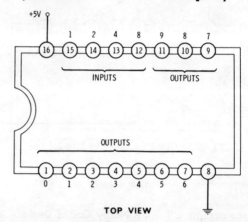

TOP VIEW

This package accepts a 1-2-4-8 Binary Coded Decimal (BCD) input code and provides a *grounded* output for the selected state. All other outputs remain an open circuit. For instance, a 0111 input or "1" = 1, "2" = 1, "4" = 1, and "8" = 0 gives output line No. 7 a *low* state; all others remain open circuited.

Outputs can sink up to 80 milliamperes in the low state and withstand up to 30 volts in the off state. An output-high condition can only be obtained by a resistor or lamp load pulling up to some voltage less than 30. Note that the *supply* voltage for this package must be +5 volts.

The package can serve as a binary to 1-of-8 decoder by grounding pin No. 12.

Slight settling glitches and overlaps during address (input) changes are possible. Any input code over 1001 sends all inputs to the *open-circuit* condition.

Propagation delay . . . . 45 nanoseconds

Current per package . . . . 43 milliamperes

BCD TO 7-SEGMENT DECODER-DRIVER
(Low = on, 40-mA, 30-Volt Outputs)

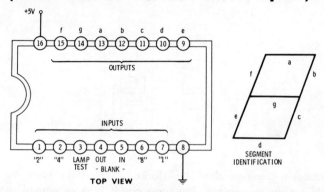

SEGMENT IDENTIFICATION

TOP VIEW

This package accepts a 1-2-4-8 positive-logic Binary Coded Decimal input and converts it to the proper pattern to light a 7-segment display. A *low* output is intended to light the segment.

The outputs can sink 40 milliamperes in the low state and can withstand 30 volts in the high state. Note that the *supply* must remain at +5 volts. An output-high state can be obtained only if a display device or resistor pulls the output to some positive voltage less than 30 volts.

Current-limiting resistors, typically 330 ohms, must be used when drving a light emitting diode display with this package. Incandescent or fluorescent readouts can be directly driven.

The Lamp Test input should remain high. Bringing the Lamp Test to ground simultaneously brings all the outputs to ground.

A low on the Blanking *input* will extinguish only character "0." A low on the Blanking output is provided to extinguish the character "0" of the next stage if leading-edge blanking is desired.

A low on the Blanking *output* will extinguish the display. It is permissible to short this output to ground.

Propagation delay .... 45 nanoseconds

Current per package .... 43 milliamperes

DUAL JK LEVEL-TRIGGERED FLIP-FLOP
(With Preclear Only)

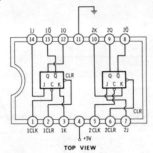

TOP VIEW

Contains two independent level-clocked JK flip-flops. Note the un-usual supply connections. The same circuit in more normal supply pinouts is the 74107.

This is a clocked logic block and is covered in detail in Chapter 5. There are two outputs: Q, and its complement $\overline{Q}$.

Under certain input conditions, Q and $\overline{Q}$ can change whenever the Clock input goes to a low level. The Q and $\overline{Q}$ outputs do not change for a change in the J and K inputs; the only time they can change is as the input clock goes to a low level.

If J and K are grounded, the clock does *nothing*. If J and K are made positive, the clock changes the output states on Q and $\overline{Q}$, or *binarily divides*. If J is high and K is low, clocking makes Q high and $\overline{Q}$ low. If J is low and K is high, clocking makes Q low and $\overline{Q}$ high.

Information on the J and K inputs can be changed only once, immediately after clocking. Further changes can bring about invalid operation (See Chapter 5). The clock must be conditioned to drop only once and then very rapidly.

The Clear input should be left or tied positive for normal operation. If the Clear input is grounded, the flip-flop immediately goes or stays in the state with the Q output low and the $\overline{Q}$ output high.

Maximum toggle frequency .... 20 megahertz

Current per package .... 20 milliamperes

DUAL D EDGE-TRIGGERED FLIP-FLOP
(With Preset and Preclear)

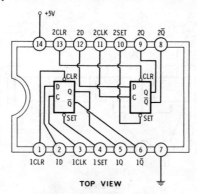

TOP VIEW

Contains two independent positive-edge-clocked D flip-flops. This is a clocked logic block and is covered in detail in Chapter 5. There are two outputs: Q, and its complement $\overline{Q}$.

The information presented to the D input goes on to the Q output whenever the clock input changes from a low to a high level. The *only* time the output can change is when the clock goes positive; changes on the D input are not passed on if the circuit is not clocked.

If D is high, on clocking, Q goes high and $\overline{Q}$ goes low. If D is low, on clocking, Q goes low and $\overline{Q}$ goes high.

Information on the D input can be changed at any time. It is only its value at the instant of the positive clock edge that matters; this is what is entered into the flip-flop.

The Clear and Set inputs should be left or tied positive for normal operation. If the Clear input is grounded, the flip-flop *immediately* goes into the state with Q low and $\overline{Q}$ high. If the Set input is grounded, the flip-flop *immediately* goes into the state with Q high and $\overline{Q}$ low. Set and Clear should *never* be simultaneously grounded or a disallowed state will result.

Maximum toggle frequency .... 25 megahertz

Current per package .... 17 milliamperes

QUAD LATCH (Level-Sensitive)

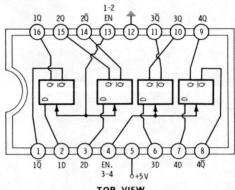

TOP VIEW

This package contains four memory elements. Note the unusual supply connections.

The memories are controlled in pairs with an *Enable* control. If the Enable control is high, the memories *follow* the input, thereby providing the input signal at Q and the complement of the input at $\overline{Q}$. A low at the D input appears as a low at Q and a high at $\overline{Q}$.

For use as a quad storage latch, both Enables are paralleled. Enable-high follows the input. Enable-low holds the previous value.

Note that this is *not* a clocked system and cannot be used as a shift-register element. Stages cannot be cascaded.

Propagation delay .... 24 nanoseconds typical

Current per package .... 32 milliamperes

7476

DUAL JK LEVEL-TRIGGERED FLIP-FLOP
(With Preset and Preclear)

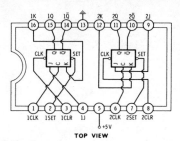

TOP VIEW

Contains two independent level-clocked JK flip-flops. Note the unusual supply connections.

This is a clocked logic block and is covered in detail in Chapter 5. There are two outputs: Q, and its complement $\overline{Q}$.

Under certain input conditions, Q and $\overline{Q}$ can change whenever the Clock input goes to a low level. The Q and $\overline{Q}$ outputs do not change for a change in the J and K inputs; the only time they can change is as the input clock goes to a low level.

If J and K are grounded, the clock does *nothing*. If J and K are made positive, the clock changes the output states on Q and $\overline{Q}$, or *binarily divides*. If J is high and K is low, clocking makes Q high and $\overline{Q}$ low. If J is low and K is high, clocking makes Q low and $\overline{Q}$ high.

Information on the J and K inputs can be changed only once immediately after clocking. Further changes can bring about invalid operation (see Chapter 5). The clock must be conditioned to drop very rapidly per desired operation.

The Clear and Set inputs should be left, or tied positive for normal operation. If the Clear input is grounded, the flip-flop *immediately* goes into the state with Q low and $\overline{Q}$ high. If the Set input is grounded, the flip-flop *immediately* goes into the state with Q high and $\overline{Q}$ low. Set and Clear should *never* be simultaneously grounded, or a disallowed state will result.

Maximum toggle frequency .... 20 megahertz

Current per package .... 20 milliamperes

4-BIT FULL ADDER

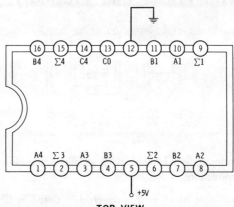

TOP VIEW

This is an arithmetic unit that provides the sum of two 4-bit binary numbers. Note the unusual supply connections.

The A number is weighted A1 = 1, A2 = 2, A3 = 4, A4 = 8 and is used as one input.

The B number is weighted B1 = 1, B2 = 2, B3 = 4, B4 = 8 and is used as a second input.

The sum of these two numbers, A and B, appears as $\Sigma1 = 1$, $\Sigma2 = 2$, $\Sigma3 = 4$, and $\Sigma4 = 8$.

If the answer exceeds decimal 15 (binary 1111), a 1 also appears on the C4 line as a Carry Output.

When used only with 4-bit numbers, the C0 input should be grounded. When used as the upper 4 bits on an 8-bit number, the C0 input is connected to the C4 output of the previous (less significant) four stages.

Positive logic with 1 being at high level is used.

Propagation delay . . . . 16 nanoseconds typical per package

Current per package . . . . 60 milliamperes average

4-BIT MAGNITUDE COMPARATOR

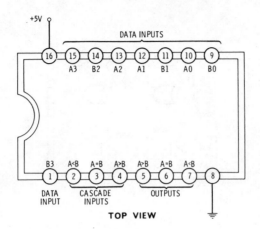

This package compares two 4-bit words and provides an output indicating whether they are equal or which is larger.

Usually the input data words to be compared are weighted $A1 = 1$, $A2 = 2$, $A3 = 4$, and $A4 = 8$, while the second word is weighted $B1 = 1$, $B2 = 2$, $B3 = 4$, and $B4 = 8$.

If only 4-bit words are being compared, the $A = B$ Cascade input should be wired *high*. The $A > B$ and $A < B$ Cascade inputs should be *grounded*.

If the two words are equal, the $A = B$ goes high. If $A > B$, the $A > B$ output goes high. If $A < B$, the $A < B$ output goes high. Thus, a high state appears at the proper output; the other two remain low.

To work with 8-bit words, the outputs of the first 4-bit comparison (least significant bits) are connected to the Cascade Inputs of the second stage. The final answer appears as the outputs of the most significant 4-bit comparator, with the proper output going high.

Propagation delay .... 23 nanoseconds

Current per package .... 55 milliamperes

QUAD EXCLUSIVE-OR GATE

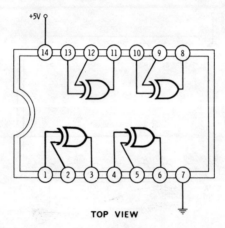

TOP VIEW

The package contains four independent EXCLUSIVE-OR gates. They may be used separately.

On any one gate, when one, *but not both, inputs are high,* the output is *high.* When *both inputs are high* or *both inputs are low,* the output is *low.*

Propagation time .... 18 nanoseconds

Current per package .... 30 milliamperes

64-BIT (16 × 4) MEMORY

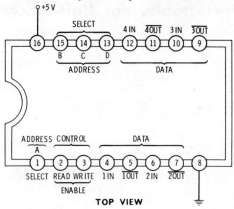

TOP VIEW

This package contains a memory arranged as sixteen different words of four bits each. It keeps its internal information as long as power is applied.

To place information in the memory, a 4-bit word is placed on the 1 In, 2 In, 3 In, and 4 In lines. This is the information to be stored. Next, a *location* in the memory is selected by using Select or Address lines A, B, C, D. These are binarily weighted A = 1, B = 2, C = 4, D = 8. The Write Enable line is then brought low to enter the data. Information that was in the four storage locations corresponding to the selected address is destroyed. The Write Enable line is left high unless new information is to be entered in the memory.

The Read Enable line is normally left in the low condition, and the *complement* of the selected word will appear as an output. Do not change addresses with *Write Enable* low.

If both Read Enable and Write Enable are held high, the output goes to an open-circuit condition. The memory may be expanded by connecting package outputs together, so long as all packages but one have their Write Enable and Read Enable outputs held high at any given time.

Read time	33 nanoseconds
Write time	48 nanoseconds
Current per package	75 milliamperes

DECADE COUNTER (÷10) (Ripple, not Presettable, not Unit-Cascadable)

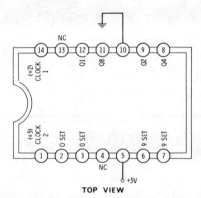

TOP VIEW

This is a divide-by-2 and a divide-by-5 counter in a single package. They may be used together as a divide-by-10 or separately. It ripple-counts in the BCD-up direction. Note the unusual supply pinouts.

For a BCD counter, weighted 1-2-4-8, enter via Clock 1, and jumper Q1 to Clock 2. Both 9-Set and both 0-Set inputs must be *grounded* for normal counting.

The counter advances on the negative-going clock edge. The clock must be properly conditioned and made bounceless and noise free. If a conventional decade counter is needed, *all set terminals must be held at ground.*

The counter may be reset to zero by bringing either or both 0-Set inputs positive. The counter may be preset to 9 by bringing either or both 9-Set inputs positive.

An external jumper must be provided between counter halves. If entry is via Clock 2, and Q8 is jumpered to Clock 1, a counter weighted 1-2-4-5 results, with Q1 as the most significant output and a symmetrical square wave at the output. More details on this device appear in Chapter 6. The circuit is not unit-cascadable.

Typical maximum toggle frequency . . . . 18 megahertz

Current per package . . . . 32 milliamperes

BASE-TWELVE (÷12) COUNTER (Ripple, not Presettable, not Unit-Cascadable)

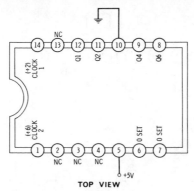

TOP VIEW

This is a divide-by-2 and a divide-by-6 counter in a single package. They may be used together as a divide-by-12 or separately. It ripple-counts in the BCD-up direction. Note the unusual supply pinouts. Note also the pin connections are not the same as the 7490 or 7493.

For a base-12 counter, weighted 1-2-4-6, enter via Clock 1 and jumper Q1 to Clock 2. The 0-Set inputs must be *grounded* for normal counting. The output is low for six counts and high for six.

The counter advances on the negative-going clock edge. The clock must be properly conditioned and made bounceless and noise free. If a conventional base-12 counter is needed, *both 0-set terminals must be held at ground*.

The counter may be reset to zero by bringing either or both 0-Set inputs positive.

An external jumper must be provided between counter halves. If entry is via Clock 2, and Q6 is jumpered to Clock 1, an unweighted counter with a different sequence results. Q1 becomes the most significant output and has a symmetrical square wave. This other connection also allows the use of the divide-by-6 section as a divide-by-3.

Typical maximum toggle frequency . . . . 18 megahertz

Current per package . . . . 31 milliamperes

BINARY (÷16) COUNTER
(Ripple, not Presettable)

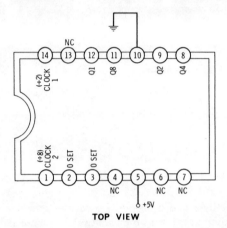

TOP VIEW

This is a divide-by-2 and a divide-by-8 counter in a single package. They may be used together as a divide-by-16 or separately. It ripple-counts in the binary-up direction. Note the unusual supply pinouts. Note also the pin connections are not the same as the 7490 or 7492.

For a base-16 counter, weighted 1-2-4-8, enter via Clock 1 and jumper Q1 to Clock 2. Both 0-Set inputs must be *grounded* for normal counting.

The counter advances on the negative-going clock edge. The clock must be properly conditioned and made bounceless and noise free. *Both set terminals must be held at ground for normal counting.*

The counter may be reset to zero by bringing either or both 0-Set inputs positive.

An external jumper must be provided between counter halves.

Typical maximum toggle frequency . . . . 18 megahertz

Current per package . . . . 31 milliamperes

7495

SHIFT REGISTER, 4 BITS
(Right-Left, Parallel In, Parallel Out)

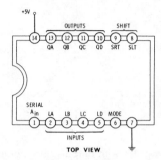

This is a 4-bit shift register with outputs and inputs on all stages. Depending on how you use it, you can parallel-load data or shift information to the right or to the left.

There are two modes, Shift and Load. You enter the Shift mode by placing the Mode input *low*. A high-to-low transition on the SRT input clock moves the data one stage to the right. A high-to-low transition on the SLT backs up the data and moves it one stage to the left. Note that there are two clocks—one to move data to the left and one to move it to the right.

During the shift-right mode, information at the Serial A_{in} input is entered into the first register stage (stage A). On a shift-right, the contents of A_{in} go to QA. The contents of QA go to QB; the contents of QB go to QC, the contents of QD are destroyed or passed on to a following package.

During the Load mode, the Mode control is made *high,* and information on the Load inputs LA, LB, LC, and LD is entered into the package by using the positive-to-ground transition of a command on the shift-left input.

Thus, the shift-left does double duty. It shifts left with the Mode input low and loads data with the Mode input high.

Maximum operating frequency . . . . 36 megahertz

Current per package . . . . 39 milliamperes

SHIFT REGISTER, 5 BITS
(Shift Right, Parallel In, Parallel Out)

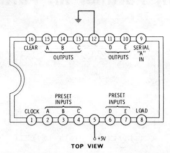

TOP VIEW

This is a 5-bit shift register with outputs and inputs on all stages. Depending on how you use it, you can parallel-load data or serial-shift data to the right. Stage A is nearest the Input; stage E is nearest the output. There are two modes, Load and Shift.

To clear the register to all zeros, the normally high Clear input should be briefly brought to ground.

To load data into the register, the desired pattern is set up on the A, B, C, D, E, inputs and the normally low Load input should be briefly brought high. *This register must be cleared before loading. You cannot change a 1 aready in the register to a 0 with the Load inputs.* The load inputs can only enter 1's or leave 0's already present as they are. A 1 is designed as a *high* state.

To shift data to the right, the Clear input should be *high,* the Load input should be *low,* and data will be shifted one stage to the right on the ground-to-high transition of the Clock input. The clock must be made bounceless and noise free so that only one ground-to-high transition occurs per desired shift. On a shift operation, the information at the Serial input goes to stage A. A goes to B. B goes to C. C goes to D. D goes to E. E goes to the next package down the line or is destroyed.

Remember, you cannot load a low state into this shift register using the parallel inputs.

Maximum operating frequency .... 10 megahertz

Current per package .... 48 milliamperes

BINARY RATE MULTIPLIER (Base 64)

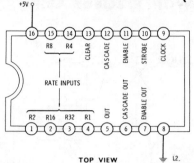

TOP VIEW

This is a specialized TTL package detailed in Chapter 7. For every 64 clock-input pulses, a selected number of 0-through-63 output pulses are provided.

For normal operation, ground the Strobe, Clear, and Enable lines. Make the Cascade input positive. Apply a square wave to the Clock input. At the Enable output you will have a 1-of-64 decoding of the input clock, i.e., one pulse for every 64 clock-input pulses.

At the normal output (pin 5), you will get as many pulses *per 64 input-clock cycles* as you select on the Rate inputs. For instance, if R32 is high, R16 is low, R8 is low, R4 is high, R2 is low, and R1 is high, you will get 37 output pulses per one enable-out pulse or 37 output pulses per 64 clock cycles.

In general, the pulses are not evenly spaced as they can occur only concidentally with a time slot on the input clock. Jitter is inherent in a rate multiplier system (see Chapter 7).

If the Clear input is made positive, the internal divide-by-64 counter is reset to zero. If the Strobe input is made high, the counter will operate, but no rate pulses will appear at pins 5 or 6. Pin 6 is the complement of pin 5 and is gated by the Cascade input. The Cascade input-low inhibits the output of pin 6. Refer to data sheet for more operation details.

Maximum operating frequency .... 25 megahertz

Current per package .... 65 milliamperes average

DUAL JK LEVEL-TRIGGERED FLIP-FLOP
(With Preclear Only)

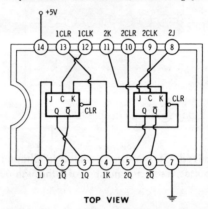

TOP VIEW

Contains two independent, level-clocked JK flip-flops. This is a clocked logic block and is covered in detail in Chapter 5. There are two outputs: Q, and its complement $\overline{Q}$.

Under certain input conditions, Q and $\overline{Q}$ can change whenever the Clock input goes to a low level. The Q and $\overline{Q}$ outputs do not change for any change in the J and K inputs; the only time they can change is as the input clock goes to a low level.

If J and K are grounded, the clock does *nothing*. If J and K are made positive, the clock changes the output states on Q and $\overline{Q}$, or *divides binarily*. If J is high and K is low, clocking makes Q high and $\overline{Q}$ low. If J is low and K is high, clocking makes Q low and $\overline{Q}$ high.

Information on the J and K inputs can only be changed once immediately after clocking. Further changes can bring about invalid operation (See Chapter 5). The clock must be conditioned to drop only once and then very rapidly.

The Clear input should be left or tied positive for normal operation. If the Clear input is grounded, the flip-flop immediately goes or stays in the state with the Q output low and the $\overline{Q}$ output high.

Maximum toggle frequency .... 20 megahertz

Current per package .... 20 milliamperes

74121

MONOSTABLE MULTIVIBRATOR
(Single, Not Retriggerable)

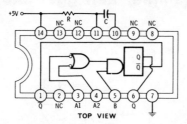

TOP VIEW

This is a monostable multivibrator or pulse generator. The circuit must be triggered.

In response to a trigger, the Q output goes high and the $\overline{Q}$ output goes low, staying there for a predetermined time and then returning to the initial state.

A capacitor connected between pins 10 and 11 determines the pulse width in combination with a resistor between pin 11 and pin 14. The resistor can range from 2 to 40K and the capacitor from 10 pF upward. Fig. 4-30 gives the time-constant curves.

There are several ways to trigger the monostable multivibrator, determined by what you do to the A1, A2, and B inputs.

If A1 and A2 are grounded, bringing B from ground to a positive level produces triggering. This is a level-sensitive input with Schmitt trigger snap action or hysteresis.

If A1 is high and B is high, bringing A2 from high to low triggers. If A2 is high and B is high, bringing A1 from high to low triggers.

Most other combinations of A1, A2, and B inhibit the operation.

Be sure to properly terminate all three Trigger inputs. The circuit cannot be retriggered during the *on* time and a duty cycle of less than 75% is recommended. Certain forms of clip-on digital testers can upset the operation of this stage, particularly on the resistor and capacitor inputs.

Unless very short times or complementary outputs are needed, the 555 is a better choice.

Current per package .... 23 milliamperes

MONOSTABLE MULTIVIBRATOR
(Single, Retriggerable)

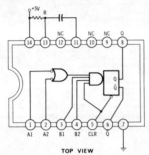

TOP VIEW

This is a monostable multivibrator or pulse generator. The circuit must be triggered.

In response to a trigger, the Q output goes high and the $\overline{Q}$ output goes low, staying there for a predetermined time and then returning to the initial state.

A capacitor connected between pins 11 and 13 determines the pulse width in combination with a resistor between pin 13 and pin 14. Fig. 4-30 gives the time-constant curves. The resistor can range from 5K to 25K and the capacitor from 10 pF upward.

There are several ways to trigger the monostable multivibrator, determined by what you do to the A1, A2, B1, B2, and Clear inputs.

If A1, A2, and B2 are high, a low-to-high transition on B1 triggers. If A1, B1, and B2 are high, a high-to-low transition on A2 triggers. The Clear input should remain high. If grounded, it inhibits triggering and returns the circuit to the state with Q low and $\overline{Q}$ high.

The circuit may be retriggered at any time. *Be sure to properly terminate all four trigger inputs.* Certain forms of clip-on digital testers can upset the operation of this stage, particularly on the resistor and capacitor inputs.

Unless very short times or complementary outputs or retriggerability is needed, the 555 is a better choice of monostable multivibrator.

Current per package .... 23 milliamperes typical

MONOSTABLE MULTIVIBRATOR
(Dual, Retriggerable)

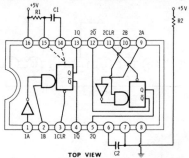

TOP VIEW

This is a dual monostable multivibrator or pulse generator. Each half of the circuit must be triggered. Each half of the circuit may be used separately.

In response to a trigger, the Q output goes high and the $\overline{Q}$ output goes low, staying there for a predetermined time and then returning to the initial state.

A capacitor and resistor connected as shown determine the pulse width. Fig. 4-30 gives the time-constant curves. The resistor can range from 5K to 25K and the capacitor from 10 pF upward.

There are two ways to trigger the monostable multivibrator. If input A is held *low,* bringing B from low to high triggers. If input B is held *high,* bringing input A from high to low triggers.

The Clear input should remain high. If grounded, it inhibits triggering and returns the circuit to the state with Q low and $\overline{Q}$ high.

The circuit may be retriggered at any time. *Be sure to properly terminate all Trigger and Clear inputs.* Certain forms of clip-on digital testers can upset the operation of this stage, particularly on the Resistor and Capacitor inputs.

Unless very short times or complementary outputs or retriggerability is needed, the 555 is a better choice of monostable multivibrator.

Current per package .... 46 milliamperes typical

BCD TO NIXIE^R DRIVER
(7-mA, 60-Volt Outputs)

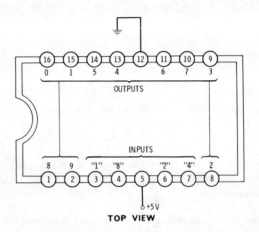

TOP VIEW

This device is intended to convert the TTL level 1-2-4-8 BCD outputs of a BCD counter to levels that will drive a Nixie^r or other neon 1-of-10 indicator.

The cathodes of the Nixie tube are connected to the outputs as indicated. The Nixie tube anode is connected to a suitable high-voltage supply, typically +175 volts dc, *through a current-limiting resistor,* typically 15K. (Consult readout data sheet for more information.)

One, and only one, output is pulled low per selected input code. Codes 10 through 15 (1010 through 1111) are considered invalid and may be used to blank the outputs, leaving all outputs high.

For non-Nixie applications, the outputs will withstand up to 60 volts and can sink up to 7 milliamperes in the low condition. The output saturation voltage is high—2.5 volts for a 7-milliampere load.

Note that the supply voltage remains at +5 V. *Be extremely careful when testing this device. A short from pins 2 to 3, however brief, will destroy the IC.*

Current per package .... 16 milliamperes

1-OF-10 COUNTING SYSTEM (BCD Counter, Latch, Decoder, Nixie^R Output) (60 V, 7 mA)

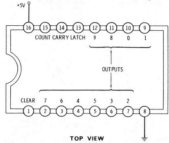

TOP VIEW

This is a one-package-per-decade counting/storage/display system intended to drive a Nixie^r or other neon high-voltage 1-of-10 indicator.

The counter advances one state on the *ground-to-high* or *positive edge* of the input Count clock. The Clear input is normally left high; bringing it to ground briefly will reset the counter to zero. The counter counts to ten. The Carry output may be directly connected to the Count input of the next stage to cascade decades.

If the Latch input is low, the output *follows* the counter. If the Latch input is high, the output *stores* the state of the counter the instant before the Latch input went high. The circuit can thus display an old answer while working on a new one.

The outputs are similar to the 74141 and directly drive a Nixie indicator whose anode is connected to a 175-volt dc source through a current-limiting resistor of 15K. Consult readout data sheet for other operating possibilities. For other applications, the outputs can withstand 60 volts and can provide up to 7 milliamperes. The saturation voltage in the *on* state is very poor: +2.5 volts.

Note that the supply voltage remains at +5 volts. *Be extremely careful when testing this device. A short from pins 1 to 2 or from pins 9 to 12, however brief, will destroy the IC.*

Typical maximum operating frequency . . . . 20 megahertz

Current per package . . . . 68 milliamperes

74148

8-BIT PRIORITY ENCODER

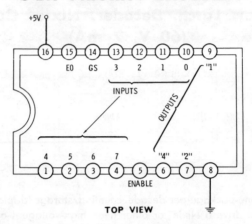

TOP VIEW

This is a specialized TTL device. It lets you rank eight inputs in order of importance. It produces as an output a binary word indicating the most important input present at any given time.

Selected inputs are placed on the 1-2-3-4-5-6-7 input lines. At the 1, 2, 4 outputs, the binary equivalent of the most significant (largest) input line selected will appear.

The Enable input must be low to get an output.

The EO output will go low if *any* input (one or more) is selected. The GS output will go high if *any* input (one or more) is selected and the Enable input is low.

The package may also be used as a keyboard encoder or as an 8-line-to-3-line encoder. It is expandable. Consult data sheet for more information.

Propagation time .... 14 nanoseconds, typical

Current per package .... 40 milliamperes

74150

1-OF-16 DATA SELECTOR

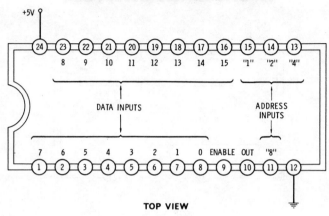

TOP VIEW

This package selects one of sixteen inputs and provides the complement of the selected input as an output. It will also generate *any* logic function of five or less input variables (see Chapter 3).

Inputs are selected by applying a code from 0000 through 1111 on the 1, 2, 4, and 8 Address inputs. The complement of the data on the selected input appears as an output.

The Enable input must be *low* for normal operation. Driving it high drives the output high, independently of the condition of the selected input.

For logic function generation, four of the variables are applied to the Address inputs. The selected Data inputs are connected low, high, to the fifth variable, or to the complement of the fifth variable per the desired truth table. See Chapter 3 for more details.

Note that this package inverts the data.

Select time .... 23 nanoseconds

Current per package .... 40 milliamperes

1-OF-8 DATA SELECTOR

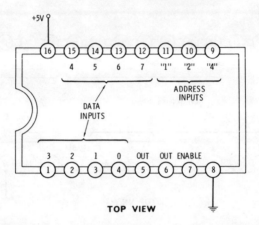

TOP VIEW

This package selects one of eight inputs and provides the data on the selected input or its complement as an output. It will also generate *any* logic function of four or less input variables. (See Chapter 3.)

Inputs are selected by applying a code from 000 through 111 on the 1, 2, and 4 Address inputs. The data on the selected input appear at pin 6; the complement of the selected data appears at pin 5. Pin 5 is faster in responding, as pin 6 is an inverter/follower.

The Enable input must be *low* for normal operation. Driving it high drives the pin-6 output *low* and the pin-5 output *high,* independently of the condition of the selected input.

For logic function generation, three of the variables are applied to the Address inputs. The selected Data inputs are connected low, high, to the fourth variable or to the complement of the fourth variable per the desired truth table. See Chapter 3 for more details.

Select time .... 19 nanoseconds

Current per package .... 29 milliamperes

74153

DUAL 1-OF-4 DATA SELECTOR

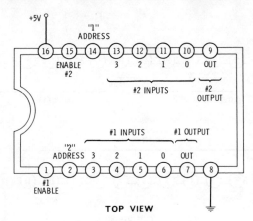

TOP VIEW

This package selects one of four inputs and provides the data on the selected input as its output. There are two separate 1-of-4 selectors with two separate outputs, but their addresses are common.

Inputs to the 1 Address and the 2 Address select the output connection for both sides simultaneously. Input data is not inverted and passed onto the output.

The Enable must be low to get an output. A high Enable drives the output low, independently of input data.

Note that both halves of this circuit have common address lines, although they have separate inputs, outputs, and enables.

Select time .... 44 nanoseconds

Current per package .... 36 milliamperes

74154

1-OF-16 DATA DISTRIBUTOR

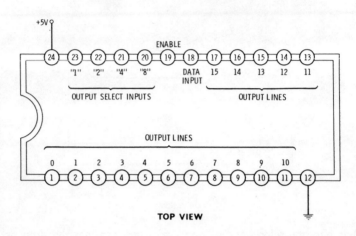

TOP VIEW

This package may be used to provide a 1-low-out-of-16 output or may be used to send input data to one selected output of sixteen, the remaining fifteen staying high.

The output address is selected with the 1, 2, 4, and 8 select lines. For instance, 1 low, 2 high, 4 high, and 8 low selects output No. 6.

If Enable and Data Input are both low, the selected output address goes low.

If Enable is low, and a Logic input is provided the Data input, the selected output address follows the Logic input.

Note that the functions of data selector and data distributor cannot be interchanged in TTL. This circuit accepts *one* input and routes it to *sixteen* outputs.

Select time .... 49 nanoseconds

Current per package .... 34 milliamperes

DUAL 1-OF-4 DATA DISTRIBUTOR

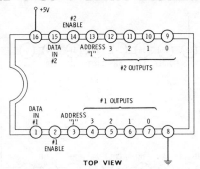

TOP VIEW

This dual package may be used to provide two 1-low-out-of-4 outputs or may be used to send input data to one selected output of four, the remaining three staying high. Both halves of the circuit are identically addressed.

The output address is selected with the 1 and 2 Address inputs. For instance, a 1 low and a 2 low input selects output No. 0 on both sides of the circuit.

If the Data input is made high and the Enable input low on circuit No. 1, the selected output address goes low. If the Data input is made low and the Enable is made low on circuit No. 2, the selected output address goes low.

If the Enable is made low on circuit No. 1, the *complement* of the input data appears at the selected output. If the Enable is made low on circuit No. 2, the input data appear at the selected output.

Note that the two halves of this circuit are not identical. Side No. 1 inverts the data. Side No. 2 does not.

The circuit is converted into a 1-of-8 data distributor by connecting the two Data input lines together and using them as a 4-address line. If both Enables are low, the selected 1-of-8 output goes low. If both Enables are paralleled and fed data, the data are routed to the selected output.

Address select time .... 21 nanoseconds

Current per package .... 25 milliamperes

QUAD 1-OF-2 DATA SELECTOR

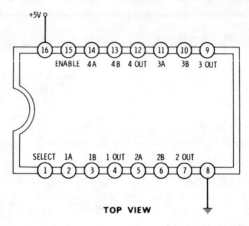

TOP VIEW

This is a four-pole double-throw data selector. All four switches are simultaneously enabled or selected.

If the Enable input is high, all outputs will be low, regardless of the input data.

If the Enable input is low, and the Select input is low, the A inputs will provide an output.

If the Enable input is low and the Select input is high, the B inputs will provide an output.

Note that this is a data selector and not a distributor. There are two inputs that may be selected to provide one output.

Select time .... 18 nanoseconds

Current per package .... 30 milliamperes

74160

DECADE (÷10) COUNTER (Synchronous, Presettable, Unit-Cascadable)

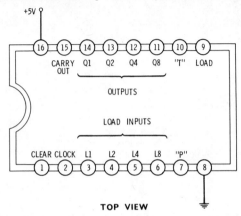

TOP VIEW

This is a synchronous, up-only decade counter. For normal counting operation, the Clear input is made high, the P and T Enables are made high and the Load input is left high.

The count advances one count synchronously every time the clock goes from the low to the high state. The circuit triggers on positive edges. Outputs at Q1, Q2, Q4, and Q8 are BCD-weighted.

To clear to zero, the Clear line is brought momentarily to ground. To load a number in parallel, the desired code is placed on the Load inputs L1, L2, L4, and L8 and the Load terminal is briefly brought to ground.

For fully synchronous operation, the Carry Out of the first stage goes to the T Enable of the second. All stages are synchronously driven from the input clock. Refer to data sheet for more design information (covered in Chapter 6).

The clock must be properly conditioned to be bounceless and noise free, providing one, and only one, positive edge per desired clocking.

Typical maximum operating frequency . . . . 25 megahertz

Current per package . . . . 34 milliamperes

74161

BINARY (÷16) COUNTER (Synchronous Presettable, Unit-Cascadable)

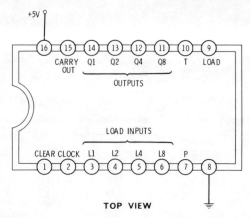

TOP VIEW

This is a synchronous, up-only binary (base-16) counter. For normal counting operation, the Clear, Load, P, and T pins are made high.

The count advances one count synchronously every time the clock goes from the low to the high state. The circuit triggers on positive edges. Outputs at Q1, Q2, Q4, and Q8 are binarily weighted.

To clear to zero, the Clear line is brought momentarily to ground. To Load a number in parallel, the desired word is placed on the Load inputs L1, L2, L4, and L8 and the Load terminal is briefly brought to ground.

For fully synchronous operation, the Carry Out of the first stage goes to the T Enable of the second. All stages are synchronously driven from the input clock. Refer to data sheet for more design information (covered in Chapter 6).

The clock must be properly conditioned to be bounceless and noise free, providing one, and only one, positive edge per desired clocking.

Typical maximum operating frequency .... 25 megahertz

Current per package .... 34 milliamperes

SHIFT REGISTER, 8 BITS
(Serial Input, Parallel Output)

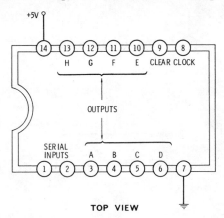

TOP VIEW

This is an eight-stage, shift-right-only shift register. It may be used as a serial-in/serial-out or serial-in/parallel-out.

For normal operation, one of the Serial inputs is held high and data is sent to the second serial input. Clear is held high. Every negative-to-positive transition (positive edge) of the clock shifts the data one stage to the right.

For instance, the data on the input gets shifted into A. A goes to B. B goes to C. C goes to D. D goes to E. E goes to F. F goes to G. G goes to H. H goes to a following stage or is destroyed.

The contents of the register may be cleared to zero by briefly bringing the Clear input low. Both Serial inputs must be *high* to enter a high-input state. Bringing either Serial input low forces a low-input condition.

The clock must be bounceless and noise free, producing one, and only one, positive transition per desired shift.

Typical maximum shift frequency . . . . 36 megahertz

Current per package . . . . 37 milliamperes

SHIFT REGISTER, 8 BITS
(Parallel Input, Serial Output)

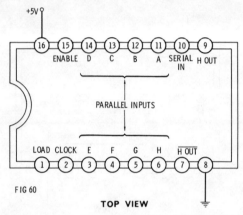

FIG 60

TOP VIEW

This is an eight-stage shift-right-only shift register. It may be used as a serial-in/serial-out or parallel-in/serial-out register.

For normal operation, the Enable is held *low* and the Load is held high. Every negative-to-positive clock transition (positive edge) shifts the data one stage to the right.

For instance, the data on the Serial input goes into A. A goes to B. B goes to C. C goes to D. D goes to E. E goes to F. F goes to G. G goes to H. H goes to the next stage or is lost. The complement of the eighth stage is also available and provides inverted data.

To parallel-load the register, the Load input is briefly brought to ground while applying the desired input word to the parallel inputs A through H.

Shifting may be inhibited by bringing the Enable input high.

The clock must be bounceless and noise free, producing one, and only one, positive transition per desired shift.

Typical maximum shift frequency . . . . 26 megahertz

Current per package . . . . 42 milliamperes

DECADE (÷10) RATE MULTIPLIER

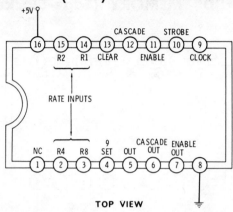

TOP VIEW

This is a specialized TTL package detailed in Chapter 7. For every ten input-clock pulses, a selected number of 0 through 9 output pulses are provided.

For normal operation, ground the Strobe, Clear, and Enable lines. Apply a square wave to the Clock input. At the Enable output, you will have a 1-of-10 decoding of the input clock, i.e., one pulse for every ten input-clock pulses.

At the normal output (pin 5), you will get as many pulses per ten input-clock cycles as you select on the Rate inputs. For instance, if R8 is low, R4 is high, R2 is low and R1 is high, you will get five output pulses per one Enable output pulse or per ten input-clock cycles.

In general the pulses are not evenly spaced as they can occur only coincidentally with a time slot on the input clock. Jitter is inherent in a rate multiplier system. (See Chapter 7.)

If the Clear input is made positive, the internal divide-by-10 counter is reset to zero. If the Strobe input is made positive, the counter will operate, but no rate pulses will appear at pins 5 or 6. Pin 6 is the complement of pin 5 and is gated by the Cascade input. The Cascade input-low inhibits the output of pin 6. Refer to data sheet for more operating details.

Maximum operating frequency .... 25 megahertz

Current per package .... 65 milliamperes

74174

HEX "D" MEMORY (Edge-Clocked)

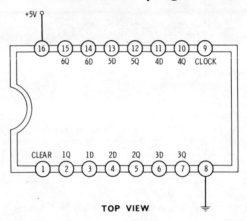

TOP VIEW

There are six separate storage latches, each with a noninverted output. All latches are simultaneously updated.

Information at the D inputs is entered into the latches on the ground-to-high (positive edge) of the clock command. The *only* time that information is entered into this package is on the positive edge of the clock.

The Clear input is normally held high. Briefly bringing it to ground will clear the memory, making all Q outputs low.

This is a fully clocked system and can be used as a shift-register element. Stages can be cascaded. Note that there is no "Follow" mode; storage is updated only on the positive-clock edge.

Propagation delay . . . . 23 nanoseconds

Maximum update frequency . . . . 35 megahertz

Current per package . . . . 45 milliamperes

QUAD "D" MEMORY (Edge-Clocked)

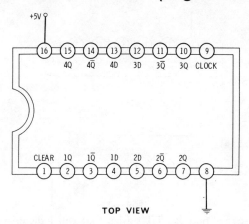

TOP VIEW

There are four separate storage latches, each with normal and complementary output. All latches are simultaneously updated.

Information at the D inputs is entered into the latches on the ground-to-high (positive edge) of the clock command. The *only* time that information is entered into this package is on the positive edge of the clock.

The Clear input is normally held high. Briefly bringing it to ground will clear the memory, making all Q outputs low and all $\overline{Q}$ outputs high.

This is a fully clocked system and can be used as a shift-register element. Stages can be cascaded. Note that there is no "Follow" mode; storage is updated only on the positive-clock edge.

Propagation delay .... 23 nanoseconds

Maximum update frequency .... 35 megahertz

Current per package .... 30 milliamperes

PARITY GENERATOR/TESTER

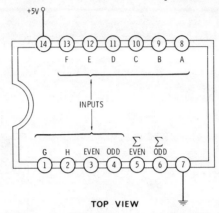

TOP VIEW

This is a special-purpose TTL device that will indicate whether the number of 1's on the inputs is even or odd. It is used as an error tester in computer systems or as a "single note" detector in electronic music.

The inputs to be tested are applied to A through H. Unused inputs are terminated either to ground or high, as needed.

If the Even input is made high and the Odd input is made low, an even number of input 1's drive the Σ Even output high and the Σ Odd output low. An odd number of 1's drives the Σ Even output low and the Σ Odd output high.

If both Even and Odd inputs are high, both outputs will go low, regardless of the A-through-H inputs. If both Even and Odd inputs are low, both outputs will go high, regardless of the A-through-H inputs.

If the Even input is made low and the Odd input is made high, an even number of input 1's drive the Σ Even output low and the Σ Odd output high. An odd number of 1's drive the Σ Even output high and the Σ Odd output low.

Maximum operating speed .... 45 nanoseconds

Current per package .... 34 milliamperes

74181

ARITHMETIC UNIT (CPU)

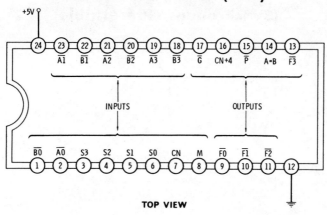

TOP VIEW

This is a versatile arithmetic element. It may be used to add, subtract, or shift two 4-bit words, make magnitude comparisons, perform numerous other arithmetic operations, and generate logic functions. It is normally used as the central processing unit for a computer. As many stages as needed are cascaded.

Refer to data sheet for more information.

Operating time .... 35 nanoseconds

Current per package .... 94 milliamperes

DECADE (÷10) UP/DOWN COUNTER
(Synchronous, Presettable)

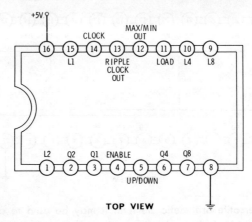

TOP VIEW

This is a synchronous decade counter that counts in either direction. One input clock is used.

For a normal up-counting sequence, Load should be high, Enable should be low, Up/Down should be low.

The counter advances one count on each ground-to-positive transition of the input clock. Outputs Q1, Q2, Q4, and Q8 are weighted 1-2-4-8 BCD. The clock must be noise free.

To count down, the Up/Down input is made high.

To load, the desired word is placed on Load inputs L1, L2, L4, and L8, and the Load input is briefly brought low. There is no separate Clear input; to clear the counter, load all zeros.

The ripple clock output can be used for cascading, along with the Max/Min output gating. Refer to data sheet for more information about applications.

Maximum counting frequency .... 20 megahertz

Current per package .... 65 milliamperes

BINARY (÷16) UP/DOWN COUNTER
(Synchronous, Presettable)

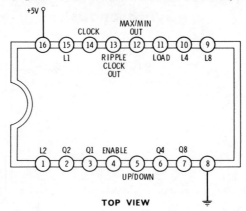

TOP VIEW

This is a synchronous binary (base-16) counter that counts in either direction. One input clock is used.

For a normal up-counting sequence, Load should be high, Enable should be low, Up/Down should be low.

The counter advances one count on each ground-to-positive transition of the input clock. Outputs Q1, Q2, Q4, and Q8 are weighted 1-2-4-8 binarily. The clock must be conditioned to be bounceless and noise free.

To count down, the Up/Down input is made high.

To load, the desired word is placed on Load inputs L1, L2, L4, L8 and the Load input is briefly brought low. There is no separate Clear input. To clear the counter, load all zeros.

The ripple clock output can be used for cascading, along with the Max/Min output gating. Refer to data sheet for more information about applications.

Maximum counting frequency .... 20 megahertz

Current per package .... 65 milliamperes

DECADE (÷10) UP/DOWN COUNTER
(Carry, Borrow, Presettable, Synchronous)

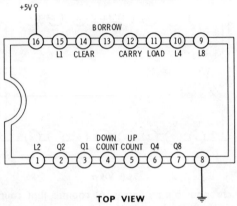

TOP VIEW

This is a synchronous decade (base-10) counter that counts in either direction. Two input clocks are used, and stages are Carry/Borrow cascaded.

For a normal up-counting sequence, Load should be high, and Clear should be low.

The counter advances one count on each ground-to-positive transition of the Up-Count input clock. It backs up one count on each ground-to-positive transition of the Down Count input clock. When up-counting, hold the Down-Count input high. When down-counting, hold the Up-Count input high.

To load, the desired word is placed on Load inputs L1, L2, L4, and L8. The Load input is then briefly brought low. To clear the counter, the Clear input is briefly made *positive*. Note that the Clear must be low for normal counting.

Stages are cascaded by connecting Carry to Up Count and Borrow to Down Count. See Chapter 6. For more details, consult data sheet.

Maximum operating frequency .... 32 megahertz

Current per package .... 65 milliamperes

5-VOLT, 750-mA REGULATOR

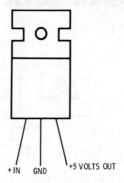

+ IN   GND   +5 VOLTS OUT

This voltage regulator is recommended for TTL supplies to 750 milliamperes.

It must have a heat sink for high currents. The minimum applied supply voltage at a ripple trough and low line voltage must be more than 7 volts. The maximum applied supply voltage at a ripple peak and high line voltage must be less than 12 volts.

A 1-microfarad, high-quality tantalum capacitor should be placed from output to ground for stability. Fig. 1-5 shows a suitable circuit.

Standby current drain .... 5 milliamperes

DM8093
(74125)

QUAD TRI-STATE DRIVER (Low Enable)

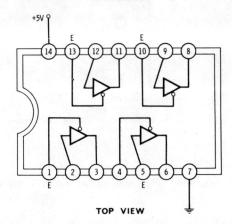

TOP VIEW

The package contains four separate drivers that may be used independently.

Unlike regular TTL, this package has three possible output states—an output-low, an output-high, and an open-circuit that presents no load either to positive or ground on the output line.

If the Tri-State Control input is low, the input gets passed to the output without inversion. If the Tri-State Control is high, the output assumes an open-circuit condition. These types of circuits are covered in Chapter 3.

Propagation delay .... 10 nanoseconds

Enabling delay .... 6 nanoseconds

Package supply current .... 32 milliamperes

DM8094
(74126)

QUAD TRI-STATE DRIVER (High Enable)

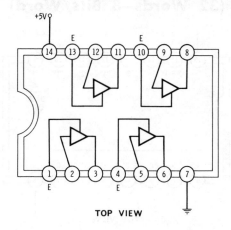

TOP VIEW

This package contains four separate drivers that may be used independently.

Unlike regular TTL, there are three possible output states—an output-low, an output-high, and an open-circuit that presents no load either to positive or ground on the output line.

If the Tri-State Enable input is *high,* the input gets passed to the output without inversion. If the Tri-State Enable is *low,* the output assumes an open-circuit condition. These types of circuits are covered in Chapter 3.

Propagation delay .... 10 nanoseconds

Enabling delay .... 10 nanoseconds

Package supply current .... 36 milliamperes

PROGRAMMABLE READ-ONLY MEMORY
(32 Words—8 Bits/Word)

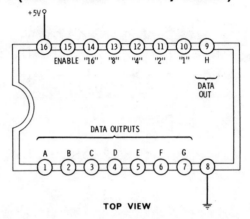

TOP VIEW

This device is a Read-Only Memory. It can be field programmed once to provide 32 different 8-bit words. See Chapter 3.

For a given input address, the word programmed at that address is output on the Data Output lines. The Enable input must be low to get an output. The memory is expanded to other packages by connecting identical outputs together and enabling only one package at a time.

ROMs may be used for random logic generation, to generate complex waveforms, or to provide a microprogrammed sequence of states. Refer to original data sheet for programming information and to Chapter 3 for more application details.

Response time .... 31 nanoseconds

Current per package .... 82 milliamperes

8280
(74176)

DECADE (÷10) COUNTER (Ripple, Presettable, not Unit-Cascadable)

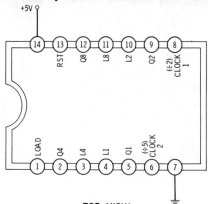

TOP VIEW

This is a divide-by-2 and a divide-by-5 counter in a single package. They may be used together as a divide-by-10 or separately. It ripple-counts in the BCD-up direction.

For a BCD counter, weighted 1-2-4-8, enter via Clock 1, and jumper Q1 to Clock 2. Outputs Q1, Q2, Q4, and Q8 will be BCD-weighted 1-2-4-8. The counter advances on the negative-going clock edge. The clock must be properly conditioned and made bounceless and noise free. If a conventional decade counter is needed, Load and Reset terminals should be held at +5 volts.

The counter may be reset to zero at any time by bringing the RST input briefly to ground. The counter may be loaded to any desired state by bringing the L1, L2, L4, and L8 Load terminals to the proper code and then briefly dropping the Load input to ground.

An external jumper must be provided between counter halves. If entry is via Clock 2 and Q8 is jumpered to Clock 1, a counter weighted 1-2-4-5 results with Q1 as the most significant output and a symmetrical square wave. More details on this device appear in Chapter 6. This circuit is not normally unit-cascadable.

Typical maximum toggle frequency .... 25 megahertz

Current per package .... 35 milliamperes

BINARY (÷16) COUNTER
(Ripple, Presettable)

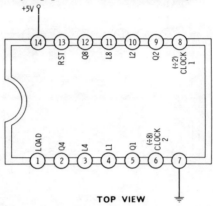

TOP VIEW

This is a divide-by-2 and a divide-by-8 counter in a single package. They may be used together as a divide-by-16 or separately. It ripple-counts in the up direction.

For a binary counter, weighted 1-2-4-8, enter via Clock 1 and jumper Q1 to Clock 2. Outputs Q1, Q2, Q4, and Q8 will be binary-weighted 1-2-4-8. The counter advances on the negative-going clock edge. The clock must be properly conditioned and made bounceless and noise free. If a conventional binary counter is needed, Load and Reset terminals should be held at +5 volts.

The counter may be reset to zero at any time by bringing the RST input briefly to ground. The counter may be loaded to any desired state by bringing the L1, L2, L4, and L8 Load terminals to the proper code and then briefly dropping the Load input to ground.

An external jumper must be provided between counter halves and normally is placed between Q1 and Clock 2. More details on this device appear in Chapter 6. This circuit is not normally unit-cascadable.

Typical maximum toggle frequency .... 25 megahertz

Current per package .... 35 milliamperes

8288

BASE-12 (÷12) COUNTER (Ripple, Presettable, not Unit-Cascadable)

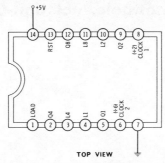

TOP VIEW

This is a divide-by-2 and a divide-by-6 counter in a single package. They may be used together as a divide-by-12 or separately. It ripple-counts in the up direction.

For a base-12 counter, weighted 1-2-4-8, enter via Clock 1 and jumper Q1 to Clock 2. Outputs Q1, Q2, Q4, and Q8 will be binary-weighted 1-2-4-8. The counter advances on the negative-going clock edge. The clock must be properly conditioned and made bounceless and noise free. If a conventional divide-by-12 is needed, Load and Reset terminals should be held at +5 volts.

The counter may be reset to zero at any time by bringing the RST input briefly to ground. The counter may be loaded to any desired state by bringing the L1, L2, L4, and L8 Load terminals to the proper code and then briefly dropping the Load input to ground.

An external jumper must be provided between counter halves and normally is placed between Q1 and Clock 2. More details on this device appear in Chapter 6. This circuit is not normally unit-cascadable.

Note that the Q8 output is low for the first eight counts and high for the last four. If entry is made via Clock 2 and Q8 is jumpered to Clock 1, an output will be obtained at Q1 that is high for six counts and low for six counts.

Typical maximum toggle frequency . . . . 25 megahertz

Current per package . . . . 35 milliamperes

8290
(74196)

DECADE (÷10) COUNTER, 50 MHz
(Ripple, Presettable, not Unit-Cascadable)

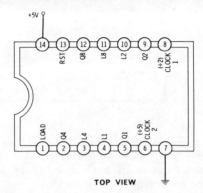

TOP VIEW

This is a divide-by-2 and a divide-by-5 counter in a single package. They may be used together as a divide-by-10 or separately. It ripple-counts in the BCD-up direction.

For a BCD counter, weighted 1-2-4-8, enter via Clock 1 and jumper Q1 to Clock 2. Outputs Q1, Q2, Q4, and Q8 will be BCD-weighted 1-2-4-8. The counter advances on the negative-going edge. The clock must be properly conditioned and made bounceless and noise free. If a conventional decade counter is needed, Load and Reset terminals should be held at +5 volts.

The counter may be reset to zero at any time by bringing the RST input briefly to ground. The counter may be loaded to any desired state by bringing the L1, L2, L4, and L8 Load Data terminals to the proper code and then briefly dropping the Load input to ground.

An external jumper must be provided between counter halves. Only the divide-by-2 can operate at 50 megahertz, so it *must be used first in high-speed applications.*

This package is similar to the 8280, except it is faster, consumes more power, costs more, and is more noise susceptible.

Typical maximum toggle frequency . . . . 50 megahertz

Current per package . . . . 48 milliamperes

8291
(74197)

BINARY (÷16) COUNTER, 50 MHz
(Ripple, Presettable, not Unit-Cascadable)

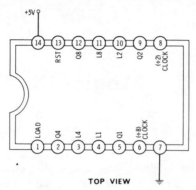

TOP VIEW

This is a divide-by-2 and a divide-by-8 counter in a single package. They may be used together as a divide-by-16 or separately. It ripple-counts in the binary-up direction.

For a binary counter, weighted 1-2-4-8, enter via Clock 1 and jumper Q1 to Clock 2. Outputs Q1, Q2, Q4, and Q8 will be binarily weighted 1-2-4-8. The counter advances on the negative-going clock edge. The clock must be properly conditioned and made bounceless and noise free. If a conventional binary counter is needed, Load and Reset terminals should be held at +5 volts.

The counter may be reset to zero at any time by bringing the RST input briefly to ground. The counter may be loaded to any desired state by bringing the L1, L2, L4, and L8 Load Data terminals to the proper code and then briefly dropping the Load input to ground.

An external jumper must be provided between counter halves. Only the divide-by-2 can operate at 50 megahertz, so *it must be used first in high-speed applications.*

This package is similar to the 8281, except it is faster, consumes more power, costs more, and is more susceptible to noise.

Typical maximum toggle frequency .... 50 megahertz

Current per package .... 48 milliamperes

CHAPTER 3

Logic

A *logic* circuit has digital inputs and digital outputs. The one or more outputs follow a rule or a set of rules that are determined by the conditions placed on the input leads and by the specific function desired of the circuit.

There are two basic types of logic. Circuits that respond immediately to changes in the inputs are called *direct* or *asynchronous* logic. Circuits that wait until a system-clocking pulse arrives are called *clocked, synchronous,* or *sequential* logic circuits. In this chapter, we will look at the direct logic techniques.

We will start with some simple 1-gate circuits and follow this up with a powerful logic trick that can save on system packages and connections. Then, we will examine some advanced logic design techniques. One is a medium-power tool called *data-selector logic.* A second is a heavyweight approach called *Read-Only Memory,* or ROM logic design. Both of these techniques are new methods that work directly with a state chart or *truth table* and immediately give workable results. Usually the result is a 1-package solution, low in cost, and easy to change. Best of all, design time with these techniques is measured in seconds rather than hours!

Finally, we will end up with two design examples: a code converter from 5-level Baudot teletype systems to modern ASCII 8-level computer teletype systems, and a keyboard encoder that will convert the single-make contacts of any keyboard into a complete 7- or 8-level computer-compatible ASCII code.

We will reserve the clocked or synchronous logic circuits for the chapters on clocked flip-flops, counters, and shift registers.

THE TWO-INPUT GATE AS A SIMPLE SWITCH

As an example of digital logic, suppose we wanted to turn a train of pulses off and on upon command. We could do this with any of the single-gate circuits of Fig. 3-1. In Fig. 3-1A, we use 1/4 of a 7400 NAND gate. If we ground the control input, the output stays high and the pulse train is blocked. If we make the control input positive, the output is an *inverted* replica of the input. Thus, our control line determines whether the pulse train is passed on by the gate.

One possible use of a circuit like this would be in the input of an electronic frequency counter. If we pass input pulses for exactly one second, the digital display will be the *frequency* of the input in hertz (cycles per second). If we pass pulses for only 1/10 of a second, the display will be 1/10 the frequency of the input, and so on. If we want only whole pulses out, a more complicated circuit is needed. The point is that we can use a gate as a simple logic switch to turn the output load on and off.

By using different gates, we can get different results. In Fig. 3-1B, a 7402 NOR gate is used. The output is still an inverted replica of the

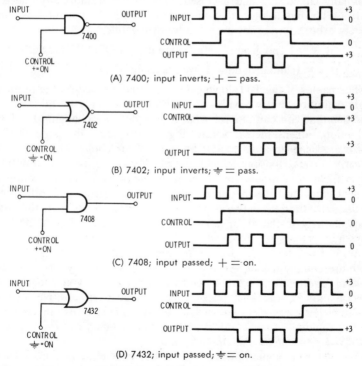

(A) 7400; input inverts; + = pass.

(B) 7402; input inverts; ⏚ = pass.

(C) 7408; input passed; + = on.

(D) 7432; input passed; ⏚ = on.

Fig. 3-1. Two-input gate used as switch.

input, only now a *grounded* control line *passes* the pulse train and a *positive* one *blocks*. In the blocked condition, the output is at ground. Figs. 3-1C and 3-1D are similar circuits that do not invert the pulse train.

STATE DEFINITIONS: WHAT IS A ZERO?

With digital logic, we have a choice of definitions. Any input, and most logic outputs, normally will have two possible conditions. With regular TTL, a positive-output state somewhere between 2.4 and 5 volts holds the output load positive, or a low or grounded state holds the load within a few tenths of a volt of ground and is capable of absorbing or sinking considerable current. A TTL input either can be held positive above 2.4 volts or can be pulled to ground and have current removed from it. The usual TTL gate can sink 16 mA in the low-output state. A gate input normally needs 1.6 mA, so the output of one gate can drive 10 inputs.

We usually call one state a "1" and the other one a "0." We have a choice. With relays and older circuits, an open contact was traditionally called a 0 and a closed contact was traditionally called a 1. But with digital logic, the choice (except for the benefits) is completely arbitrary, as shown by the following rules:

If + = 1 and ground = 0, we are using POSITIVE logic.

If + = 0 and ground = 1, we are using NEGATIVE logic.

The names of the TTL logic gates are usually based on the *positive*-logic definition, but we will see that both are equally useful. We will also see that you can change what a gate does by changing the logic definition. For instance, a positive-logic NAND gate is the same piece of hardware as a negative logic NOR gate. Your choice of positive- or negative-logic definition depends on which way the inputs and outputs are defined, and which way economizes on parts, or allows combination of gates into the minimum number of packages. It is often convenient to alternate between positive and negative logic in the same system, because the cheaper and simpler TTL gates invert the logic anyway.

With TTL, the positive-logic definition tends to predominate, but both are equally useful. As a general rule, if you find yourself adding several inverters and extra gates to a circuit, or if you end up with several unused fractional packages, a change from positive logic to negative logic or vice versa will often simplify the overall circuitry.

The logic is independent of the state definitions, but the device is 100% dependent on the state definitions.

Let us turn to some of the more popular logic circuits, remembering that they can be built either as positive- or negative-logic circuits, but that the choice of TTL components will change with the choice of logic definition. In any system, positive logic, all negative logic, or a mixture of the two can result in the simplest overall circuitry, and all possibilities should be checked.

ONE-INPUT LOGIC

Suppose that we have a logic device with one input and one output and that we require that the output always obeys some rule relating to the input in deciding what the output will be. We will further require that it changes its output immediately after the input does and without regard to the history of the input and output. With these restrictions, there are only four possible circuits of this type, as shown in Fig. 3-2.

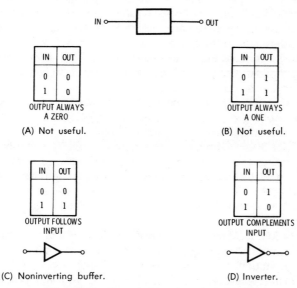

IN	OUT
0	0
1	0

OUTPUT ALWAYS
A ZERO

(A) Not useful.

IN	OUT
0	1
1	1

OUTPUT ALWAYS
A ONE

(B) Not useful.

IN	OUT
0	0
1	1

OUTPUT FOLLOWS
INPUT

(C) Noninverting buffer.

IN	OUT
0	1
1	0

OUTPUT COMPLEMENTS
INPUT

(D) Inverter.

Fig. 3-2. The four possible 1-input logic blocks.

Beside each circuit, Fig. 3-2 shows a state chart that indicates the output we can expect for all possible combinations of all possible inputs. This is called a *truth table*. It is very simple for 1-input logic, for there is only one input, which can have only two states—0 or 1.

In Fig. 3-2A, we always get a 0 out. This is not very useful. In Fig. 3-2B, we always get a 1 out. This is also worthless, for both these circuits ignore the input.

In Fig. 3-2C, we get a 1 out if the input is a 1 and a 0 out if the input is a 0. While this does not seem useful either, it can have a number of system uses. For instance, we can increase the drive level or increase the fan-out. Or we can interface with the outside world or another logic family. With some feedback, we can use it as a snap-action circuit or a rise-time improver. And finally, in high-speed systems, we may be able to use the inherent tens of nanoseconds of internal delay to make sure that timing signals end up in the right sequence and do not get ahead of each other. While logically useless, this circuit, called a *noninverting buffer,* can be handy in several ways.

Fig. 3-2D is the only circuit of the four that performs a logically useful task. It puts out a 0 if the input is a 1 and a 1 if the input is a 0. It is called an *inverter.*

Inverters are used to generate the *complement* of an input signal. Two inverters back-to-back form a simple latch with two stable states. Inverters may be used to change from positive to negative logic definitions. One capacitor and one or two resistors in front of an inverter form a simple pulser to detect either the rising or falling edge of a waveform. Three or more cascaded inverters form a high-frequency oscillator whose rate may be easily controlled. And, we can use inverters just as noninverting buffers to increase the system drive level, add delay, improve rise time, obtain snap-action, or interface with the outside world or some other logic family.

Inverters often come six per package. The 7404 is a typical example. Three open-collector versions also exist, the 7405, 7416, and 7406. These latter three devices lack an internal pull-up mechanism and can have 5, 15, or 30 volts applied to their output collectors without damage. This makes them useful for driving outside-world signals, D/A conversion, and translating to a new logic family or other circuit.

TWO-INPUT LOGIC

The situation becomes more interesting when we add a second input to the logic block. Now there are four possible input conditions (00, 01, 10, 11), and our truth table has four possible places on the output side of the chart where we could put a 1 or a 0. We could look at these four possible places, "vertically" as a 4-bit binary word. There are then apparently 16 possible truth tables for the 2-input logic block. Six are trivial or worthless. Six are common and used extensively. The remaining four are specialized but can solve a particular logic problem.

Fig. 3-3 shows the six trivial states. As with the inverter, the all-1's and all-0's outputs have little value. The remaining four ignore one input and provide either the other input or its complement as an output. What this does is degenerate a 2-input logic block into a 1-input one. This lets us provide the inverter or the noninverting buffer functions with part of a remaining 2-or-more input gate and can save us packages in a total circuit. Fig. 3-4 shows various ways we can convert

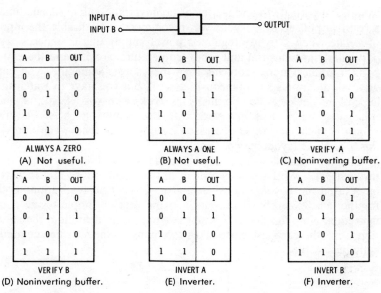

A	B	OUT
0	0	0
0	1	0
1	0	0
1	1	0

ALWAYS A ZERO
(A) Not useful.

A	B	OUT
0	0	1
0	1	1
1	0	1
1	1	1

ALWAYS A ONE
(B) Not useful.

A	B	OUT
0	0	0
0	1	0
1	0	1
1	1	1

VERIFY A
(C) Noninverting buffer.

A	B	OUT
0	0	0
0	1	1
1	0	0
1	1	1

VERIFY B
(D) Noninverting buffer.

A	B	OUT
0	0	1
0	1	1
1	0	0
1	1	0

INVERT A
(E) Inverter.

A	B	OUT
0	0	1
0	1	0
1	0	1
1	1	0

INVERT B
(F) Inverter.

Fig. 3-3. There are 16 possible 2-input logic gates. These 6 are trivial possibilities.

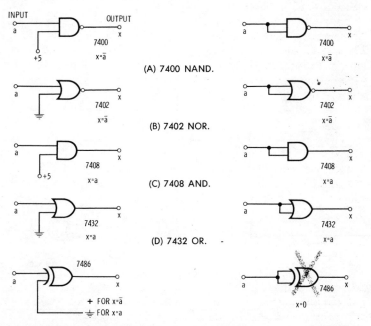

(A) 7400 NAND.

(B) 7402 NOR.

(C) 7408 AND.

(D) 7432 OR.

(E) 7486 EXCL OR. May be used either as an inverter or as a noninverting buffer.

Fig. 3-4. Inverters or buffers can be made from multiple-input gates with these typical circuits.

from a 2-input gate to an inverter or noninverting buffer. At one time, a resistive pull-up to +5 volts was recommended to disable the input of a gate. With a tightly regulated power supply this is unnecessary, particularly in industrial and room-temperature circuits, and the extra parts introduce more problems than they solve. Sometimes you can drive all the inputs simultaneously as well, but you have to watch the logic of the device as you do this. This works with AND, NAND, OR, and NOR gates, but it does *not* work with EXCLUSIVE OR gates. Fan-out from the signal source is decreased by one input load when you do this, but the pc layout may be simpler.

The most useful 2-input logic functions are shown in Figs. 3-5 through 3-12. We have shown them in truth-table form, and then we have listed the possible positive- and negative-logic realizations both for the least-expensive TTL gate and the best or simplest gate configuration. Note that if we choose the wrong logic definition, the solution using the cheapest parts takes too many of them to be economically reasonable.

A	B	X
0	0	0
0	1	1
1	0	1
1	1	1

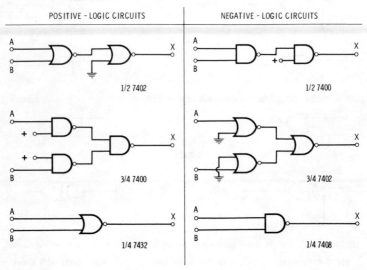

Fig. 3-5. The OR gate.

These circuits are called the OR, the NOR, the AND, the NAND, the correlator or EXCLUSIVE NOR, and the EXCLUSIVE OR circuit.

The OR circuit of Fig. 3-5 provides a 1 out if either or both inputs are 1's and a 0 out if both inputs are 0's. The OR circuit normally is used if you want to detect or use the presence of *any* input. The NOR circuit of Fig. 3-6 does the opposite—the presence of *any* input drives

A	B	X
0	0	1
0	1	0
1	0	0
1	1	0

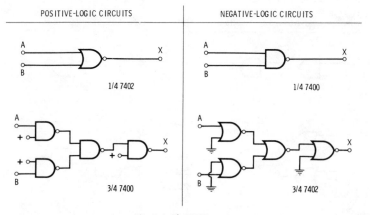

Fig. 3-6. The NOR gate.

the output to ground. Generally, the inverting logic gates either take less hardware or have less circuitry inside the package—therefore, they are preferred for system design to save cost and power. Thus, the NOR and the upcoming NAND functions are preferrable to the AND and OR in TTL systems design.

The AND gate appears in Fig. 3-7. It is used to detect the coincidence or presence of 1's on *both* inputs. The NAND gate of Fig. 3-8 is the complementary device—it provides a 0 out for a coincident pair of 1's on the input. Note that there are at least three good ways to realize most of these logic functions. They may be built out of 7400 NAND gate parts, out of 7402 NOR gate parts, or out of fancier 7400 ICs that directly realize the desired function. Note further that the choice of whether to use a 7400 or 7402 is usually clear—one will be more complicated in the final circuit. The chosen route depends on the economics of the circuit and the remaining unused parts from other logic in the system.

The EXCLUSIVE OR gate of Fig. 3-9 is more complex than the common AND, NAND, OR, and NOR functions and has a number of useful

A	B	X
0	0	0
0	1	0
1	0	0
1	1	1

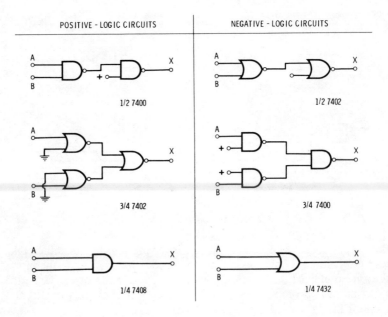

Fig. 3-7. The AND gate.

and interesting applications. It provides a 1 out if only *one* input is 1. Looking at it slightly differently, it gives a 0 out if the inputs are *identical* and a 1 out if the inputs are *different*.

The EXCLUSIVE OR gate is extremely versatile, as the variety of different ways of applying this device (Fig. 3-10) indicate.

In Fig. 3-10A, the gate is treated as a controllable complementer. On command it will either invert a logic signal to be controlled or else pass it on noninverted. If the control is a 0, the output follows the input. If the control is a 1, the output complements the input. In Fig. 3-10B, the EXCLUSIVE OR is used as a dc to ac converter, a function that is particularly handy in liquid-crystal displays, motor controls, and some instrumentation circuits. A square wave that is equal in amplitude to both the supply voltage (usually 5 volts with TTL) and the

A	B	X
0	0	1
0	1	1
1	0	1
1	1	0

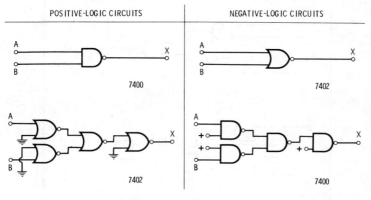

Fig. 3-8. The NAND gate.

zero-to-peak needs of the load resistor is applied to both one side of the load and one of the OR gates. If the other input to the EXCLUSIVE OR gate is a 0, the square wave at the output of the EXCLUSIVE OR gate will be identical to the source, and the same square wave will be applied to both sides of the load. The net load voltage will be zero since the voltages on both sides of the load go up and down together. Thus, a logic 0 at the input puts zero voltage on the load. Now, if a logic 1 is the input, the square wave is inverted going through the gate. Its output will be out of phase with the original square wave, and the full supply power will appear across the load, alternating in polarity each cycle. Note that the peak-to-peak load voltage will equal *twice* the supply voltage, for if you monitor one end of the load resistor, the other end is first made positive by the supply voltage and then is made negative by the same amount.

Fig. 3-10C shows the traditional use of an EXCLUSIVE OR gate—as a binary adder. The rules of binary addition (Chart 3-1) are statements that are identical to those in the EXCLUSIVE OR truth table. We apply two inputs A and B, and the sum appears as an output. This is called a *half adder,* because we have neither generated a carry nor

A	B	X
0	0	0
0	1	1
1	0	1
1	1	0

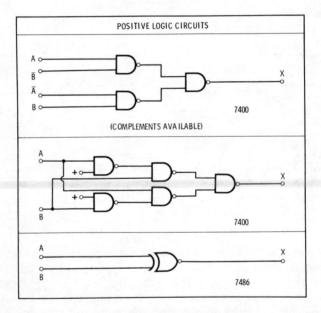

Fig. 3-9. The EXCLUSIVE OR gate.

allowed for the carry from the lower stage. To build a *full adder,* you sum A and B and derive an output. This output is then summed with a possible carry from the previous stage, and the main output is formed. The generation of a new carry is accomplished by ANDing the A and B inputs, ANDing the *carry* in and A and B outputs, and ORing the two possible carry sources. The circuits for one possible half adder and a full adder appear in Fig. 3-11.

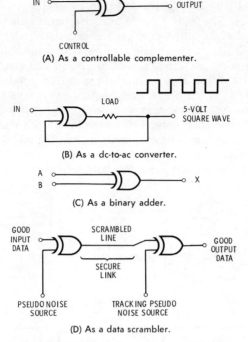

(A) As a controllable complementer.

(B) As a dc-to-ac converter.

(C) As a binary adder.

(D) As a data scrambler.

Fig. 3-10. The EXCLUSIVE OR gate is extremely versatile. Here are some typical applications.

EXCLUSIVE OR gates are often combined into larger standard circuits. It is common to add at least four binary bits at a time in a system, or else to work with cascaded 4-bit *bytes* of an 8-, 12-, or 16-bit *word*. Thus a 4-bit full adder is a versatile device and is available as the 7483. More complex addition, along with other shifting and housekeeping functions are handled by a more elaborate unit, the 74181. Another use for cascaded EXCLUSIVE OR gates is as a *parity* generator or checker. The cascaded gates can tell whether the total number of 1's in a digital word is *even* or *odd*. By tacking a new 1 or 0 onto the input, you can transmit words that are always even parity, or else that are always odd parity. If the parity is rechecked at the other end of the system and is *different* from what you sent, a transmission error has

Chart 3-1. Rules of Binary Addition

$0 + 0 = 0$
$0 + 1 = 1$
$1 + 0 = 1$
$1 + 1 = 0$, plus carry 1

been made. Parity is a simple and highly useful way of error testing and indication. The 74180 is one available parity generator.

A final use of EXCLUSIVE OR gates is as a data coder or scrambler, as Fig. 3-10D shows. Good data is mixed with a random stream of 1's and 0's from a pseudo-random noise generator and combined with an EXCLUSIVE OR circuit to form a chain of mixed good and bad data. This is transmitted. At the far end, another EXCLUSIVE OR gate driven from the same pseudo-random noise source, or a copy of it that is in sync, extracts the good data. The reason for all this elaborate mixing is security and secrecy—unscrambling data in the middle is very difficult. The circuitry finds use in cryptography, electronic locks, and security measures for computer data banks.

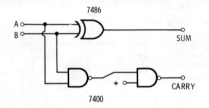

B	A	SUM	CARRY
0	0	0	0
0	1	1	0
1	0	1	0
1	1	0	1

(A) Half adder.

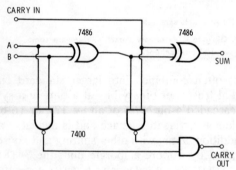

C_{in}	B	A	SUM	C_{out}
0	0	0	0	0
0	0	1	1	0
0	1	0	1	0
0	1	1	0	1
1	0	0	1	0
1	0	1	0	1
1	1	0	0	1
1	1	1	1	1

(B) Full adder.

Fig. 3-11. EXCLUSIVE OR circuits used in binary addition.

Fig. 3-2 is the EXCLUSIVE NOR circuit, otherwise known as a *correlator*. It puts out a 1 if the inputs are identical and a 0 if they are different. When cascaded with an AND gate, the correlator can compare all the bits of a pair of words and provide an output if they are identical. One elaborate version is the 7485, which contains four correlator gates and some support logic.

Correlators and EXCLUSIVE OR gates are also used in various forms of code generation and sequence setups. A *Barker code* is one possibility. Another is the *Pseudo Random Sequence* (see Chapter 7).

A	B	X
0	0	1
0	1	0
1	0	0
1	1	1

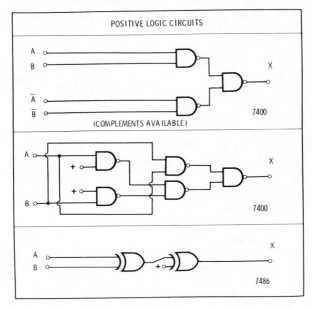

Fig. 3-12. The EXCLUSIVE NOR gate.

OTHER TWO-INPUT LOGIC FUNCTIONS

The remaining four 2-input logic functions are shown in Fig. 3-13. While they are theoretically just as useful as the previous six functions, they simply are not used as much and do not have common names. They are A AND $\overline{B}$, B AND $\overline{A}$, $\overline{A}$ AND B, and $\overline{B}$ AND A. Note that one variable is always inverted with respect to the other. You can work up the circuits of these four functions on your own as an exercise.

THREE AND MORE INPUTS

The number of possible logic functions for three and more inputs becomes astronomical. There are eight possible states of a 3-input asynchronous gate. Thus, there are apparently 2^8, or 256, different truth tables you can write. For a 4-input gate, there are 2^{16} possibilities, or 65536. And for people who like big numbers, the 5-input gates number 4,294,967,296.

Obviously many of these see little use. What generally happens is that the common AND, OR, NAND, and NOR functions carry over to the larger numbers of inputs, with 3-, 4-, and 8-input NAND circuits being common. Other many-input systems go by their functional names, like an 8-position data selector, a BCD-to-Binary converter, a Decimal Decoder/Driver, a True-Complement element, and so on.

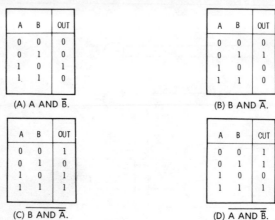

A	B	OUT
0	0	0
0	1	0
1	0	1
1	1	0

(A) A AND $\bar{B}$.

A	B	OUT
0	0	0
0	1	1
1	0	0
1	1	0

(B) B AND $\bar{A}$.

A	B	OUT
0	0	1
0	1	0
1	0	1
1	1	1

(C) $\overline{B \text{ AND } \bar{A}}$.

A	B	OUT
0	0	1
0	1	1
1	0	0
1	1	1

(D) $\overline{A \text{ AND } \bar{B}}$.

Fig. 3-13. The remaining 2-input logic functions are workable but seldom used.

Some older logic families made extensive use of *Gate Expanders* that let you arbitrarily extend certain logic functions to any reasonable number of inputs. While one or two TTL gates are expandable, this is neither a common nor a popular practice. With TTL, you are usually limited to what is available in package form. For instance, a 24-input AND gate is obtained by cascading three 8-input NAND gates with a 4-input *negative logic* NAND gate and disabling the one unused input. Generally speaking, logic that is this complex is almost never needed. If an excessive amount of hardware appears to be required, often rethinking the problem will allow the use of one falling edge somewhere, or preloading a number or changing some other factor will eliminate the complexity through a different approach to the problem. The rule is simple—if the logic you are about to use seems unwieldy or complex, stop and try to find a different way to do the same thing. This almost always works.

A TRICK CALLED DEMORGAN'S THEOREM

We can easily change what a TTL device does by changing our logic definitions. This simple and powerful logic trick can greatly reduce system complexity if it is properly used; almost always it will simplify circuitry. The rules for logic conversion are as follows:

A positive logic AND	is a negative logic OR
A positive logic NAND	is a negative logic NOR
A positive logic OR	is a negative logic AND
A positive logic NOR	is a negative logic NAND
A positive logic EXCLUSIVE OR	is a negative logic EXCLUSIVE NOR
A positive logic EXCLUSIVE NOR	is a negative logic EXCLUSIVE OR

Inverters are independent of logic definition.

These rules may seem hard to believe until you go back to the truth tables and substitute 1's for 0's and see what the hardware does. Thus, a 7400 is a NOR gate—if you are using negative logic. A 7402 is a NAND gate—if you are using negative logic. Remember that the title in the catalog of a TTL component is its *positive logic* function. It will do other things for you if you change the logic definition.

The usual trick is to use inverting logic and change the definition with each successive stage. Thus, the first logic stages might be positive logic. Since their outputs invert, there is negative logic on the next successive stage, and so on. Remember that both positive and negative logic definitions are equally useful, and that the proper combination of both in a system will usually drastically simplify the overall circuitry.

OPEN-COLLECTOR LOGIC

Some TTL gates are available with open-collector outputs. These may be safely connected to other open-collector output gates to perform additional logic provided one pull-up resistor, typically 2.2K, is included. This is sometimes called the WIRED OR or IMPLIED OR connection and, while free, it is not really as handy as you might suspect. With ordinary TTL gates, there is a totem-pole output structure. The gate either pulls the output high or pulls the output low. Put two outputs together and you can have a fight if one of them decides 0 and the other decides 1. The output logic would be indeterminate, supply power would be excessive, and one of the devices might be destroyed. On the other hand, if you tie one load resistor to +5 volts and attach as many open-collector gates as you want, the gates can only pull the output down, not up. Only when none of the gates are pulling down does the load resistor swing positive. Thus, we have a positive-logic NOR function, and it is apparently free.

While this works nicely with such things as a 7405, which is an open-circuit hex inverter and can give us a 6-input NOR gate, it is easy to get in trouble if the same thing is tried with NAND logic. For instance, tying four 7401 open-collector NAND outputs together would work, but the logic would be (A and B) OR (C and D) OR (E and F) OR

$(\overline{G \text{ and } H})$, instead of the simpler 8-input NAND or NOR you may have expected to get. The wired or implied OR function is primarily useful for expanding positive-logic NOR or negative-logic NAND functions. It always provides a NOR combination for positive logic, regardless of what happens previously inside the gate.

Two open-collector logic circuits are shown in Fig. 3-14.

System designers do not like open-collector logic for several reasons that become important if lots of ICs are in use. First, there is an increased noise problem. Second, system speed can suffer, as a pull-up resistor cannot hope to be as fast as an active totem-pole output

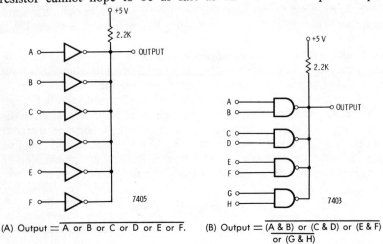

(A) Output = $\overline{\text{A or B or C or D or E or F}}$.

(B) Output = $\overline{\text{(A \& B) or (C \& D) or (E \& F)}\atop\text{or (G \& H)}}$

Fig. 3-14. Examples of the "wired NOR" function of open-collector TTL logic.

pull-up. Third, and worst of all, there is no reasonable way to service a point that has several open-collector gates tied to it. If one gate is defective, the entire circuit appears defective. There is no easy, reasonable way to find the faulty part—short of a lot of foil cutting, device removal, or wire unwrapping. For larger systems, Tri-State Logic is recommended to overcome these problems, but at a somewhat higher price and with either larger packages or fewer functions per packages.

Open-collector logic is a neat trick that only rarely can be used—and then on systems that are inherently simple or small.

Incidentally, there is a possibility for creative logic expansion by gating the ground line to an entire IC package. For instance, if you lifted the ground off a 7400 gate, you would have four 3-input logic gates in a single package, because to get the output to go to ground, the package ground would have to be present and both inputs would have to be positive. Obviously, the four functions will have one common logic line—the one controlling the package ground. This can simplify things, but it takes careful consideration of what is going on inside the package. Also, higher-power devices are normally needed to control an entire package at once. Simply running a whole package through the open collector of another one generally is very bad practice.

As an example, if you wanted to enable 12 lines simultaneously, you could do this normally with three gate packages, or else you could use two hex inverters and key the ground line. Since TTL is a current-sinking logic, removing the supply power is *not* the same as a grounded output. To get an output-low state (positive-logic 0), you must provide a low-impedance current path to ground. This technique is handy sometimes, particularly in small systems, but you have to be very careful how you use it.

TRI-STATE LOGIC

To overcome the limitations of open-collector logic, such as limited speed, poor noise immunity, and difficulty of servicing, Tri-State logic was invented. National Semiconductor has been responsible for much of the development and application of Tri-State logic. It has turned out to be a very powerful tool for any application where many logic gates have to "talk" to each other over a common "party line" or *system buss.* One obvious application is in minicomputers where any number of input and control devices must be able to selectively talk to each other in any combination, over a single group of buss rails.

The third state in Tri-State logic is an *open circuit.* It is not a level halfway up, nor does it have anything to do with 3-input gates or majority logic. Any Tri-State device has an output enable control. With the enable control activated, the output behaves as an ordinary TTL gate, either with active totem-pole pull-up for a logic 1 (positive logic) and current-sinking pull-down for a logic 0. In the third state, the internal circuitry is essentially *disconnected* from the output. The output is then free to assume any value it likes, and the integrated circuit is essentially *transparent* to anything connected to the output.

Fig. 3-15 shows two applications in Tri-State logic. In the first (Fig. 3-15A) we can use the enable controls on Tri-State packages to replace several data selectors. Suppose we have four lines that are to obtain digital data from any of four possible sources. Done traditionally, this would take two dual 4-input data selectors. Each selector would be taught with a 4-state code (00, 01, 10, 11) which input to select. With Tri-State logic, we simply short four outputs together and then selectively enable only that output we want to use. The three outputs not selected are essentially transparent to the output, pulling it neither up nor down. Of course, we have to be careful to enable only one output at a time, but this is what Tri-State is all about. Enabling two at a time would be the same as shorting conventional TTL.

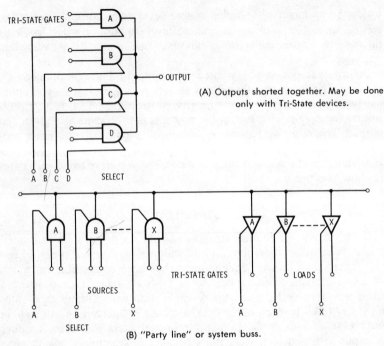

(A) Outputs shorted together. May be done only with Tri-State devices.

(B) "Party line" or system buss.

Fig. 3-15. Using Tri-State logic to simplify system connections.

If the source of the logic signals can be converted to Tri-State, the operation is essentially free, and we have replaced a group of data selectors with nothing. The only price paid is a small one—Tri State gates cost slightly more than regular ones, are available in fewer functions, and take either a larger package or fewer functions per package to make room for the enable commands.

In Fig. 3-15B, we have a buss-oriented system, such as is typical of a minicomputer. Here, any one of the devices can talk to any other one over the same line, provided, of course, that only one source is enabled at a time.

The hallmarks of the Tri-State system are its use to eliminate selectors, to combine signals, or to build a buss-oriented system. Tri-State logic is normally reserved for only these applications and normal logic should be used elsewhere. The rule is that Tri-State logic solves a number of design problems, but you do not use it where you do not need it.

ADVANCED LOGIC DESIGN: DATA-SELECTOR LOGIC

We will look at some logic design examples shortly and try to formulate a set of rules of logic design. Generally, for a simple logic task, you pick the few TTL devices needed to provide the function. If the task is more complex, a standard piece of MSI may do the job or be readily adapted to do the job. For very complicated tasks, several advanced logic techniques are available to solve the problem.

In the past, standard procedure was to learn all about Boolean Algebra, minimization techniques, subsets, Karnaugh mapping, and related time-consuming horrors. After hours of labor, the end product was a circuit that was "minimum" in a sense of using the minimum possible number of gates.

Today this approach is no longer reasonable. A logic problem should be solved in the least possible time, using the most reasonable combination of TTL packages to get the job done. Preferably, it should be easy to alter, unlike the complex logically minimum network of the past that required extensive reworking. The name of the game is changed; today you use the simplest and most direct method to get the job done.

There are two 1-package solutions to any logic design problem, and the design time is measured in seconds with either technique. One is a middleweight technique called *data-selector logic*. The second is a heavyweight block buster, called *Read-Only Memory* logic. A third technique, called *programmable logic arrays* also exists, but it is reserved for special problems and is not readily available to the average designer.

A *data selector* is a TTL version of a one-way selector switch. On proper command, it routes a selected input to its own output line. It is normally used to sequentially sample a number of logic inputs. You can get four SPDT units per package (74157), two 4-position selectors (74153), one 8-position selector (74152), and, finally, one 16-position data selector (74150). This last circuit, being a little more complex, requires a 24-pin package.

An obvious way to use data selectors is to put 1's and 0's where they are needed on the inputs to directly generate the logic truth table. The *select lines* become the logic inputs, and the output goes to the proper position for each combination of inputs and picks a 1 or a 0 as called for in the truth table.

A nonobvious way to obtain the same result, with only half the hardware is to apply a 1, a 0, a new variable, or the complement of that new variable to each successive input. The only restriction here is that one of the logic inputs must have its complement available for the majority of truth tables.

With this "folding" technique, you can realize one function of four variables with one 8-position data selector. In this manner, any desirable logic function can be achieved in a single-package solution. What is even better is that it will always work, it is easy to change, and it takes only seconds to design.

The best way to show the process is with an example. Suppose we had four variables as inputs and we wanted the truth table shown in Fig. 3-16.

At first inspection, there is no apparently reasonable way to obtain a single-package solution to this truth table by conventional means. But, with data selector logic, the results are obvious and instantaneous. All it takes is a single 8-position data selector.

D	C	B	A	OUT
0	0	0	0	0
0	0	0	1	1
0	0	1	0	1
0	0	1	1	0
0	1	0	0	0
0	1	0	1	1
0	1	1	0	1
0	1	1	1	0
1	0	0	0	1
1	0	0	1	0
1	0	1	0	1
1	0	1	1	0
1	1	0	0	1
1	1	0	1	1
1	1	1	0	0
1	1	1	1	0

Fig. 3-16. Truth table for problem stated in the text.

Of course, a 16-position data selector could be used instead. We connect A to the 1 Select logic line, B to the 2 Select logic line, C to the 4 Select logic line, and D to the 8 Select logic line. The data selector then sequentially scans the truth table, and all we do is put the desired output at each input sample point, or a 0-1-1-0-0-1-1-0-1-0-1-0-1-1-0-0. The circuit is shown in Fig. 3-17A.

Even with the obvious solution, we end up with one package and an instant design that changes as quickly as you can write down your truth table. Let us now consider the "folding" technique that needs only a half-size data selector.

Suppose we use the A, B, and C lines to step an 8-position data selector and temporarily set aside input D. We then look at our truth table and check *pairs* of entries with identical A, B, and C values.

Starting at the top, 0-(000) is a 0, while 1-(000) is a 1 on our particular truth table. Evidently we need an output that is a 1 when D is a 1 and a 0 when D is a 0, so we connect D to this input. This takes care of two states in the truth table.

We continue. 0-(001) is a 1, while 1-(001) is a 0. Here, we need a 0 when D is a 1 and vice versa, so we connect the complement of D, or $\overline{D}$, to the input corresponding to C = 0, B = 0, A = 1. And two more states of the truth table are resolved.

Going on further, the (010) state is a 1 output regardless of D, and the (011) state is a 0 regardless of D, so we put a 1 and a 0 on these respective inputs.

We go on down the list, checking each pair of truth-table entries, providing either 0, 1, D, or $\overline{D}$ as inputs to generate the entire truth table. The final circuit appears in Fig. 3-17B.

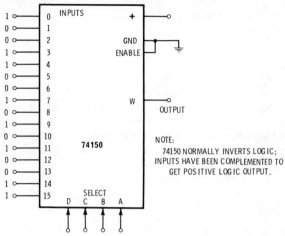

(A) Direct solution (obvious method).

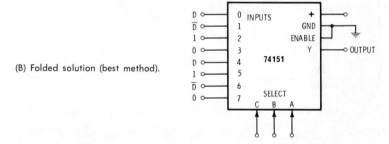

(B) Folded solution (best method).

Fig. 3-17. Data selector logic solutions to problems.

Had the truth table been different, the position and combination of 1, 0, D, and $\overline{D}$ on the inputs would be redistributed. Thus any truth table is equally easy to do this way.

The design rules are simple. You write down the truth table. Then you pick a data selector having *one less* position logic line than you have variables in your truth table. You then look at the truth table and apply the 1, 0, D, or $\overline{D}$ to the right inputs. To make any changes, just change the truth table and repeat the process. Any medium-sized logic problem should take less than 30 seconds this way.

You use data-selector logic if the complexity of the problem is such that a 1-package or a 2-package "gates only" solution to the logic problem will not work, or if you find yourself spending a lot of design time on a system that probably will be changed later. Cost is another factor. Sometimes it is a comparison of IC prices, with data selectors costing more than simple gates. Most of the time, the extra design time, extra pc board space, and extra installation costs of the conventional system make the data-selector route attractive. Obviously, if the logic is simple enough to be handled with a basic NAND or NOR gate or perhaps two packages, the conventional route is better; above this, consider this powerful advanced-logic technique.

In summary, a logic block with a tremendous amount of *redundancy* has been limited to performing only the specific task desired. This solution is by no means logically "minimum," in that it can handle all possible logic problems. But a "minimum" solution takes more parts and more design time, is difficult to change, and costs more.

The number of functions that can be obtained per package is shown in Table 3-1.

For logic designs above five inputs or with a number of different outputs, we have to consider a stronger tool, the Read-Only Memory.

Table 3-1. Data-Selector Logic

Input Variables	Selector Positions per Output	Packages per Output
2	2	¼
3	4	½
4	8	1
5	16	1*
6	32	2*
7	64	4*

*24-pin package.

ADVANCED LOGIC DESIGN: THE READ-ONLY MEMORY

For major design problems, perhaps eight outputs of six variables each, we can use a group of ICs called Read-Only Memories, or ROMs. A Read-Only Memory is a *table look-up* type of device. A truth table is decided upon and then the initially blank memory is "taught" the needed truth table. This teaching process can be done by the manufacturer with a masking step for volume use, or it can be done in the field either by yourself or with any of the programming services available at many electronic distributors. Chart 3-2 lists some of the leading Read-Only-Memory manufacturers and one source of programming machines.

A ROM can be thought of as a universal logic block with A inputs and B outputs. For each unique combination of A inputs, a selected

Chart 3-2. Some Read-Only-Memory Manufacturers

Circuits:

Harris Semiconductor Box 883 Melbourne, Florida 32901	Motorola Semiconductor Products Box 20912 Phoenix, Arizona 85036
Intel Corp. 3065 Bower Avenue Santa Clara, California 95051	National Semiconductor Corp. 2900 Semiconductor Drive Santa Clara, California 95051
Intersil, Inc. 10900 N. Tantau Avenue Cupertino, California 95014	Signetics 811 East Arques Avenue Sunnyvale, California 94086
Microsystems International Box 3529, Station C Ottawa, Canada	Solitron Devices 8808 Balboa Avenue San Diego, California 92123
Monolithic Memories, Inc. 1165 East Arques Avenue Sunnyvale, California 94086	Texas Instruments, Inc. Box 1443, Station 612 Houston, Texas 77001

Programmers:

Spectrum Dynamics
2300 East Oakland Park Blvd
Ft. Lauderdale, Florida 33306

and programmed series of outputs appears on the B lines. As with data-selector logic, the Read-Only Memory has an incredible amount of redundancy. During programming, the ability to realize any logic task is reduced to the particular job for which it is programmed. With most ROMs, the training is permanent. Once programmed, it retains the information forever. Since the programming is physical, loss of supply power has no effect; when power is returned, the ROM again provides the right information in the proper place.

Fig. 3-18 shows how a "semidiscrete" Read-Only Memory might be built. Suppose we took four input lines (A = 4) and routed them to a 4-line to 16-line decoder such as a 74154. We now have 16 intermediate output lines. Only one of these lines will go to ground at a time; the rest will remain high. For instance on input code 0000, the top line will go to ground. On code 1001, the "9" line or the tenth line from the top goes to ground, and so on.

We now arrange a diode array on eight possible output lines (B = 8). The diodes perform a negative-logic OR function. This means that those output lines we select by connection of diodes will also go low when the intermediate output lines do; the remainder will stay high. By inserting or omitting diodes, any truth table we wish can be generated. The particular truth table shown is for a 7-segment hexidecimal display decoder. Any desired truth table, consistent with the number of available inputs and outputs or less, can be built this way.

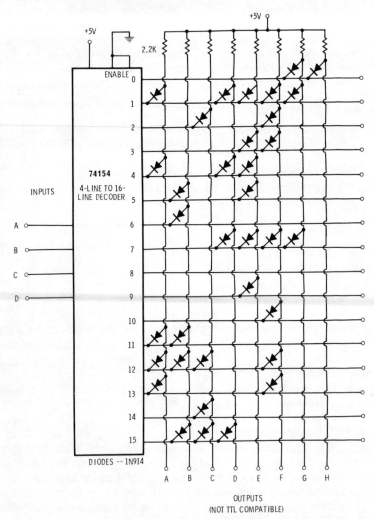

Fig. 3-18A. "Do it yourself" Read-Only Memory shows how the fully integrated ones work. Program shown is for a hexidecimal 7-segment decoder.

146

To change the logic, only the number of diodes used and their location need be changed.

In commercial ROMs, holes in a mask, a buried charge layer, or fuses that can be blown are used instead of diodes. The *organization* of a Read-Only-Memory determines how it is internally arranged. This particular version has four input lines capable of 16 possible individual output combinations. There are eight output lines. This is called a ROM of sixteen 8-bit words, a 16×8 or a 128-bit ROM. The number of bits equal the number of potential diode, fuse, or buried charge points.

While building a custom-integrated circuit may seem complicated and expensive, its 1-package solution and instant design make it very attractive. As of January, 1977, PROM prices start at $1.95 and average half a cent per bit for larger sizes. Many "ordinary" integrated circuits are really preprogrammed ROMs in disguise, and a wide variety of functions are available as stock items. Typical devices are decoders, character generators, trig look-up tables, code converters, and keyboard encoders. While you can do the programming your-

INPUT				OUTPUT								PATTERN
D	C	B	A	A	B	C	D	E	F	G	H	
0	0	0	0	1	1	1	1	1	1	0	0	*0*
0	0	0	1	0	1	1	0	0	0	0	1	*1*
0	0	1	0	1	1	0	1	1	0	1	1	*2*
0	0	1	1	1	1	1	1	0	0	1	1	*3*
0	1	0	0	0	1	1	0	0	1	1	1	*4*
0	1	0	1	1	0	1	1	0	1	1	1	*5*
0	1	1	0	1	0	1	1	1	1	1	1	*6*
0	1	1	1	1	1	1	0	0	0	0	1	*7*
1	0	0	0	1	1	1	1	1	1	1	1	*8*
1	0	0	1	1	1	1	1	0	1	1	1	*9*
1	0	1	0	1	1	1	1	1	0	1	1	*d*
1	0	1	1	0	0	1	1	1	1	1	1	*b*
1	1	0	0	0	0	0	1	1	0	1	1	*C*
1	1	0	1	0	1	1	1	1	0	1	1	*d*
1	1	1	0	1	1	0	1	1	1	1	1	*E*
1	1	1	1	1	0	0	0	1	1	1	1	*F*

```
    A
  F   B
    G
  E   C
    D
```

+ = LIT
SEGMENT

FOR LAMP TEST, MAKE ENABLE ON 74154 POSITIVE.
FOR BLANKING, REMOVE +5 VOLTS FROM TOP OF RESISTORS.

Fig. 3-18B. Truth table and pattern for "do it yourself" Read-Only Memory. By rearranging diode positions, 2^{256} different truth tables can be handled.

self—all it takes is a power supply and a meter—the "zero defects" nature of the job and its tediousness makes distributor programming services a bargain. Their results are guaranteed—provided your truth table is correct. Charges vary somewhat, ranging from free to nominal.

We will save a design example on ROM use for the next section. The design process is almost trivial. The use of a ROM should be considered anytime the circuit complexity is too much for simple gate combinations or data-selector logic. Next, a check should be made to see if some standard product, maybe a ROM in disguise, is already available as a stock item that will do the job, or perhaps the task can be suitably modified to fit an available device.

When a custom ROM is called for, a truth table should be generated. If the first truth table seems to require a very large ROM or a group of ROMs, you must attack the problem of minimizing the essential functions of the ROM. If the truth table seems too large, it can usually be reworked into a smaller form by the use of folding, multiple quadrants, or symmetry, or by factoring, eliminating don't-care states, or omitting functions that are trivial or easy to do with one or two external ICs. Some minimization and rethinking can be applied to virtually all ROM applications, especially if a very large ROM or more than one is needed.

A ROM is then selected, programmed either by you or by a programming service, and proven out. Should you need a large quantity of ROMs, factory-programmable units are cheaper as they use a mask instead of fuses. The breakeven point is typically several hundred units. Field-programmable units should always be used in applications that are likely to change or need customizing in the future.

A few ROMs are erasable, but the majority are not. One popular unit is the Harris HPROM 0512 (now the 74186). This was one of the earliest units available. It is a 512-bit unit, arranged as sixty-four 8-bit words, giving you six input lines and eight output lines. It works on the same supply as the TTL does and is essentially a TTL device. Operating speed is around 50 nanoseconds. A second ROM is the *Signetics* 8223, arranged as thirty-two 8-bit words.

Read-Only Memories are by no means limited to table look-up and logic applications. If you go through the inputs sequentially, you can generate waveforms with them. If you latch the outputs and let the output of one state determine the next *input address,* the ROM can be made to *sequence* in any way you like. Obvious applications are in special sequence and special length counters, and in minicomputer control circuitry. In minicomputers, ROM sequencing is called *microprogramming.* Loops are done by returning a ROM to its initial address, and branching is done by using an additional input line to break out of a loop or make a decision.

Output enable controls are normally provided on a Read-Only Memory. Besides letting you turn the output load on and off, this lets you combine several ROMs for a bigger truth table. Note that the number of fixed-organization ROMs equals 2^x, where x is the number of extra inputs you need. Thus, to use 512-bit, 6-input ROMs, you need one for six inputs (zero extra inputs), two for seven inputs (one extra input), four for eight inputs (two extra inputs), eight for nine inputs (three extra inputs), and sixteen for ten inputs (four extra inputs). Truth tables that seem excessive can almost always be reduced to manageable size by suitably rearranging or rethinking the problem. Unless you are using a simple truth table and a small ROM, always assume your initial truth table is 4 to 64 times bigger than is really needed to do that part of your problem which is handled best by a ROM. Always rethink and recombine truth tables to the minimum possible size.

SOME EXAMPLES AND LOGIC DESIGN RULES

In this chapter we have examined four good approaches to logic design. We can build our own logic blocks out of simple combinations of gates. We can make use of already available stock devices and functions wherever possible. We can use a data-selector logic for intermediate, nonstandard problems, and, finally, we can use Read-Only Memory logic for complex problems.

The first step in any logic design is to ask if the design is needed at all. Is there some easier way of thinking out the problem or an additional or fresh approach that will be simpler or will completely eliminate the need for a design? This step is often eliminated—the result is a costly design, a waste of time, and possibly a later reworking. If it appears that a logic problem is going to take a number of parts, chances are the problem can be eliminated or greatly minimized. In fact, the *more* parts it seems to need, the greater the possibility of doing away with it entirely.

Once you are convinced that a solvable problem does exist, a thorough search should be made for any stock ICs that will do the job or that can be adapted for use. Be sure to check cost and availability as well as technical suitability for the job. Only if you are absolutely convinced that the logic design is necessary and then are further convinced that no inexpensive, available IC in stock will do the job, should you consider your own custom design. Having made this decision, the complexity of the problem will decide whether it is best to use gate combinations, data-selector logic, or a full ROM design. The best solution will often be a combination of the techniques—for instance, a ROM with several attached gates or a stock item with some added logic. The obvious solution to a logic problem is rarely the best.

We have already seen how to use data-selector logic. Let us look at two examples that show the use of ROMs, standard parts, and multiple gates:

Problem No. 1—Redesign an old surplus teletype to speak modern computer language.

Problem No. 2—Modify a single-contact keyboard assembly to speak modern computer language.

Note that these problems are real-world ones, not generate-the-following-logic ones. We will try to show the thought processes as well as the final solutions.

THE ASCII COMPUTER CODE

We obviously have to start with the modern computer code. It is called ASCII, short for *A*merican *S*tandard *C*omputer *I*nformation *I*nterchange code. The code is shown in Fig. 3-19. (In the real world,

BIT NUMBERS								$0\,0_0$	$0\,0_1$	$0\,1_0$	$0\,1_1$	$1\,0_0$	$1\,0_1$	$1\,1_0$	$1\,1_1$
b_7	b_6	b_5	b_4	b_3	b_2	b_1	COLUMN → ROW ↓	0	1	2	3	4	5	6	7
			0	0	0	0	0	NUL	DLE	SP	0	@	P	\	p
			0	0	0	1	1	SOH	DC1	!	1	A	Q	a	q
			0	0	1	0	2	STX	DC2	"	2	B	R	b	r
			0	0	1	1	3	ETX	DC3	#	3	C	S	c	s
			0	1	0	0	4	EOT	DC4	$	4	D	T	d	t
			0	1	0	1	5	ENQ	NAK	%	5	E	U	e	u
			0	1	1	0	6	ACK	SYN	&	6	F	V	f	v
			0	1	1	1	7	BEL	ETB	'	7	G	W	g	w
			1	0	0	0	8	BS	CAN	(	8	H	X	h	x
			1	0	0	1	9	HT	EM	)	9	I	Y	i	y
			1	0	1	0	10	LF	SUB	*	:	J	Z	j	z
			1	0	1	1	11	VT	ESC	+	;	K	[	k	{
			1	1	0	0	12	FF	FS	,	<	L	\	l	l
			1	1	0	1	13	CR	GS	-	=	M	]	m	}
			1	1	1	0	14	SO	RS	.	>	N	^	n	~
			1	1	1	1	15	SI	US	/	?	O	—	o	DEL

Fig. 3-19. ASCII standard computer code.

we would consult the *Reference Data for Radio Engineers** or try some American Standards Association publications or back issues of computer magazines, particularly *Communications of the A.C.M.,* as well as computer handbooks or textbooks.)

---

*Published by Howard W. Sams & Co., Inc.

The code is thought of in *subsets*. Sixty-four of the possible words are reserved for upper-case alphabet, numbers, a blank, and often-used punctuation marks. Thirty-two more words are reserved for *transparent* or *machine* commands: such as starts and stops, carriage returns, line feeds, etc. These never appear in a message or in print; they control and communicate between hardware at both ends. A final 32 words are saved for lower-case alphabet and some little-used punctuation. These are rarely used.

The total number of words is 128, so we can use seven bits to represent all of the code. In practice, an eighth bit is added for *parity* and error detection, or is left blank. Eight bits make up the normal complete code. These may be sent either in serial form, one bit at a time, or in parallel, all bits at once.

We will attack problem No. 1 first. The "old" teletype is probably a 5-level machine using the *Baudot* code of Fig. 3-20. This was a 5-bit

CODE	LETTERS	FIGURES	CODE	LETTERS	FIGURES
00000	BLANK	BLANK	10000	T	5
00001	E	3	10001	Z	+
00010	LINEFEED	LINEFEED	10010	L	)
00011	A		10011	W	2
00100	SPACE	SPACE	10100	H	#
00101	S	'	10101	Y	6
00110	I	8	10110	P	Ø
00111	U	7	10111	Q	1
01000	CAR RET.	CAR RET.	11000	0	9
01001	D	ACKNOWLEDGE	11001	B	?
01010	R	4	11010	G	&
01011	J	BELL	11011	FIGURES	FIGURES
01100	N	,	11100	M	.
01101	F	!	11101	X	/
01110	C	:	11110	V	=
01111	K	(	11111	LETTERS	LETTERS

Fig. 3-20. Baudot (five-level teletype) code.

code that had "case" shift commands. If you hit the LETTERS key, a mechanical flip-flop was set, and 30 letters and punctuation were printable. If the FIGURES key was pressed, 30 numbers and punctuation were printable, with machine commands mixed in for good measure.

We first decide whether we need any logic at all. If the task must be done with an old teletype, and if we are to have all commands and be able to touch-type, the answer is probably yes. We next ask if any commercial unit is available to do the job. You can get ROMs that go from ASCII to SELECTRIC and back again, and ASCII to EBCDIC converters; but at this writing, no BAUDOT to ASCII ROM is readily available at low cost.

So, we can consider a custom design. It is fairly obvious that the task is well beyond what is reasonable with either simple gates or data selectors, although we will need some simple gates to straighten out the figures-letters problem. A ROM seems to be a solution, and since we apparently need sixty-four 8-bit words, a 512-bit, 64 × 8 ROM would be ideal. There also is no obviously good way to reduce these requirements, so this is the size we will use.

Five inputs from the teletype go directly to the ROM (assuming they have been conditioned and made TTL compatible). From these five lines we decode the letters state and the figures state and use them to set and reset a set-reset flip-flop (see next chapter), so that LETTERS gives us a 0 and FIGURES gives us a 1. We use this lead from the flip-flop as a sixth ROM input line.

We then generate a truth table. Each address is determined by the input code, and each output is determined by the equivalent ASCII code we want. Although we will leave the eighth bit all 1's, we could put odd or even parity in instead. For instance, a Baudot R is coded 01010. Letters would be a 0, and the input address is then 0-01010 or simply 001010. An ASCII R has an output code of 101-0010. To this we add an eighth bit 1, for an output of 1101-0010. After completing

ROM TRUTH TABLE							
	IN	OUT		IN	OUT		IN	OUT
NUL	0-00000	1000-0000	0	0-11000	1100-1111	,	1-01100	1010-1100
E	0-00001	1100-0101	B	0-11001	1100-0010	!	1-01101	1010-0001
LF	0-00010	1000-1010	G	0-11010	1100-0111	:	1-01110	1011-1010
A	0-00011	1100-0001	FIG	0-11011	1000-0000	(	1-01111	1010-1000
SP	0-00100	1010-0000	M	0-11100	1100-1101	5	1-10000	1011-0101
S	0-00101	1101-0011	X	0-11101	1101-1000	+	1-10001	1010-1011
I	0-00110	1100-1001	V	0-11110	1101-0110	)	1-10010	1010-1001
U	0-00111	1101-0101	LET	0-11111	1000-0000	2	1010011	1011-0010
CR	0-01000	1000-1101	NUL	1-00000	1000-0000	#	1010100	1010-0011
D	0-01001	1100-0100	3	1-00001	1011-0011	6	1-10101	1011-0110
R	0-01010	1101-0010	LF	1-00010	1000-1010	Ø	1-10110	1011-0000
J	0-01011	1100-1010	—	1-00011	1010-1101	1	1-10111	1011-0001
N	0-01100	1100-1110	SP	1-00100	1010-0000	9	1-11000	1011-1001
F	0-01101	1100-0110	'	1-00101	1010-0111	?	1-11001	1011-1111
C	0-01110	1100-0011	8	1-00110	1011-1000	&	1-11010	1010-0110
K	0-01111	1100-1011	7	1-00111	1011-0111	FIG	1-11011	1000-0000
T	0-10000	1101-0100	CR	1-01000	1000-1101	.	1-11100	1010-1110
Z	0-10001	1101-1010	ACK	1-01001	1000-0110	/	1-11101	1010-1111
L	0-10010	1100-1100	4	1-01010	1011-0100	=	1-11110	1011-1101
W	0-10011	1101-0111	BEL	1-01011	1000-0111	LET	1-11111	1000-0000
H	0-10100	1100-1000						
Y	0-10101	1101-1001	NOTE THAT THE LETTERS (LET) AND FIGURES (FIG)					
P	0-10110	1101-0000	COMMANDS ARE CONVERTED TO AN ASCII NULL (NUL) OR					
Q	0-10111	1101-0001	"DO NOTHING" STATE					

Fig. 3-21A. Building a Baudot to ASCII converter, using a Read-Only Memory.

the truth table, we program the ROM. The truth table and final circuit are shown in Figs. 3-21A aand B.

If we wanted to approach the problem in the opposite way, we would reverse the process and design a new ROM that accepted ASCII for inputs and produced BAUDOT outputs. To avoid needing eight bits of input, we could use the ROM only with the six bits of letters/numbers ASCII and somehow route the machine commands around the ROM. Since there are only three commands (Linefeed, Carriage Return, and Bell), only simple external logic is needed. This is a good example of cutting what would initially appear to need a 2048-bit ROM down to a 512-bit one. Some additional simple logic would take care of figures/letters shifting. Try it as an exercise.

The keyboard problem is obviously easy. All we need to do the job is eight 64-input gates! The challenge is to accomplish it with a few low-cost integrated circuits and simple wiring instead of a complex system. This is an outstanding example of the obvious way to do things being a very poor route indeed.

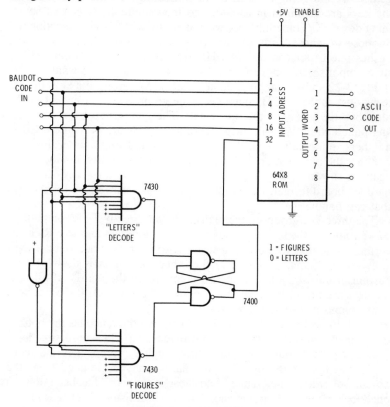

Fig. 3-21B. Baudot to ASCII circuit.

We first check for full ASCII encoder availability. At this writing, we find that they are available, but are expensive and relatively difficult to get. One interesting encoder we would probably find is the *Harris* HD0165 keyboard encoder. It is low in cost and encodes 16 lines into a 4-bit code, as well as generating internal Key-pressed and "ERROR—there are two keys pressed" commands. The practical method is to use this as a nucleus for our encoder.

Two of these keyboard encoders could be arranged to obtain the full 8-bit code. Some thought would indicate that we would either need several diodes or else some double-pole keyswitches for each key. Neither of these routes is attractive, although either one would certainly be better than our initial brute-force attempt. What can we do?

We can forget about the eighth bit completely. If we need parity on it, an external single IC parity generator, such as the 74180, can be added.

A further observation is that if we tie one end of all the keys together, we are going to need 64 of something. On the other hand, if the keys are arranged in a *matrix* so they simultaneously pull something down *and* something up, we can get by with fewer "somethings." Suppose we chose a matrix that pulls one of three things down and pushes one of sixteen up. The HD0164 is a current-sourcing (RTL style) input so current can be delivered to any input we want.

Fig. 3-22 shows one possible key matrix. We group the keys by sixteens, just as the ASCII code does. One group is the lower half of the alphabet, the second is the upper half. The final group is the numbers and punctuation. We will further assume that we are only interested in numbers, punctuation, machine commands and upper-case alphabet, and that the punctuation will mostly be shared as shifted number keys, again as shown in Fig. 3-22. This closely follows an American Standard keyboard format. Lower-case alphabet is easily added for systems that can handle it.

The three key groups in the matrix are not directly TTL compatible, so we translate the logic by using two pnp transistors and two RTL inverters. Note that we do not need three transistors, since we can logically conclude that if neither of the other transistors is drawing base current, it must be a key in the third column of the matrix. If none of the keys are pressed, the key-pressed detector in the HD0165 does not activate and it does not matter.

What do we have so far? We have a system that encodes the bottom four bits of a 48-key keyboard and provides two TTL-compatible logic signals, an "A through O" and a "0 through 9." We can further conclude that the "P through Z" information may be implied from the absence of either other signal. And most of the work has been done in one stock integrated-circuit encoder, two transistors, and a RTL inverter. Note that this is one instance where we cannot use TTL effec-

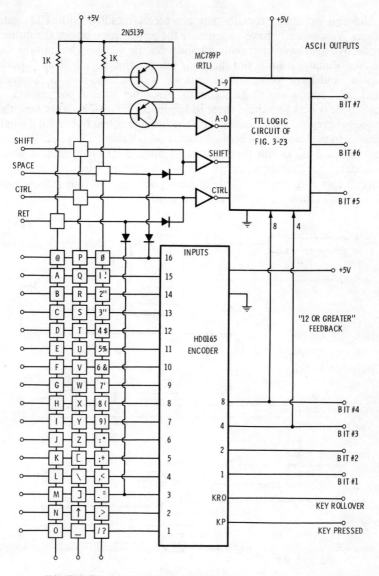

Fig. 3-22. Keyboard encoder using combination of stock integrated circuits and TTL logic design.

tively with its current-sourcing inputs. Another benefit is that we should be able to use higher impedance (conductive foam, etc.) contacts if we wish.

155

Several problems remain that are nicely handled with TTL gate logic. We obviously have to generate the upper three bits of the output code. We also have to provide for shifts for the numbers but not for the letters. Finally, it turns out that four punctuation keys will be "upside down" and have to be shifted backwards somehow, if both the code and the keytops are to be standard. Since we have a progression of details, it is best to handle them in sequence. Fig. 3-23 shows how the logic progresses, from dealing with the basic problem to handling small details to perfecting it. The final circuit adds three TTL gates. We end up with a 5-IC circuit that, at this writing, is far cheaper than commercial 1-package equivalents, yet is still easy to wire and use. This circuit can even be simplified further by leaving the four punctuation keys upside down from the U.S. standard.

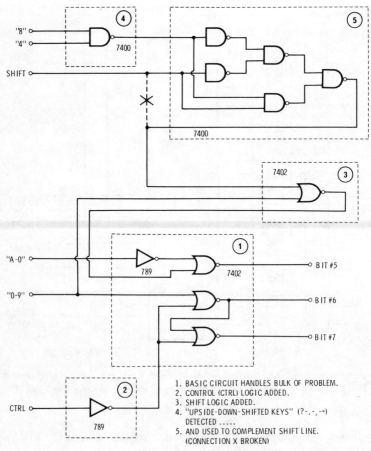

1. BASIC CIRCUIT HANDLES BULK OF PROBLEM.
2. CONTROL (CTRL) LOGIC ADDED.
3. SHIFT LOGIC ADDED.
4. "UPSIDE-DOWN-SHIFTED KEYS" (?-.-,-=) DETECTED .....
5. AND USED TO COMPLEMENT SHIFT LINE. (CONNECTION X BROKEN)

Fig. 3-23. Completing the TTL logic design of the ASCII keyboard encoder through a successive approximation technique.

We might choose to use data-selector logic to replace the three TTL ICs, or we might prefer to use a single EXCLUSIVE OR gate to replace the one we built with a 7400 (step 5, Fig. 3-23). In this case, economy favors the simple gate construction. With only slight additional complexity, data-selector logic would be the better choice.

These examples show how logic design can be integrated into a system, taking the best parts of the best techniques to reach an overall solution that represents a reasonable, and hopefully the best possible, circuit you can build.

CHAPTER 4

Gate and Timer Circuits

Whenever two inverting logic gates are cross coupled, we can get a circuit with two states, both of which are stable. This may be called a latch, a memory, a bistable multivibrator, or a reset-set flip-flop. They are useful by themselves and also lead to a variety of *interface* or *conditioning* circuits, as well as being developable into the more complex and much more useful clocked flip-flops of Chapter 5. The same types of circuits are used in phase detectors, tachometers, frequency meters, D/A converters, and other variable-duty-cycle circuits.

Three cascaded gates and a capacitor or two form a high-frequency oscillator or signal source, but there are better ways of generating a test signal or reference for use with TTL; many of these methods are centered around the MC4024 and 555 timers. The 555, particularly, is unique in solving a number of pulse and timing problems that are easily interfaced with TTL. Rounding out the signal sources is a crystal-oscillator circuit that is more easily constructed with another logic family called CMOS.

Monostable circuits are a group of pulsers that act only when acted upon and produce an output of fixed time duration. Again, the 555 and MC1555 devices form ideal solutions to many medium- to long-time pulse applications, while several of the conventional TTL monostable circuits remain useful at higher frequencies or in applications needing faster operation.

Pulse and edge-sensitive techniques are a second form of monostable circuits that often take only a single resistor or capacitor, but have very definite limitations on duty cycle and stability.

Some of the astable and monostable circuits lead naturally to applications such as 2-tone alarms, temperature measurement, direct-reading digital capacitance displays, dimmers for digital displays, and a wide variety of other applications.

That is what this chapter is about.

TWO CROSS-COUPLED INVERTERS

Fig. 4-1 shows how two inverters can be connected so that one drives the other and vice versa. Assume that the input of inverter A is low. The output will be high. This in turn makes the input to inverter B high, which in turn makes the output of inverter B low, completing the loop. The circuit is stable and will remain that way unless we break the connection, remove supply power, or trigger the circuit into doing something else.

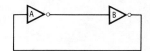

Fig. 4-1. Two cross-coupled inverters form a latch with two stable states.

Note that the input on inverter A could just as well be high, and that this state is also stable. We have a circuit that can be forced into one of two equally stable conditions. This is called a *bistable multivibrator*. Unlike the logic circuits of Chapter 3, this circuit has a *memory* capability—it remembers what state it has been put into, and thus the history of the circuit enters into its present condition. Other names for this circuit are a *latch*, a *memory*, or a *set-reset* flip-flop. A somewhat similar electromechanical equivalent would be that of a relay latching on its own make contact.

One limitation of the 2-inverter circuit is that there is no easy and obvious way to force it into one or the other state. We can overcome this with the two push buttons of Fig. 4-2A or the SPDT push button of Fig. 4-2B. This latter circuit is called a *contact conditioner* or a *contact debouncer*. Circuits of this type are also called *bounceless push buttons* and are absolutely essential if a mechanical contact is going to be used to cycle any of the clocked logic blocks of Chapter 5 through 8.

Mechanical contacts normally produce noise during their settling time. They also bounce and make repeated contact for the first few milliseconds of actuation. TTL is normally so fast that it will recognize each and every bounce or noise pulse as a separate input command. Push the button once, and instead of adding one count, you can add as many as several hundred, unless proper conditioning is used.

With the circuit of Fig. 4-2B, the very first bounce or noise pulse flips the circuit over into the other state, and it stays there till the contact is once again released. On release, the first time the upper contact is made, the circuit flips back the other way. The output is a clean, single square wave that lasts for the time the button is pressed. A small box with several bounceless push buttons in it (you can build three with a single hex inverter) is very handy and is an almost essential piece of TTL test gear, second only to a state checker in usefulness.

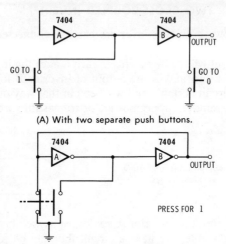

(A) With two separate push buttons.

(B) Mechanical contact conditioner using spdt push button or switch.

Fig. 4-2. Mechanically triggering a two-state latch.

This ultrasimple circuit will draw rather high supply current during the inverter transition times, so a good bypass capacitor very close by is essential to prevent generating extra noise on the supply lines.

IMPROVED TRIGGERING

Any means of forcing a bistable into its other state is called *triggering*. The simple triggering circuit of Fig. 4-2 is useful for switches, but it is not electronically compatible with TTL, and the momentary short on the device does not look like good practice, even if it is more or less harmless. We can overcome both of these problems by using any of the two input-inverting gate circuits of Fig. 4-3.

In Fig. 4-3A, we use a 7400 NAND gate. One input of each gate is cross coupled to the output of the other gate. The second input drives its own output positive if it is briefly grounded. Thus, we ground one input to set the bistable to one state and ground the other to reset the bistable to the other state.

We are no longer restricted to mechanical contacts because we are working with a TTL input now, not an output. As Fig. 4-3B shows, we can electrically set and reset the device by keeping both trigger inputs positive and briefly grounding either one when a change is needed.

In Fig. 4-3C, we use a 7402 NOR gate. Both trigger inputs are normally held at ground with the 330-ohm resistors, and one of them is pulled positive to provide triggering. Note that a 7400 gate needs both inputs positive to get a ground, while a 7402 needs only one input positive to get an output ground. Fig. 4-3D is the same circuit with electronic-TTL-compatible triggering rather than mechanical. Fig. 4-3B triggers with a low pulse; Fig. 4-3D triggers with a high pulse; the choice of IC is determined by the type of triggering you need.

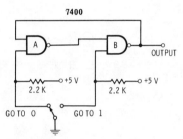

(A) NAND gate contact conditioner.

(B) Electrically triggered NAND latch; inputs must normally be held high.

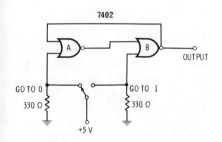

(C) NOR gate contact conditioner.

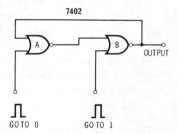

(D) Electrically triggered NOR latch; inputs must normally be held low.

Fig. 4-3. Latches made from two-input gates.

Either Fig. 4-3A or Fig. 4-3C may also be used as bounceless push buttons or contact conditioners, depending on whether a positive ground or common ground on the switch is desired.

THE SET-RESET FLIP-FLOP

We can look at the 2-gate pair as a 1-piece logic block called the set-reset flip-flop, whose truth table is shown in Fig. 4-4 for the 7400 and Fig. 4-5 for the 7402.

The 7400 circuit of Fig. 4-4 obeys these rules:

1. If both inputs are left positive, the circuit stays in the original state.
2. If the Set input is momentarily grounded, the circuit goes to the state with the Q output positive and the $\overline{Q}$ output grounded.
3. If the Reset input is momentarily grounded, the circuit goes to the state with the Q output grounded and the $\overline{Q}$ output positive.

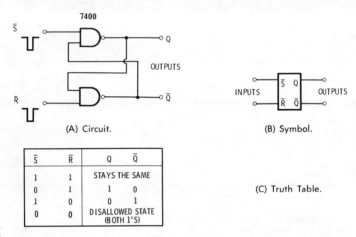

(A) Circuit.

(B) Symbol.

$\overline{S}$	$\overline{R}$	Q	$\overline{Q}$
1	1	STAYS THE SAME	
0	1	1	0
1	0	0	1
0	0	DISALLOWED STATE (BOTH 1'S)	

(C) Truth Table.

Fig. 4-4. A Set-Reset flip-flop made from two NAND gates.

4. If both Set and Reset are simultaneously grounded, the flip-flop goes into a *disallowed state condition* in which both outputs are simultaneously positive. The last input to go positive determines the final state. This condition is normally avoided.

The Q and $\overline{Q}$ outputs are normally *complements* of one another in that Q is 1 when $\overline{Q}$ is 0 and vice versa. State No. 4 should be avoided as it is not a valid part of normal circuit operation.

Similarly, the rules for the 7402 circuit of Fig. 4-5 are as follows:

1. If both inputs are left grounded, the circuit stays in the original state.
2. If the Set input is made positive, the flip-flop goes into the state with the Q output positive and the $\overline{Q}$ output grounded.
3. If the Reset input is momentarily made positive, the circuit goes to the state with the Q output grounded and the $\overline{Q}$ output positive.
4. If both Set and Reset are simultaneously made positive, the flip-flop goes into a *disallowed state condition* in which both outputs

are simultaneously grounded. The last input to go to ground determines the final state. This condition is normally avoided.

The choice of which circuit to use is determined by how you want to trigger the circuit. In both cases, condition No. 4 is disallowed and normally avoided.

Note that neither of these circuits can be made to binary divide or go to alternate output states with sequential triggering unless extra circuitry is added to them. There will be more about this in Chapter 5 when we talk about clocked flip-flops which can be made into binary dividers and other more elaborate circuit applications.

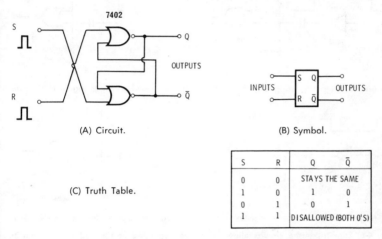

(A) Circuit.

(B) Symbol.

(C) Truth Table.

S	R	Q	$\bar{Q}$
0	0	STAYS THE SAME	
1	0	1	0
0	1	0	1
1	1	DISALLOWED (BOTH 0'S)	

Fig. 4-5. A Set-Reset flip-flop made from two NOR gates.

EDGE TRIGGERING

Sometimes we might like to use only the beginning or the end of a signal to trigger a flip-flop. This is done with any of the *edge-triggering* circuits of Fig. 4-6. Note that the Set command must go away before the Reset appears and vice versa, unless these commands are suitably shortened with the edge-trigger circuits. With edge triggering, only the beginning or the end of the event matters; its duration does not.

USING RS FLIP-FLOPS

The RS flip-flop (for some reason it is called a "set-reset" but it is normally spelled "RS") is one of the simplest logic blocks that have a memory. We can use them anywhere that we want to store a single *bit* of information. We will see in the next chapter that there are ways of modifying the basic RS flip-flop to let us count, store, shift, or synchronize information. One way to do this is to use the RS flip-flops as *master-slave* pairs.

An electronic stopwatch might use an RS flip-flop to start and then stop a train of pulses being routed to a counter; by picking the right pulse frequency, the number of pulses is made to equal the time between the start and stop commands, expressed in microseconds, milliseconds, seconds, or any other selected base.

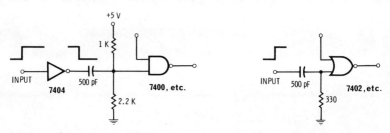

(A) Positive-edge triggering a NAND gate.   (B) Positive-edge triggering a NOR gate.

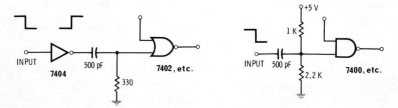

(C) Negative-edge triggering a NOR gate.   (D) Negative-edge triggering a NAND gate.

Fig. 4-6. Edge-triggering circuits allow either the beginning or the end of an event to initiate a flip-flop.

An alarm might use an RS flip-flop such that it is set by the alarm line being tripped and is not reset until help arrives. The same technique works in computer interface circuits where a brief input command may arrive and then be held by one or a group of RS flip-flops until the computer can properly use the command or data; it then releases the flip-flop for a new command. This is often called data or command *buffering,* and the request to make use of the new information is sometimes called an *interrupt.*

Fig. 4-7 shows two ways an RS flip-flop can be used as a power-line conditioner to convert the 60-cycle power line into a TTL-compatible, noise-free square wave, useful as a time reference for medium-accuracy (less than 0.05%) digital measurement tasks. Remember that a TTL 0-input state needs a low-impedance path to ground that can sink 1.6 mA, while its 1 state needs very little sourcing current but must be held above 2.4 volts. In Fig. 4-7A, we use a center-tapped filament

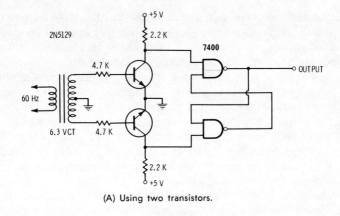

(A) Using two transistors.

(B) Using a CMOS gate.

Fig. 4-7. Power-line conditioning circuits to obtain a clean 60-Hz TTL square wave.

transformer and two npn transistors. On the positive cycle, one transistor turns on and sets the flip-flop. On the negative cycle swing, the other transistor turns on and resets the flip-flop. The output is a clean square wave whose duty cycle is 50-50 and whose repetition frequency equals the power-line frequency. Fig. 4-7B does the same thing with a CMOS gate from another logic family as shown; it works the same way. One TTL input may be driven but only if both CMOS input gates are paralleled as shown.

The output of the power-line conditioner usually goes to a divide-by-6 or divide-by-60 counter (see Chapter 7) to get a 0.1-second time reference for digital measurements or a 1-second time reference for electronic clocks. The center-tapped transformer can often be the same one as the power supply or an additional winding.

Besides building your own RS flip-flops out of simple gates, a quad flip-flop package exists as the 74279.

THE SCHMITT TRIGGER

Another type of cross-coupled inverter circuit is called the *Schmitt trigger* and appears in Fig. 4-8. Here we add a resistor between the output and input and add a second resistor that sums an input signal with it. This gives us a snap-action circuit that is useful for converting a low-frequency sine wave into a fast-rise square wave, or for contact conditioning or interfacing slower logic families.

As the input goes positive, it reaches a point where the output of the first inverter starts to go low. The instant this happens, the second inverter starts to go high and reaches around and pulls the input further positive. If the signal once again starts to go low, nothing happens until it is well below the point where it sent the inverter high. Making it more negative starts an opposite action. The output of the first inverter starts to go positive, and the second one reaches around and accelerates the grounding process.

The two trip points are called the *upper trip point* and the *lower trip point;* the area between is called the *deadband* or the *hysteresis zone.* The trip points for this circuit are at 0.7 volt and 0.95 volt. Note that once the upper trip point is hit, noise in the deadband or above it will have no effect. Similarly on the downswing, once the lower trip point is reached, noise in the deadband or below it will have no effect.

This new circuit gives us another way to condition outside-world signals for TTL use by cleaning them up. Another contact debouncer

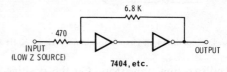

(A) Basic circuit. Input must have low impedance to ground.

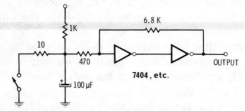

(B) A contact conditioner for a single-make contact.

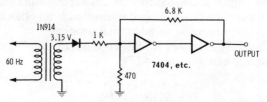

(C) Single-ended power-line conditioner. Output frequency is 60Hz, but the duty cycle is not exactly 50%.

Fig. 4-8. Schmitt trigger circuits add snap action and condition low-frequency inputs.

is shown in Fig. 4-8B; this one works with a single make contact instead of a SPDT pair. In Fig. 4-8C, a single-ended 60-Hz power-line reference is used for a new power-line gate. Note that the time width of this circuit is *not* one half of the power-line cycle—the only accurate reference is that the leading edges will follow each other at the power-line frequency. Similar circuits may be used in keyboard-conditioning circuits for electronic calculators.

A Schmitt trigger can be built out of a single noninverting gate such as the 7408 or 7432, or with noninverting buffers such as the 7406 or 7416. A quad Schmitt trigger package is also available as the 7413 and 7414. These latter two need no resistors and also offer a higher input impedance (around 6K) so they are easier to use. They may be used for interfacing logic families as well as for converting sine waves and other low-frequency signals to TTL-compatible logic levels.

Note that in any interface circuit, the input signal must *not* be allowed to go below ground, especially if it is from a low-impedance source. Most TTL gates have clamping diodes on their inputs to eliminate a high-frequency ringing problem. A below-ground input signal will forward-bias these diodes. If the input source impedance is low enough, it will also damage the diode and ruin the package. If input swings that go below ground ever do occur, they must be limited to only a volt or so at maximum and must be current-limited so the maximum input diode current is only 10 mA or less. This problem is shown in Fig. 4-9.

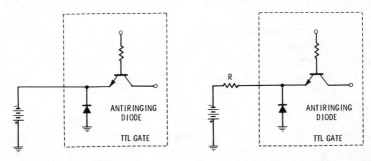

(A) With no limiting resistor, excess current may flow.

(B) Limiting resistor holds current under 10 mA. (This circuit works but should be avoided.)

Fig. 4-9. Reverse (below-ground) input current to a TTL gate can destroy it unless current is limited.

A HIGH-IMPEDANCE INTERFACE

Fig. 4-10 shows how we can drive a single TTL input with a CMOS gate that has both its inputs paralleled. The input impedance to the CMOS gate is essentially an open circuit, so it will not load outside-world signals at all, yet will still provide the needed current-sinking 0 current for a TTL input. Once again, there are input diodes that can be damaged if the input swing exceeds the positive supply or goes below ground. Around 10 mA of diode current can be safely handled; more than that will damage or latch the device.

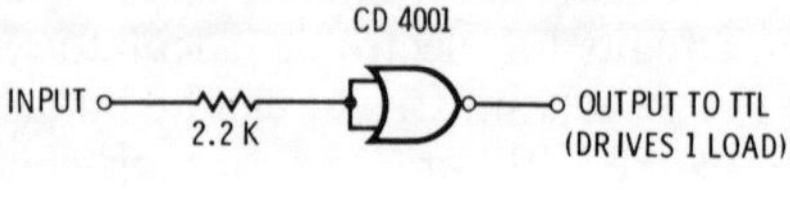

Fig. 4-10. This CMOS interface gives an infinite impedance and drives one TTL medium-power load.

CD 4001

INPUT o——/\/\/——[>o——o OUTPUT TO TTL
2.2 K   (DRIVES 1 LOAD)

OTHER INTERFACE CIRCUITS

CMOS will directly interface TTL with the circuit shown, but it is limited to driving one TTL load. Similarly, RTL and DTL may be directly connected to a TTL input. Current-mode logic such as MECL and 10,000 Series ECL works with negative supplies, and translators are available to make the two systems compatible. MOS devices can usually be made compatible if so noted in their data.

In a large-systems environment, transmission lines, cables, or their twisted-pair equivalents must be used to connect different parts of the circuit. If long lines are needed, integrated circuit pairs called *line drivers* and *line receivers* may be used. Ordinary analog comparators can also be used for interface work if their output is specified as being TTL compatible. The National LM311 is one such device.

The general rules of interfacing say that a snap action must be provided if the input signal is a sine wave, or is slowly changing, or is noisy or bouncy. A low-impedance source must be provided to sink 1.6 mA for a TTL output "0" and a high voltage, above 2.4 volts must be provided to guarantee a TTL output "1." Further, the current that the input signal swings must be restricted or suitably limited so it does not go below ground or above the supply voltage, in order to protect the input antiringing diodes.

One final approach to interfacing uses optical couplers. These are usually LED-photodetector pairs that are now fairly low in price and can be made TTL compatible. They have the advantage of completely isolating the input and its ground from your TTL circuit and its ground. This is particularly useful in a noisy industrial environment or when the input may be on a high-voltage line or have rf associated with it.

SIGNAL SOURCES

We can cascade three open-collector inverters as shown in Fig. 4-11 to obtain a high-frequency *ring oscillator* that generates TTL-compatible square waves in the 1- to 10-MHz region. The output fre-

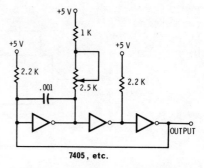

Fig. 4-11. TTL ring oscillator is a simple, reasonably stable source of high-frequency square waves.

7405, etc.

quency is not particularly stable, but it is genuinely useful for test purposes and for such applications as setting the spacing of the dots on a video time display. Varying either the resistor or the capacitor changes the operating frequency as noted.

A WIDE-RANGE VOLTAGE-CONTROLLED OSCILLATOR

If test signals in the 1-Hz to 33-MHz range are needed, the MC4024 can be used in any of the circuits of Fig. 4-12. Fig. 4-12A is a voltage-controlled oscillator whose frequency may be changed over a 3:1 range. Fig. 4-12B is a simpler circuit where a fixed-frequency output can be used that is not very accurate. Fig. 4-12C shows how a crystal can be used for direct crystal control. Crystals in the 2-MHz to 33-MHz range work best in this circuit. Lower-frequency crystals may need some tailored capacitance loading to ensure starting and non-squegging operation. There are two separate oscillators per package, each with its own supply and ground lines. This lets you decouple the two oscillators for minimum interaction. Be sure all the needed ground and + pins are connected if you experience any difficulty with circuit operation. The 4024 can be gated by applying or removing *ground;* it cannot be gated by applying or removing the positive supply voltage because of a "sneak path" back through the voltage control input.

ANOTHER CRYSTAL OSCILLATOR

We might be tempted to bias a TTL inverter or gate into its active region and try to use it as a linear amplifier. While this works in theory, the linear range is limited and the very high-frequency capability of the gate usually adds to high-frequency stability problems. The input impedance to these circuits tends to be low and the gain somewhat limited, so the process is neither recommended nor widely used.

Fig. 4-13 shows a CMOS oscillator circuit that works so well and so simply that it is recommended for use with TTL whenever a crystal-stable reference is needed. The CMOS gate is biased into its active

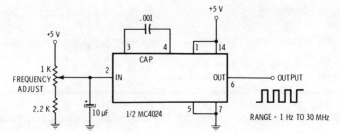

(A) Variable frequency, 3:1 range.

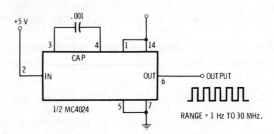

(B) Fixed frequency set by capacitor.

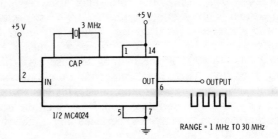

(C) Fixed frequency set by crystal.

Fig. 4-12. TTL signal sources using the MC4024.

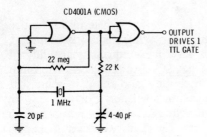

Fig. 4-13. This simple, reliable crystal oscillator drives one TTL load.

region and negligibly loads the crystal. The series resistor and shunt capacitor may need to be adjusted somewhat for wide variations in crystal frequency, but the circuit is not at all critical, is low in cost, and easy to use. One TTL gate can be driven, provided both inputs to the final MOS gate are driven in parallel.

THE 555 AND MC1555

The MC4024 of Fig. 4-12 can be used down to subaudio frequencies if desired, and one typical application might use the first half of the circuit as a video oscillator and the second as a cursor winker in a computer terminal or tv typewriter.

A newer device that has a very wide range of astable (signal source) and monostable (pulse source) possibilities is the 555 (also known as the MC1555), which is now available in some dual versions as well.

The 555 is unique in that it simply, cheaply, and accurately serves as a free-running *astable multivibrator,* square-wave generator, or signal source, as well as being useful as a pulse generator and serving as a solution to many special problems. When connected to a 5-volt supply, the circuit is directly compatible with TTL. It may also be used with any supply from 4 to 15 volts and can source or sink several hundred mA at the output if needed.

In 555 circuits, the timing capacitor always has one end connected to ground, and a positive-only current is applied. This lets you use large electrolytics for long timing periods. The input is also a very high impedance, which lets you use high-value resistors and small capacitors for a given time constant. You can easily get a 1000:1 frequency range out of a single capacitor simply by changing the series resistor.

A block diagram of the 555 is shown in Fig. 4-14. Depending on how you use the circuit, you can make it into a free-running astable multivibrator, a pulse generator or *monostable multivibrator,* or any of a number of specialized circuits.

The astable or signal-source connection appears in Fig. 4-15. Assume that the output is high (1), the charge on the capacitor low, and the "discharge" transistor is not conducting. The capacitor now begins charging through R1 and R2 in series toward the +5-volt supply. When the voltage across the capacitor gets to $\frac{2}{3}$ of the supply, the "threshold" comparator senses this and flips the internal circuitry to the other state. The output now goes low (0), and the discharge transistor turns on. The capacitor now discharges through resistor R2. Discharge continues until the capacitor voltage drops to $\frac{1}{3}$ of the supply voltage. At this instant, the "trigger" comparator senses the capacitor voltage and flips the circuit back to its initial state. The cycle continuously repeats, and the output is a rectangular waveform.

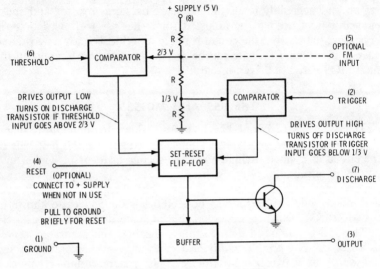

Fig. 4-14. Block diagram of the 555.

The output is high while the capacitor is charging and low while the capacitor is discharging.

Fig. 4-16 shows how to choose the timing resistors. With a TTL 5-volt supply, these can range from 1K (minimum value—R1 or R2) through 3.3 megohms (maximum value—R1 and R2 in series). This gives a potential adjustment range of 3300:1. Best results are obtained with capacitors of 1000 pF or larger, but smaller values can be used with lower values of R1 and R2. The maximum operating frequency is around 1 megahertz, but best operation is obtained below

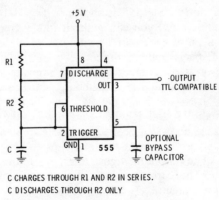

C CHARGES THROUGH R1 AND R2 IN SERIES.
C DISCHARGES THROUGH R2 ONLY

OUTPUT IS POSITIVE WHILE C IS CHARGING.
OUTPUT IS GROUNDED WHILE C IS DISCHARGING.

Fig. 4-15. The 555 connected as an astable multivibrator or signal source.

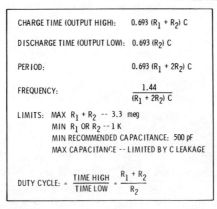

(A) Graph of R_1, R_2, C, and operating frequency.

FREE RUNNING FREQUENCY

CHARGE TIME (OUTPUT HIGH):	$0.693 (R_1 + R_2) C$
DISCHARGE TIME (OUTPUT LOW):	$0.693 (R_2) C$
PERIOD:	$0.693 (R_1 + 2R_2) C$
FREQUENCY:	$\dfrac{1.44}{(R_1 + 2R_2) C}$

LIMITS: MAX $R_1 + R_2$ -- 3.3 meg
MIN R_1 OR R_2 --1 K
MIN RECOMMENDED CAPACITANCE: 500 pF
MAX CAPACITANCE -- LIMITED BY C LEAKAGE

DUTY CYCLE: = $\dfrac{\text{TIME HIGH}}{\text{TIME LOW}} = \dfrac{R_1 + R_2}{R_2}$

(B) Design equations.

Courtesy Signetics

Fig. 4-16. Picking component values for a 555 astable multivibrator.

300 kHz. The minimum operating frequency is limited only by the size and leakage of the capacitor you use. For instance, a 10-μF capacitor and a 3.3-megohm resistor will give a time interval of 23.1 seconds if the leakage of the capacitor is low enough.

By making R2 large with respect to R1, we can get an essentially symmetrical square-wave output. For instance, if R1 is 1K and R2 is 1 megohm, the difference in charging and discharging resistance is only 0.1%, and good symmetry results. Any symmetry you want from 50 through 99.9% can be obtained by a selection of the ratio of R1 and R2. Since the 1 time always charges through two series resistors, it is always longer than the 0 time.

Fig. 4-17 shows how we can achieve a perfectly symmetrical output by adding a clocked flip-flop binary divider (see Chapter 5) to the output. The output of the clocked flip-flop will be one-half the frequency of the 555 and the symmetry will be 50-50, independent of the

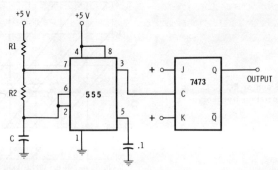

Fig. 4-17. A perfectly symmetrical output of half frequency, independent of the ratio R1 to R1, is obtained with a clocked flip-flop binary divider added to output. (See Chapter 5.)

ratio of R1 to R2. This technique works with any signal source and may be used where a constant or exact symmetry is needed.

We can extend the duty cycle below 50% by using the circuit of Fig. 4-18. Two diodes are added to make the charge and discharge paths independently controllable. This gives us any selected output duty cycle at a slight loss in temperature stability.

The circuit of Fig. 4-15 is independent of supply voltage effects because of the selection of the comparator points. As supply voltage increases, the charging current increases, but so do the comparator thresholds. Thus, *long-term* supply variations are ignored, and temperature variations are only 50 parts per million per degree C, meaning that an 18°F temperature change is needed to shift the frequency 0.05%.

Even though a circuit is this stable, it is not always suitable for precision frequency work. For instance, setting the frequency to extreme accuracy takes a multiple-turn potentiometer and highly stable com-

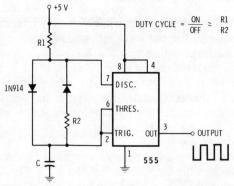

Fig. 4-18. Two diodes added to basic 555 astable multivibrator give wider control over duty cycle.

ponents for the capacitor, R1, and R2. While the 555 does make stability and a reasonably accurate frequency a practical reality in a simple circuit, more precise timing sources, such as the power line or a crystal divider, still should be considered if you need extreme accuracy in your circuit. The problem is in defining "extreme accuracy." For less than 1%, the 555 is an ideal choice. For greater than 0.1% accuracy, you should definitely consider digital or crystal techniques. In between, it depends on what you are doing. If your 555 circuit only has to hold a given frequency rather than be adjusted to a specific one, you can obtain more accuracy.

The 555 is very easy to use, but one or two possible problems should be mentioned. You will get into some jitter problems if the supply voltage variations are rapid with respect to the timing cycle, so that the average charging current is different from the instantaneous voltage at the time a comparator changes the output.

Bypassing the fm input to ground with a capacitor helps a lot, but supply filtering or regulation should be used to hold the supply voltage constant over the timing interval. One place this problem can show up is in digital battery-powered instruments, where the different multiplexed display numbers shift the supply voltage and introduce potential jitter. This specific problem is eliminated by using the fastest possible display multiplexing and adding a regulator or heavy bypassing between the 555 and the rest of the circuit.

Ac hum can also cause instability if large resistors and long leads to the timing capacitor are used. One obvious place this will be a problem is in a digital capacitance meter. The cure is to locate the timing resistor and capacitor as close to the 555 as possible.

Incidentally, you can intentionally frequency-modulate the output frequency by capacitor-coupling a signal to the fm input. Operation is nonlinear and the range is limited, but this technique is handy for such things as switching-mode power-supply designs and adding vibrato in electronic music.

When you use the 555 as an astable multivibrator, the Reset input (pin 4) should be connected to +5 volts to prevent any noise problems here.

Let us take a quick look at some typical 555 astable circuits.

TWO-TONE ALARM

By letting one 555 control the frequency of the second, or by using a dual package, you can generate a commanding alarm signal that can easily cut its way through background clutter: traffic, office, or shop noise; or, it can be used as a construction backup alarm. Fig. 4-19 shows the circuit. The first 555 runs as a 4-Hz astable multivibrator; the second runs as a 1-kHz (nominal) astable multivibrator whose

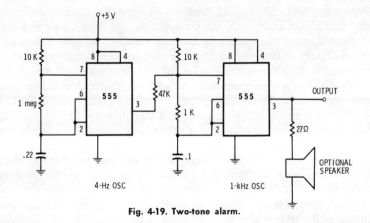

Fig. 4-19. Two-tone alarm.

actual frequency is changed eight times a second by the 4-Hz circuit. The output is a 2-note "twee-dell" "twee-dell" that is unmistakable. Resistor and capacitor values can be adjusted as needed for the best overall effects. Siren-like sounds can be obtained by letting a large capacitor slowly charge or discharge into the timing resistor portion of a 555 circuit.

TEMPO GENERATOR OR ELECTRONIC METRONOME

Fig. 4-20 shows a tempo circuit which provides a TTL output circuit that is useful as a trigger for electronic music rhythm and timing

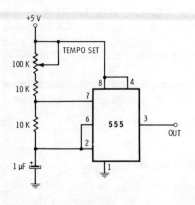

Fig. 4-20. Electronic metronome or tempo source for electronic music composer or rhythm circuit.

systems or is directly useful as a practice metronome. For downbeat emphasis or tempo generation, the circuit can drive some of the clocked flip-flops of Chapter 5 and provide the desired emphasis. The composer-synthesizer circuit of Fig. 7-22 is another typical example.

DIGITAL CAPACITANCE MEASUREMENT

We can use a 555 along with some digital test equipment to measure capacitance. One obvious way is to measure the time period of the oscillations. By choosing the right size of charging resistance, we can get a reading directly in microfarads or nanofarads. Unlike many capacitance-measuring schemes, this one easily handles electrolytics up into the tens of thousands of microfarads.

A better way is to measure only the capacitor *discharge time,* as shown in Fig. 4-21. With this method, any leakage in the capacitor under test will make the capacitor appear smaller than it really is and will be an effective indication of how the test capacitor will behave in most timing and bypass circuits. In this circuit, the 555 is used as an astable multivibrator. At the peak of the charging curve, a digital counter is reset and a clock of 100-kHz pulses is turned on and routed to the counter. When the discharge portion of the cycle is completed, the display is updated and the value of the capacitor is read out. By selecting the proper reference frequency and charging currents, you can get a direct digital display of the value of capacitance. Be sure to properly shield the leads and keep them short for low-capacity measurements, or 60-Hz hum can cause some slight instability.

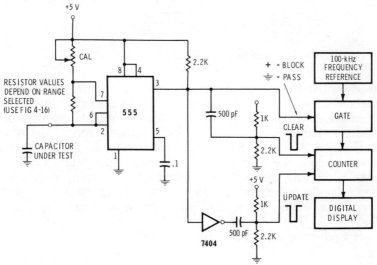

Fig. 4-21. Digital capacitance meter.

BRIGHTNESS CONTROL FOR A DIGITAL DISPLAY

The brightness of digital displays is difficult to control, for some, like neon displays, are current-operated and independent of supply voltage. Others like LEDs can be brightness-controlled by changing the supply voltage; however, the disadvantage here is the power loss associated with a resistor or resistor-transistor dropping system, particularly if the display is battery operated.

The solution to brightness control is to turn the display off and on very rapidly, and to adjust the *ratio* of the off time to the on time to get any duty cycle you want. The average brightness will equal the average duty cycle, and no power will be dissipated during the off times.

Fig. 4-22 shows how a 555 can be used to go from a duty cycle of 50% to 99.9%. By using the low portion of the output to unblank or

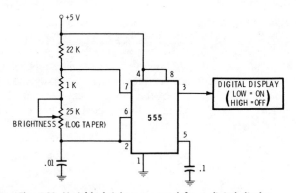

Fig. 4-22. Variable brightness control for a digital display.

to power the display, and by setting a 50% duty cycle as maximum brightness, you can control the display brightness from virtually off to maximum. A photocell can also be added to make the display adaptive, automatically adjusting the display output to match the room illumination. A second 555 could be used to reset the first for "power down" operations if a digital calculator or test equipment is not being used. In this way, the display is constant while it is being used. If you stop using the instrument, the display goes dim or blank 15 seconds later to save battery power. One final variation of all these tricks is to flash the display 0.5 second on and 3.5 seconds off. This will cut the battery power by a factor of 8 for long-term use.

ELECTRONICALLY VARIABLE TIME CONSTANT: A MUSIC ATTACK-DECAY GENERATOR

The variable-duty-cycle approach is very handy for a number of applications. The only trick to its use is that it has to happen much faster than the rate of change of the signals you are watching or controlling. One interesting example is a master attack or decay controller in an electronic music system.

The trick is to rapidly switch a resistor in and out of a circuit. A 1K resistor that is in the circuit 100% of the time looks like a 1K resistor. If it is in the circuit only 50% of the time, it looks like a 2K resistor. If it is in the circuit only 10% of the time, it behaves as a 10K resistor. If it is in the circuit 0% of the time, it looks like an open circuit.

By rapidly switching the resistor into and out of the circuit, we can make the value of the resistor appear to be anything we want, giving us an electronically variable time constant. The duty cycle of the resistor will set the time constant.

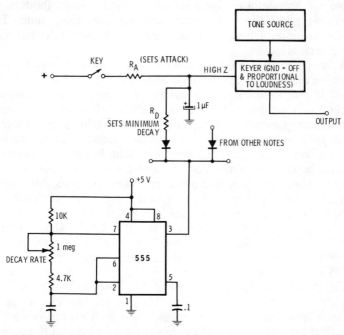

Fig. 4-23. Electronically variable time-constant circuit controls decay time in electronic music system.

Fig. 4-23 shows part of a percussion generator in an electronic music system. To control the decay rate of the notes, it is necessary to change the apparent value of resistor R_D, for this controls how fast the charge dies off capacitor C, which in turn decides how loud the note is at any given time. The faster the charge dies away, the faster the *decay* of the note. If there is only one note, we obviously can use a potentiometer here. But if there are dozens of notes as is usually the case in a polyphonic instrument, we would have to switch an unreasonable number of resistors into and out of the circuit.

Instead of this, the 555 as a variable-duty-cycle circuit rapidly switches the resistor into and out of the circuit so that the duty cycle controls the decay and time-constant rate. Only one circuit and adjustment is needed for the entire instrument, although a second one that stops "halfway" can be added for the rapid initial die-down of a plucked string or bell.

MONOSTABLE MULTIVIBRATORS AND PULSE GENERATORS

So far, we have considered circuits that have two stable states and are useful as latches or memories, and circuits that have neither state stable and are useful as signal sources or astable multivibrators. One remaining possibility is a circuit that has one stable state. These we use as pulse or time-width generators, and they are called *monostable multivibrators*.

Although monostable-type circuits are easily and cheaply made, there is a tendency to use them too often and to expect too much from them. If you need extreme accuracy of a pulse width, consider a "locked in" method such as deriving the width from system timing with decoding gates (see Chapter 5) or some other method that depends only on counting ICs and decoders, rather than on externally set time constants. One big benefit is that fewer adjustments are needed, besides the elimination of some discrete components.

There is no good way to build a true monostable multivibrator out of a basic 7400 or 7402 gate, so special-purpose circuits are needed to do the job. One simple exception is called the *half monostable* multivibrator, which takes only an inverter. It is handy when timing accuracy is not particularly important. If we need more precision or an output pulse that lasts longer than the trigger command, we can go to a 555 connected as a monostable multivibrator or we can use such special purpose monostables as the 74121, 74122, 74123, or 74221. Generally, the 555 and its dual versions are the best choice for time intervals from microseconds to hours, while the TTL versions are better suited for tens-of-nanosecond to tens-of-microsecond timing applications. Let us take a closer look at these three approaches to monostable circuits.

THE HALF-MONOSTABLE

Fig. 4-24 shows several half-monostable circuits. They are similar to the edge-triggering circuits of Fig. 4-6. Since they provide no internal feedback, the pulse width is somewhat dependent on temperature and voltage, and the falling edge might not be as fast as possible. Another limitation is that the output pulse must be shorter than the triggering command.

This circuit can be used anywhere a leading- or trailing-edge pulse of limited accuracy is needed. The time constant is determined by the two resistors and the internal TTL pull-up current in parallel, and it is adjusted by changing the capacitor. Minimum capacitor values of 330 pF are recommended. Note that the input command must last longer than the output pulse you want, and the time the input command is absent must also be long enough to allow the circuit to recover.

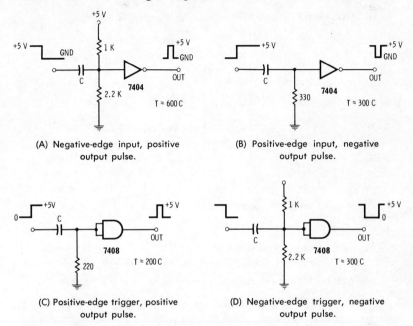

(A) Negative-edge input, positive output pulse.

(B) Positive-edge input, negative output pulse.

(C) Positive-edge trigger, positive output pulse.

(D) Negative-edge trigger, negative output pulse.

Fig. 4-24. Half-monostable circuits. Input trigger must exceed output pulse length.

One good place to use a half-monostable circuit is in a digital display where the leading edge of a command might be used for a "clear" and the trailing edge might be used for an "update." This is shown in Fig. 4-21.

Wherever the limitations of a moderate timing accuracy and an input command longer than the output pulse can be met, the half-monostable circuit is a good choice as it is cheaper and simpler than the true monostable circuits. You can get as many as six per package using a 7404 hex inverter.

THE 555 AS A MONOSTABLE MULTIVIBRATOR

The 555 can be connected as a pulse generator as shown in Fig. 4-25. An external trigger command applied to the trigger input, pin 2, starts the action. This is normally done by leaving the trigger input positive and briefly pulling it to ground to initiate the timing sequence.

When the input is triggered, the output goes positive and the discharge-clamp transistor is released from the timing capacitor. The capacitor then charges positive until ⅔ of the supply voltage is reached. At this instant, the threshold comparator flips the circuit over. The output goes to ground, and the capacitor is rapidly discharged to ground.

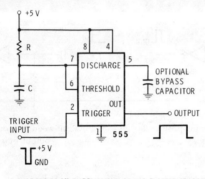

C CHARGES TO 2/3 SUPPLY VOLTAGE VIA R AFTER TRIGGERING
C DISCHARGES RAPIDLY TO GROUND AT END OF TIME CYCLE.

OUTPUT IS POSITIVE FOR TIME DURATION

TRIGGER MUST REMAIN POSITIVE UNTIL INITIATED BY
    DROPPING TO GROUND

TRIGGER PULSES MUST BE NARROWER THAN OUTPUT TIME PULSE.

Fig. 4-25. The 555 connected as a monostable multivibrator or pulse generator.

Unlike in the astable multivibrator, the cycle does not repeat by itself; an external command must be sent to the trigger to initiate a new time delay.

The design chart and key equations are shown in Fig. 4-26. As with the astable circuit, the time width is independent of temperature and supply voltage variations that are long with respect to the timing cycle. Supply variations, such as hum, glitches, or digit bobble, that are short compared to the timing cycle can introduce jitter or instability and must be suitably filtered out. Bypassing of pin 5 is also recommended.

The reset input (pin 4) may be used to hold the output low or to stop a timing cycle after it begins. This is done by bringing the reset input to ground for the length of time you wish to inhibit the operation. When not used, the reset input should be tied to the positive supply.

FREQUENCY METER OR TACHOMETER

Fig. 4-27 shows how to use the 555. This circuit serves as a frequency meter or a tachometer. The only difference between these two

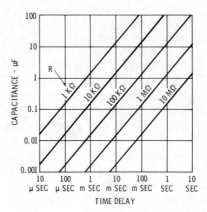

(A) Graph of on time versus R and C.

(B) Design equations.

ON TIME: T = 1.1 RC
MAX R: 3.3 meg
MIN R: 1 K
MINIMUM RECOMMENDED C: 500 pF
MAXIMUM C: LIMITED BY LEAKAGE
MAXIMUM RECOMMENDED DUTY CYCLE:
    80% WITH LARGE R; 50% WITH SMALL R.
MAXIMUM RECOMMENDED TRIGGER PULSE WIDTH:
    1/4 - ON TIME.

Courtesy Signetics

Fig. 4-26. Picking component values for a 555 monostable multivibrator.

applications is the conditioning of the input and the selection of calibration and time constants. Engine revolutions-per-minute is a frequency just as cycles-per-second is a frequency.

The circuit is normally calibrated so that a "full scale" rpm or frequency gives around a 40% duty cycle. This duty cycle is averaged or

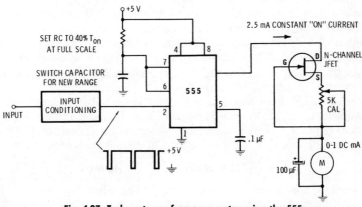

Fig. 4-27. Tachometer or frequency meter using the 555.

integrated by the meter to give you a full-scale reading. Frequencies lower than full scale change the off-on ratio linearly so that the lower the frequency, the lower the proportionate reading.

For instance, on a 1000-Hz range, the full-scale period would be 1 millisecond, so we set the 555 to around a 400-microsecond period and adjust the average meter current to get a 1-mA or "1000" reading for this frequency input. At 1000 rpm on an 8-cylinder engine, we get four distributor point closings per crankshaft revolution, or 4000 pulses per minute. This in turn is equal to 66.6 pulses per second with an equivalent period of 15 milliseconds. If we want a 1000-rpm full-scale reading, we set our monostable circuit to around 6 milliseconds (40% of the period) and adjust the meter to get a full-scale reading of 1000. With the circuit shown, the time period will be fairly independent of supply voltage, but the applied meter voltage will not. This is the purpose of the constant-current-source FET in the meter line; it provides a constant and adjusted current independent of supply voltage. A constant-current diode such as the 1N5307 or a regulated supply may be used instead.

Regardless of how you use this circuit, be sure to get one, and only one, brief, negative-going trigger pulse for each cycle of the input. An input filter and possibly an amplifier followed by a Schmitt trigger is one ideal route. As a frequency counter, the accuracy is pretty much limited to that of the meter movement. With a 3% meter accuracy, you can get an instrument with 3% accuracy. One simple calibration source is the 60-Hz power line, although accurate decade-related capacitors would be needed if this calibration is carried over to other ranges.

DIGITAL THERMOMETER

Another application of a 555 as a monostable multivibrator is the digital-thermometer circuit of Fig. 4-28. We obtain a pulse width that is linearly related to a temperature and then use this to gate a selected number of 100-kHz reference counts into an electronic counter and display. System constants are easily adjusted to get a direct reading in either degrees F or C, and negative as well as positive temperatures can be read to a potential accuracy of 0.1 degree.

One possible thermistor with a linear resistance versus temperature characteristic is the Yellow Springs 44203. It has a resistance at 0 degrees C of 12,175 ohms and linearly decreases at a rate of 127.096 ohms per degree. We use two 555s. The first is driven by the thermistor, and its pulse width is proportional to temperature. The second is a constant-width pulse equal to the time width of the temperature monostable multivibrator at zero degrees. The difference between the two will be proportional to temperature, and the capacitor values are

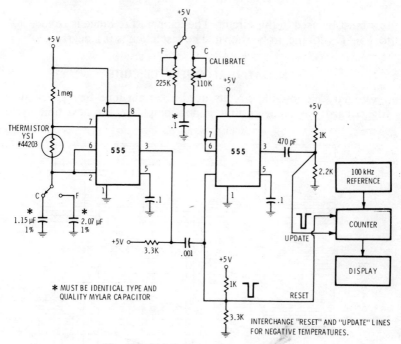

Fig. 4-28. Digital thermometer using 555s.

chosen such that each degree of change gives a 100-microsecond time change, or ten "1.0" pulses of a 100-kHz clock. At zero degrees C, the two time widths are identical and the output width is zero. Above zero, the time width is set to 100 microseconds per degree C with the

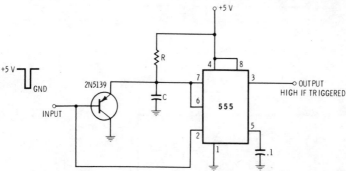

Fig. 4-29. Negative-recovery monostable multivibrator can be retriggered at any time.

right selection of the capacitor value. Below zero, you simply interchange the reset and update lines and provide a "−" on the display, and negative numbers turn out as expected. High-quality Mylar capacitors must be used in this circuit. The temperature range is from $-30°$ to $+50°C$ with the probe shown. The resolution is 0.1 degree.

NEGATIVE-RECOVERY CIRCUITS

Ordinary monostable circuits need a certain time to recover after triggering. If the recovery time is not completed, the next time cycle

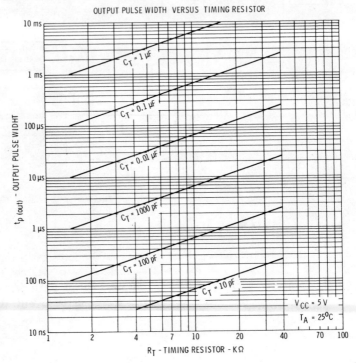

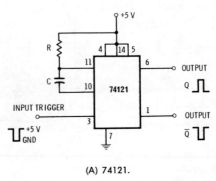

(A) 74121.

Fig. 4-30. Monostable circuits

might be shortened, and an inaccuracy or jitter can result. As a general rule, monostable circuits operate best if the recovery time exceeds the ON time, although you can operate with ON times of 90% if you are careful and choose the right resistor values.

Some special circuits let us retrigger the monostable circuit at any time. These are called *negative-recovery monostable circuits.* They are used for missing-pulse detection, voice-controlled systems, code anal-

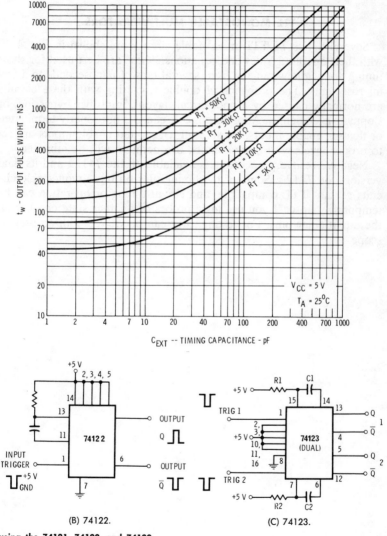

OUTPUT PULSE WIDTH VS TIMING CAPACITANCE

C_{EXT} -- TIMING CAPACITANCE - pF

(B) 74122.

(C) 74123.

using the 74121, 74122, and 74123.

ysis, and other similar functions. So long as trigger pulses keep arriving at a certain rate, the monostable circuit stays triggered and the output remains high. Should a trigger pulse be missed, the output drops until the next trigger pulse arrives. Usually, the monostable ON time is set approximately ⅓ longer than the expected time between triggers. An external transistor may be added to the 555 as shown in Fig. 4-29 to provide a negative-recovery circuit. Other component values are selected per the design equations of Fig. 4-26.

TTL MONOSTABLE MULTIVIBRATORS

Several Series 74 TTL monostable circuits are shown in Fig. 4-30 with their operating rules and equations. These are best used for short timing applications ranging from several tens of nanoseconds to a few microseconds. The problems of double triggering with these circuits are normally caused by a poor circuit layout, improper bypassing, or sloppy trigger signals. Another possible cause is improperly terminated or floating enable inputs. Be sure all trigger and enable inputs are set to proper levels with these circuits, or operation will be inhibited.

Negative-recovery operation is available on the 74122 and its dual version, the 74123. Some of the timing pins on these monostable circuits are not TTL compatible, and circuit timing or operation can be temporarily upset if you use logic probes or another state checker on these particular pins. For testing, they can be viewed with an oscilloscope.

CHAPTER 5

Clocked Logic — the JK and D-Type Flip-Flops

Clocked, synchronous, or *step-by-step* logic systems make up the bulk of the sophisticated digital circuits of today, particularly at package or device level. Instead of providing an output immediately after input conditions change, clocked-logic packages wait till the arrival of a system *clock* pulse or command; only then do they respond and provide an output.

There are several advantages to clocked logic. The first is that unchecked transitions cannot wildly run through a circuit. Instead, changes can only progress one stage at a time in an orderly manner. This one-step-at-a-time action makes devices like shift registers and elaborate counters possible. The second advantage of clocked logic is that everything in a system happens more or less at the same time. This often eliminates or greatly minimizes race conditions, glitches, and timing sequence mixups.

The cornerstones of clocked logic are the JK flip-flop and the D-type flip-flop, with the 7473 and 7474 being typical prototype examples. In this chapter, we will take a closer look at how these devices may be used in clocked-logic systems and how they work internally. This will be followed with the major clocked-logic applications and a look at some of the more complex TTL devices. Two groups of applications are so numerous and so important that they deserve separate chapters. Counters are thus reserved for Chapter 6 and shift registers for Chapter 7.

HOW DOES THE CLOCK WORK?

On any clocked-logic block, a change of clock conditions initiates or else completes what is happening inside the block.

One of the greatest problems in understanding TTL and in making it work properly is realizing exactly what the clock does and what the sequence is. This is especially true of early devices in the TTL line. It is trivially easy to get the 7473 or 74107 to appear faulty ("one-swallowing," wrong data entries, etc.), simply because the designer thinks the device works one way and it actually is behaving quite differently.

There are two basic types of clocking, *level* and *edge*. In level clocking, the *state* of the clock being a 0 or a 1 carries out a transfer or completes an action. In edge clocking, the *change* of the clock from a 1 to a 0 or vice versa completes the action. Traditionally, shift registers operate on the positive level or *positive-edge* clocking, thus letting a positive logic 1 on the clock line do something. Ripple counters normally operate on the negative level or *negative-edge* clocking, thus allowing the dropping and "carrying" of a previous stage to continue the count sequence.

If the data is allowed to change more than once or randomly, problems can occur with level-clocked logic. Before we find out the reason, let us state the rule that causes all the problems:

On any level-clocked logic block, the input data or information cannot be changed or altered except immediately after clocking happens. At that time, it can be changed only once. An edge-clocked logic block may have its input data changed at any time.

Normally, if the device is called a Master-Slave type, it is *level* clocked. If it is called a D-type or edge-triggered device, it is *edge* clocked. Many of the later TTL devices minimized the data-changing problem, but the early versions did not. The rule is thus a bit conservative—if there is any doubt, consult the actual device data sheet.

The use restrictions on the rule are: Level-clocked devices should be provided with continuous logic inputs only (hard-wired 1's or 0's) or should come from a source that is clocked identically to the one you are working with. If input data is continuously changing at a random rate or is coming from some other source, one that is uncontrolled, an edge-triggered device should always be used for the first stage.

THE MASTER-SLAVE FLIP-FLOP

Fig. 5-1 shows how we can build up some flip-flops with progressively more circuit capabilities. Fig. 5-1A is the Set-Reset flip-flop of Chapter 4. As with all bistable flip-flops, it has two stable states. It usually has two outputs, a Q output and a $\overline{Q}$ output which is normally

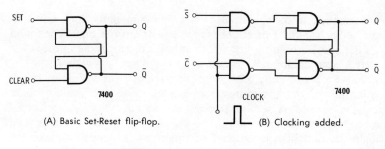

(A) Basic Set-Reset flip-flop.

(B) Clocking added.

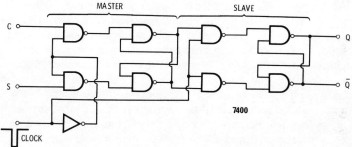

(C) Converted to Master-Slave flip-flop.

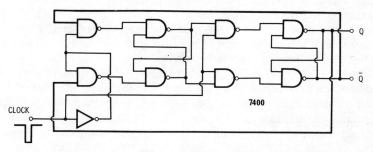

(D) Binary divider or T flip-flop made from (C) with feedback shown.

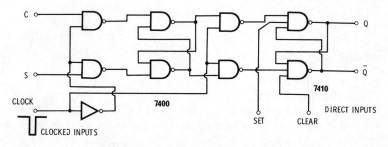

(E) Direct Set and Clear added to slave flip-flop.

Fig. 5-1. Improving the basic Set-Reset flip-flop so it can safely be used as a binary divider or shift register element.

complementary to the Q output. It is a simple memory device, in that it can be Set ($Q = 1$) or Reset ($Q = 0$) with a brief input command on its Set and Reset input lines. It then holds or stores the information after the input commands go away.

There are several obvious system limitations to this simple circuit. One is that the outputs change immediately instead of waiting for a clocked command. A second problem is that a *disallowed state* condition occurs if the device is simultaneously told to set and reset. A final problem is that there is no easy or direct way to reliably make the device behave as a binary divider or a sequential storage element.

In Fig. 5-1B, some input gating has been added to produce a clocked RS flip-flop. The outputs will not change except when the clock line goes positive. We now have a clocked system, but the rest of the problems still remain. Note that if we cascaded several identical sections like this and attempted to build a *shift register,* a mad race would take place when all the clocks simultaneously went positive and the data would run through all the sections instead of transferring only one stage forward. Perhaps we could "beat" this problem by a careful choice of a very narrow clock width, selecting a clock wide enough to let the data through, but not so wide that the inherent delay in the set-reset action causes a more-than-one-stage transfer. While this works, it is critical and temperature dependent.

By the same token, we cannot get this stage to act as a binary divider simply by cross-coupling outputs to inputs, for again, a mad race takes place when the clock is positive.

In Fig. 5-1C, we have cascaded two stages but driven their clocks complementary, so that when the clock is low, data is accepted on the first, or master, stage. When the clock goes high, the contents of the master stage are transferred to the following slave stage. Any possibility of an unchecked race or of indeterminancy is now gone, for the second stage cannot change until long after the first one has completed its changing. Stages of this Master-Slave type may easily be cascaded (two circuits per data transfer stage) to pass data on one, and only one, circuit group per clock interval.

By the same token, we can now safely cross couple the outputs to the input and perform binary division, forming the T or *Toggle* flip-flop of Fig. 5-1D. The output stays steady the entire time the clock is low, so a mad back-and-forth race is not possible. At every clock interval, the inputs are told to change the state of the output, caused by the cross-coupled feedback from Q to Reset and $\overline{Q}$ to Set. Since there are two changes per cycle of a square wave, this circuit divides by two or performs *binary division*. Since a T flip-flop turns out to be easily built from either a JK or D flip-flop, it is not offered separately as a TTL component, except as part of a larger binary divider, the 7493, 8281, and 74161.

The T flip-flop may be considered a *two-phase* logic system, with the "clock low" being a time of loading or accepting data, and the "clock high" being a time of transferring data to the output.

Any clocked-logic system must have these two phases of operation, for if the output is allowed to change at the same instant the input is enabled, the wild race results. The second phase may be a clock level. In other systems, it can be merely the charge on a capacitor, or a stored charge holding a transistor on for a brief interval. To build an edge-clocked system, you provide a brief memory that lasts only for an instant after the clock rises or falls. At that instant, the input is disabled so that a race cannot result, and the stored information is transferred to the output stage.

In Fig. 5-1E, we have added a refinement. The slave flip-flop has two new inputs brought out, called the direct *Set* and direct *Reset* inputs. These let us immediately and dominantly set or reset the flip-flop, *independent* of clocking. They are normally used to clear a shift register or return a counter to zero or set it in some predetermined position.

Direct inputs are normally only used at the beginning or end of a clocking sequence and are disabled during normal operation. Only one direct input can be used at a time or a disallowed output state will result.

THE JK FLIP-FLOP

In the sequence of improvements of Fig. 5-1, clocking and a second delay stage have been added to the set-reset flip-flop and a provision made for direct setting and clearing. This has improved the circuit so that it can safely binary divide and shift information one stage at a time without any problems of racing or possibilities of multiple stage shifts.

About all we could do to further improve operation is to eliminate the disallowed input condition. Better yet, we could recognize the disallowed input condition and convert the flip-flop into a T flip-flop whenever this happens. Now, instead of only three out of a possible four meaningful input combinations, we have four—do nothing, enter a 1, enter a 0, or change. And this is about as versatile as you can get.

This is called a *JK* flip-flop. People still argue over what the *J* and *K* stand for. Chances are the letters were chosen at random to separate the more versatile new flip-flop from the older RS one.

Rather than further improve the circuit of Fig. 5-1, let us look at a "real" JK flip-flop, the 7476. It is shown in Fig. 5-2.

At the top of the drawing, the cross-coupled gates form the slave portion of the flip-flop. The master flip-flop is shown at the bottom. Logic from the J and K inputs and the Q and $\overline{Q}$ outputs is used to determine the state this flip-flop goes into when the clock is high. The transistors in the middle form a *transmission gate* that routes the proper command to the slave flip-flop when the clock goes low.

The internal logic lets the JK flip-flop do something meaningful for all four possible conditions on the J and K inputs. The rules are as follows for the *clocked* inputs:

1. If the J input is grounded and the K input is grounded, *nothing* happens when the clock goes to the low level.
2. If the J input is positive and the K input is grounded, the Q output goes or stays positive when the clock goes to the low level. The 1 on the J line is passed directly to the Q output.

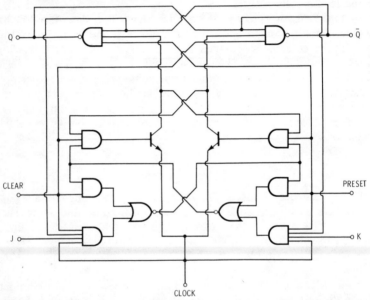

Fig. 5-2. Internal schematic of one-half of a 7476. This is a TTL, level-triggered, Master/Slave flip-flop.

3. If the J input is grounded and the K input is positive, the Q output goes or stays grounded when the clock goes to the low level. The 0 on the J line is passed directly to the Q output.
4. If the J input is made positive *and* the K input is made positive, the Q output *changes* when the clock goes to the low level. The circuit becomes a T flip-flop, or binary divider.

If we are using the *direct* inputs, they will obey the following rules:

5. If both the Set and Clear inputs remain positive, the clocked sequence 1 to 4 above works normally and is not interfered with.
6. If the Set input is grounded and the Clear input remains positive,

the flip-flop *immediately* goes into a state with the Q output positive and the $\overline{Q}$ output grounded.

7. If the Clear input is grounded and the Set input remains positive, the flip-flop *immediately* goes into a state with the Q output grounded and the $\overline{Q}$ output positive.

8. If the Set and Clear inputs are simultaneously grounded, a disallowed state condition exists, and Q and $\overline{Q}$ will no longer be complementary. This condition should be avoided.

The direct inputs dominate; clocking will have no useful effects so long as the Set or Clear is held grounded, although some output glitches or noise can result.

Fig. 5-3 summarizes the JK flip-flop operation. Direct inputs are tied positive unless used. J and K grounded disables; J and K positive binarily divides; complementary data on J and K are passed on directly across the flip-flop.

CLOCKED INPUTS:

J	K	CLOCK	OUTPUT Q
0	0	⎍	STAYS THE SAME
0	1	⎍	0
1	0	⎍	1
1	1	⎍	CHANGES TO OPPOSITE

DIRECT INPUTS

PRESET	PRECLEAR	OUTPUT Q
0	0	DISALLOWED STATE -- DO NOT USE
0	1	1
1	0	0
1	1	NORMAL CLOCKED OPERATION

CLOCKING OCCURS WHEN CLOCK LINE GOES TO LOW LEVEL. DATA ON J AND K LINES MAY NOT BE CHANGED EXCEPT IMMEDIATELY AFTER CLOCK GOES LOW. ONLY ONE CHANGE PER CLOCK CYCLE IS PERMITTED.

(A) Clocked inputs.   (B) Direct inputs.

Fig. 5-3. Operating rules for the 7473, 7476, and 74107 level-triggered, JK Master/Slave flip-flop.

The 7476 shown needs a 16-pin package to get two independent flip-flops. A 14-pin package may be obtained by leaving off the Preset inputs, resulting in the 7473 or 74107. These latter two differ only in power-supply connections and pinouts. The 74107 has the more reasonable pin connections (identical to 99% of the other TTL circuits), but the 7473 somehow seems more available and more popular. If you have a choice, use the 74107.

All these devices will operate at a 20-MHz typical maximum clock frequency, with correspondingly higher or lower speeds of operation for low-power, high-power, and Schottky versions. There is no low-frequency limit. It takes about 25 nanoseconds to transfer data, and both the clock and clear pulses must be at least 25 nanoseconds wide.

While there are no restrictions on clock rise and fall times, noise problems can be expected for extremely slow-rising or falling clocks that bias the input devices into their active regions. A good practice is to keep the rise times and fall times to 5 microseconds or less; this is very easy to do in most cases.

Clocked logic is generally more sensitive to supply-line noise. All the bypassing and layout techniques covered in Chapter 1 are absolutely essential when you are using clocked flip-flops. This includes a supply that is tightly regulated to within a quarter of a volt of 5 volts and short-leaded bypass capacitors of 0.01 to 0.05 μF, at least one for every three clocked-logic packages.

The 7473, 74107, and 7476 are level-sensitive clocked devices. From the rule given at the beginning of the chapter, we can only change the J and K inputs immediately after clocking, and then only once. These devices are well suited for binary dividers, counters, internal shift-register stages, and anywhere else the inputs remain stationary or change only once after a clocking. They are *not* suited for synchronizers, one-and-only-one circuits, and the first stage of a shift register accepting randomly changing data. These restrictions will become more obvious when we discuss applications. The 74107 remains a good choice for the bulk of TTL internal circuitry.

THE D-TYPE FLIP-FLOP

If we add an inverter to a JK flip-flop (Fig. 5-4) so that the K input is always the complement of the J, we have a D-type flip-flop, the D

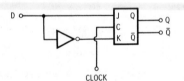

Fig. 5-4. Adding an inverter to a JK flip-flop converts it to a D flip-flop.

standing for *data* or *delay*. Its main uses are as a memory, storage, and shift-register element. Only one connection is needed between cascaded stages for serial shift registers, a very handy layout feature. *If* a level-clocked D flip-flop were available to you, you still would be restricted by rule to when and how you changed the input data. It turns out that an edge-clocked D-type flip-flop is far more versatile—it is available as the 7474, or appears in quadruplicate in the 74175 and by sixes in the 74174. A logic diagram of the 7474 appears as Fig. 5-5.

In this diagram, the Slave portion of the flip-flop appears on the right and the Master portion is on the left. If you go through the left-half portion of the logic, you will find that the state of the D input *at the instant the clock line goes positive* determines the state the slave portion goes into. There are also two overriding direct inputs.

The rules are as follows:

1. If the D input is positive, the Q output goes or stays positive when the clock suddenly changes from grounded to positive; a 1 is loaded into the stage.

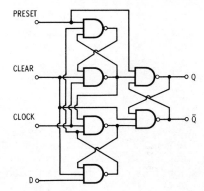

Fig. 5-5. Internal schematic of one-half of a 7474.

2. If the D input is grounded, the Q output goes or stays grounded when the clock suddenly changes from grounded to positive; a 0 is loaded into the stage.

The direct inputs once more dominate and obey the following rules:

3. If the Preset and Clear inputs remain tied positive, they do not interfere with the normal clocked operation.
4. If the Preset input is grounded, the flip-flop *immediately* goes to a state with $\overline{Q}$ grounded and Q positive, independent of the clocking.
5. If the Clear input is grounded, the flip-flop *immediately* goes to a state with Q grounded and $\overline{Q}$ positive, independent of the clocking.

The chart of Fig. 5-6 summarizes these rules. Since the TTL D-type flip-flops are edge clocked, the input data can be changed at any time. This makes them ideal for input synchronization, one-and-only-one circuits, and first shift register stages. Fig. 5-7 shows how to make a binary divider or T flip-flop out of a D-type. Unlike the JK flip-flop, you cannot readily obtain a "do-nothing" state, nor can you rapidly switch into or out of the binary division mode.

The choice of which type of flip-flop to use will become more obvious in the next section when we talk about flip-flop applications. D flip-flops tend to be easier to lay out, take less power, and accept

CLOCKED INPUTS:

D	CLOCK	OUTPUT Q
0	⌐_	0
1	⌐_	1

DIRECT INPUTS:

PRESET	PRECLEAR	OUTPUT Q
0	0	DISALLOWED STATE – DO NOT USE
0	1	1
1	0	0
1	1	NORMAL CLOCKED OPERATION

CLOCKING OCCURS ON THE POSITIVE EDGE. DATA ON THE D LINE MAY BE CHANGED AT ANY TIME INDEPENDENTLY OF THE CLOCK LEVEL.

Fig. 5-6. Operating rules for the 7474 edge-triggered type-D flip-flop.

random input data, but they are not as versatile a logic block as the JK flip-flop.

One problem that comes up if you mix JK and D flip-flops in a system is that the one clocks on the positive clock transition and the other completes its clocking on the level following a positive-to-ground transition. The clock lines must be inverted if the two types are being mixed in a given system. Table 5-1 is a summary comparison of the

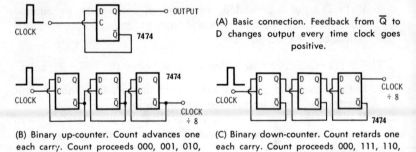

(A) Basic connection. Feedback from $\overline{Q}$ to D changes output every time clock goes positive.

(B) Binary up-counter. Count advances one each carry. Count proceeds 000, 001, 010, 011, 101, 110, 111, and back to 000.

(C) Binary down-counter. Count retards one each carry. Count proceeds 000, 111, 110, 101, 100, 011, 010, 001, and back to 000.

Fig. 5-7. Converting a D flip-flop into a T flip-flop or binary divider.

7473, 7476, and 74107 JK versus the 7474 D-type. There are, of course, a wide variety of other flip-flops in the line, some with properties that feature the best of both worlds. These may be expensive, unavailable, or available only from a single source. Checking with a data sheet will readily show you what you can and cannot do with the more exotic flip-flops. Devices in this category are the 7470, 7472, 74104, 74105, 74110, and 74111. These are generally harder to use and harder to get; they also usually cost more and offer fewer functions per package. Stick with the 74107, the 7474, or larger MSI blocks as much as possible unless you have an out-of-the-ordinary problem that these other devices can solve for you.

Table 5-1. Comparing the Four Most Popular TTL Flip-Flops

	7473	7474	7476	74107
Type	JK	D	JK	JK
Clocking	Negative level	Positive edge	Negative level	Negative level
Supply pinouts	Unusual	Standard	Standard	Standard
Package	14 pin	14 pin	16 pin	14 pin
Devices per package	2	2	2	2
Direct set?	No	Yes	Yes	No
Restrictions on when input can be changed?	Yes*	No	Yes*	Yes*
Usable as synchronizer?	No	Yes	No	No

*See rule at beginning of chapter

USING THE DIRECT INPUTS

The *direct* inputs on flip-flops and more complex TTL logic blocks are normally used to clear the circuit to a 0000 state or to enter a fixed number at the beginning of a calculation. They are normally disabled (usually to +5 volts) during the actual clocked logic operation.

Direct set and clear functions cannot be obtained by using expanders or shorting the outputs of a TTL flip-flop, at least not reliably. If both a direct set and a direct clear are needed, you go to the dual D-type flip-flop (7474) or the 7476 dual JK in a 16-pin package.

If you only need a Set input, simply redefine the stage so that it turns "upside down." Q becomes $\overline{Q}$. J becomes K. K becomes J. Clock stays clock. $\overline{Q}$ becomes Q. And Clear becomes Set. This is handy in some sequences where the first flip-flop in a string goes in upside down. Instead of initializing a sequence to 0000000 this way, it gets initialized to 100000 instead.

If several stages have their Clear or Set input lines tied together, they must be returned to +5 volts via a small resistor or another active TTL stage. Floating these leads creates an antenna effect that can introduce noise and erratic operation into the system. Reset lines should never leave a circuit board or go through a connector without an inverter or some other form of buffering.

The *rise time* of the Reset pulse was very critical on certain early TTL counters, particularly the 8280 (74176) style devices. While production changes have minimized the problem, a pull-up resistor of not more than 330 ohms is still recommended on the reset lines. As the reset signal goes through its active region, oscillation can occur if the transition occurs too slowly, ending in an erratic count or a partial reset. Even with known well-behaved devices, it is still good practice to have the reset lines rise and drop very sharply from a solid low-impedance source.

System reset pulses should also be as wide as practical—at least 10 microseconds in slow systems. A very brief reset operation can produce a trigger or a carry at an output that can arrive at a new logic block after the reset pulse has gone away. This can produce a wrong or erratic count, or a partial reset. Maximum possible reset width is usually determined by system clocking speed; obviously the reset has to go away, and the circuit has to settle before the next clock pulse arrives. Good practice is to use the widest possible reset pulses of the fastest possible rise time.

WHERE DO WE USE FLIP-FLOPS?

Many of the more complex TTL logic blocks consist of internally connected groups of JK or D flip-flops, particularly all the counter and shift-register devices. So far, we have only hinted at the many different things you can do with the JK and D flip-flops. Let us look at some applications in more detail.

DIGITAL READOUT MEMORY

Clocked flip-flops can be asked to store information at a selected instant. With the D flip-flop, that instant occurs on the positive-going clock edge. With the JK level-triggered flip-flop, that instant occurs the entire time the clock is positive and the input information must *not* change during that time. We can store data with either device.

One good example of simple storage is in a digital-readout system, where we might like a display to accept a measured value and hold the result for an entire new measuring interval. To do this, a group of latches are placed between the counting system and the decoder/drivers needed for the readouts. Fig. 5-8 shows one possible circuit. For a 4-bit binary or decimal BCD number, we can use the 74175 quad D flip-flop. At the instant the contents of the counter have the right answer in it, we transfer the information to the D flip-flops by applying a positive-going clock pulse. The D flip-flops then keep the number for as long as you like, and the counter is free to go onto a new measuring cycle or sequence. The display continuously puts out answers, instead of being a blur during counting times. Many second-generation TTL devices include counter/decoder/latch combinations in a single package. As with Fig. 5-8, the internal latch holds the data to get a stationary display during a new measuring time.

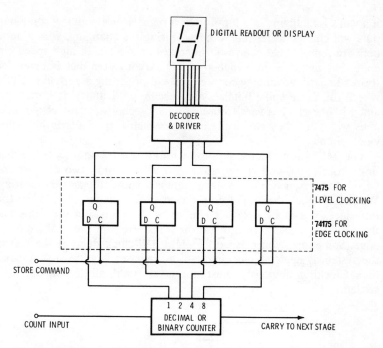

Fig. 5-8. Storage latch used to hold count for a stationary digital display while count continues on next measurement.

A good general-purpose system latch is the 74174 Hex D flip-flop. It can store six bits of information in one package in parallel form. Being edge clocked, the data can change at any time. Further, the stages can be cascaded in depth if needed for multiple-number storage.

The 7475 and 74100 are also called bistable latches, and some data sheets show them with D-type inputs These are a different sort of device. They are level-sensitive clocking. If the clock is high, the latches follow the input. If the clock is low, the latches store previous information. These packages are low in price and handy for readouts. Note that they can *not* be cascaded, for a wild race through them will result. Their performance is identical to a single-stage, gated RS flip-flop. There is no practical way to let these devices behave as a shift register or counter, although they are ideal for output storage.

HIGH-SPEED DEGLITCHER

Another simple storage application involves high-speed D/A converters, where a digital waveform is to be converted into its analog equivalent. It turns out that practically all TTL digital logic has different propagation times from a 1 to a 0 than from a 0 to a 1. Thus, if a word is changing in a flip-flop or a register or a counter, some outputs will change faster than others. During the changing, wrong numbers are put out that can result in spikes or glitches in high-speed circuits. For instance, in a high-speed D/A converter that is being fed from a linearly advancing counter, instead of getting a perfect stairstep waveform, large spike glitches may occur, particularly at steps 4, 8, and 12. The glitches vary from a few nanoseconds to tens of nanoseconds wide, but they can really cause problems, particularly in analog video circuits.

The 74S74 is a Dual-D flip-flop with identical 7-nanosecond transitions from 1 to 0 and vice versa. Fig. 5-9 shows how two of these can be used to resynchronize a 4-bit number whose 1's and 0's overlap. We simply clock the 74S74 on the next system clock pulse. While this introduces a 1-clock delay, it eliminates the transition problems and the glitches go away. Information is transferred on the positive clock edge. Sometimes you can work only a half-clock delay if the rest of the system is negative clocking or if an inverter is added to the clock line. Clocking obviously must not occur until all the inputs have settled.

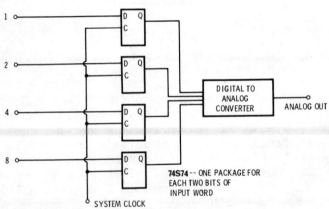

(A) Circuit to make 1–0 and 0–1 transitions fast and equal.

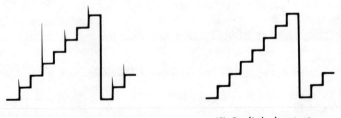

(B) Typical result without deglitching.　　　(C) Deglitched output.

Fig. 5-9. An effective deglitcher for high-speed digital-to-analog converters.

KEYBOARD DEBOUNCER

Data-entry keyboards present several circuit problems that are nicely eliminated with the debouncing and storage circuit of Fig. 5-10. When key contact is first made, the output code tends to be noisy and erratic until a *settling time,* usually less than 10 milliseconds, has allowed both the key contacts to make firm contact and the encoder to set up and deliver to proper code. Further, there is the possibility that the key could be released before the data could be entered into the rest of the circuit. The cure is to use a 10-millisecond delay from the Key

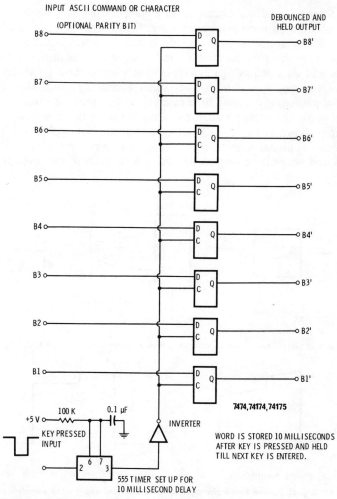

Fig. 5-10. Using type-D flip-flops to debounce and hold a data entry keyboard.

Pressed output to store or latch the code word being put out at that instant. The 555 timer provides the time delay as detailed in Chapter 4; the two 74175 latches provide the storage. The new code, corresponding to an ASCII command, is entered 20 milliseconds after the key is pressed and is held till the next key is entered. Edge-sensitive type-D latches work best in this application. Refinements are easily added to the circuit to provide for two or more keys down at the same time. These are called *2-key-rollover* and *n-key-rollover* schemes.

DIGITAL SAMPLE AND HOLD

A *Sample-and-Hold* circuit is an analog circuit that measures the value of an input for a brief instant and then keeps the value for later usage. These are sometimes called "boxcar" circuits and have seen wide use in the past in military radar signal processing, electronic music, and data-acquisition systems. Regardless of how good the design of the analog system is, the circuit eventually "runs down" or *droops,* particularly if long time intervals occur between samples. We can obtain a zero-droop circuit by doing the same thing digitally. The circuit is shown in Fig. 5-11A. Input signals are either obtained in or converted to digital form. A digital latch then stores the value on command and keeps it as long as needed. There is no droop, even if the

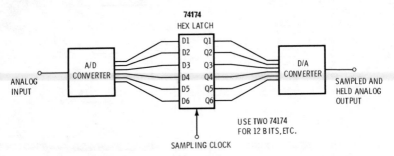

(A) Circuit converts analog signal to digital, then samples and stores at sampling time.

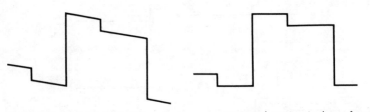

(B) Typical analog sample-hold has droop.   (C) Digital version is droop free.

Fig. 5-11. Digital storage forms the equivalent to a zero-droop analog sample-and-hold circuit. Output can be held for months without changing.

value is held for years. The output signal can either be used in digital form or converted back to analog. In the majority of systems, the A/D and D/A conversion processes turn out to be simpler and cheaper than the original Sample/Hold circuit, particularly if low droop is essential. The circuit shown samples on the positive-going clock edge. It has a resolution of 1 part in 64. Two circuits can be used for 12-bit accuracy; 1 part in 4096, and so on.

GARBAGE ELIMINATOR

Clocked flip-flops set up as simple storage devices also let you remove bad or unwanted portions of data in high-speed systems. For instance, if you are using data selectors to sample many different inputs, there will be a settling time when the data selector is putting out the wrong answer or when glitching by other inputs is occurring until the final selected input is obtained. During the settling time, the output is *garbage* (or any of a wide selection of unprintable names). These bad-data intervals can make up most of the time on a high-speed system. The trick is to sample the data with a storage latch when the data is known to be good. This eliminates completely any garbage and at the same time introduces a one-clock or one-half clock (using an inverter) system delay. Besides eliminating the garbage, the outputs

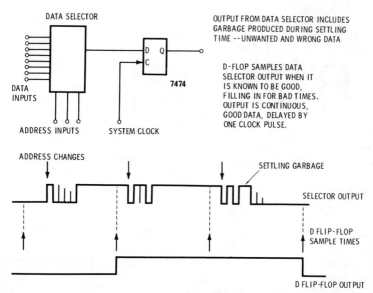

Fig. 5-12. A type-D flip-flop samples system data only when the data is known to be good, thus eliminating any "garbage" produced during settling and address change times earlier in the system.

are also *resynchronized* and locked into system timing. Fig. 5-12 shows details.

ELECTRONIC MUSIC KEYBOARD STORAGE

Before we go on to some other configurations, let us look at one more example of a flip-flop used for simple storage. Fig. 5-13 shows how we can place a storage latch between the keyboard and the digital note generator of a monophonic digital music synthesizer. The storage remembers what the note was after the key is released, allowing the completion of the decay portion of the note after key release.

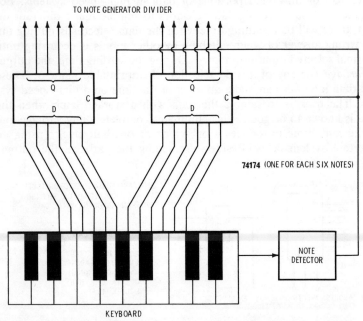

Fig. 5-13. In this monophonic music synthesizer, storage latches are used to hold the note after key release so the decay envelope can be completed.

SHIFT REGISTERS

The basic shift-register connection is shown in Fig. 5-14. Shift registers are used to *format* data from serial to parallel or back again, to shift data back and forth so it can be used, and to generate *sequences*. Two examples of sequences are the *walking-ring counter,* and the *pseudo-random sequence generator*.

There are so many possible shift-register applications that we have reserved Chapter 7 for them.

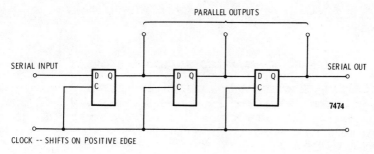

PARALLEL OUTPUTS

SERIAL INPUT

SERIAL OUT

7474

CLOCK -- SHIFTS ON POSITIVE EDGE

(A) Using type-D flip-flops.

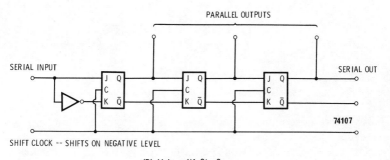

PARALLEL OUTPUTS

SERIAL INPUT

SERIAL OUT

74107

SHIFT CLOCK -- SHIFTS ON NEGATIVE LEVEL

(B) Using JK flip-flops.

Fig. 5-14. Clocked flip-flops used as shift registers.

BINARY DIVIDERS AND COUNTERS

The basic binary division circuits are shown in Fig. 5-15. You can cascade sequential stages to divide by 2, 4, 8, 16, 32, and so on. By selectively interfering with the count sequence or by preloading, we can count by any number we choose. Once again, there are so many possibilities, that we saved this topic for Chapter 6.

Generally, the JK flip-flop is more versatile than the type D for the majority of counter applications. Note that the D flip-flops clock on the positive edge; the JKs on the negative clock state. Inverters or a two-phase clock should be used if both types are mixed in one system.

GATE SYNCHRONIZER

Synchronizers in general are a way of aligning random outside-world commands and then getting them to exactly fit a time slot in a timing system. A *gate synchronizer* takes an external time command and produces an output that lasts for an even number of clock pulses; it starts with the first pulse after the command arrives and ends with the first

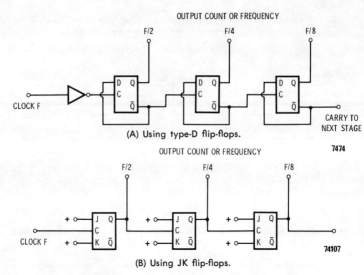

OUTPUT COUNT OR FREQUENCY

(A) Using type-D flip-flops.

OUTPUT COUNT OR FREQUENCY

(B) Using JK flip-flops.

Fig. 5-15. Binary counters or dividers using clocked flip-flops.

pulse after the command goes away. The circuit is shown in Fig. 5-16A.

The length of the synchronized output command will approximately equal the length of the outside-world command. It will precisely begin with a system clock pulse and end with one.

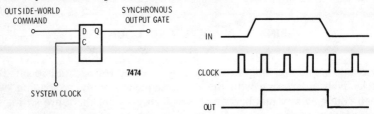

(A) Output gate exactly a whole number of clock cycles in length and approximately equal to input command length.

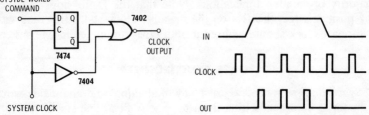

(B) Gating added to put out a whole number of clock cycles approximately equal to input command length.

Fig. 5-16. Two basic circuits of synchronizers used to tie-in outside commands to a system.

When the input command arrives, it sets up the D input. The output does not change until after clocking. Output follows input until the input drops. The output stays high until the next clock pulse and then it drops.

As a general rule, D edge-clocked devices should be used for *all* synchronizer applications. JK devices that are level clocked *cannot* normally be used to synchronize random data.

CLOCK SYNCHRONIZER

Fig. 5-16B shows a simple modification of the gate synchronizer. By adding a gate, we can get a whole number of system clock pulses out. These are equal approximately to the length of the input pulse but are always a whole number of clock cycles that begin and end synchronously with the clock. Again, only edge-sensitive D flip-flops should be used.

THE ONE-AND-ONLY-ONE

A very useful synchronizer is the *One-and-Only-One* circuit of Fig. 5-17. It is used to convert a single outside-world command, such as a pulse or a pushed button, into a precise time gate that lasts for one, and exactly one, whole interval between system clock pulses. The outside-world trigger sets the Set-Reset flip-flop on the left half of the circuit. Note that the direct inputs are used, so this half of the circuit responds immediately. The output of the Set-Reset flip-flop enables the D input of the clocked D flip-flop. Its Q output goes positive immediately after the next system clock pulse. This resets the Set-Reset flip-flop, which in turn places a ground on the D input. At the next clock pulse, the ground is transferred to the Q output. The net result is a positive output pulse on the Q output of the D flip-flop that lasts for one, and only one, whole clock interval, the interval immediately following the input command.

For instance, if you have a 1-hertz square wave for a clock, pushing the button at any time generates an output waveform that lasts precisely one second. This is independent of when the button was pushed with respect to system timing.

THE N-AND-ONLY-N

We can add a counter to the one-and-only-one circuit and come up with a circuit that delivers a burst of whole-length clock pulses of any number we like. For instance, if n = 7, pushing the button delivers 7 clock pulses. Fig. 5-18 shows details. The circuit starts off just like the one-and-only-one, but instead of resetting the input flip-flop im-

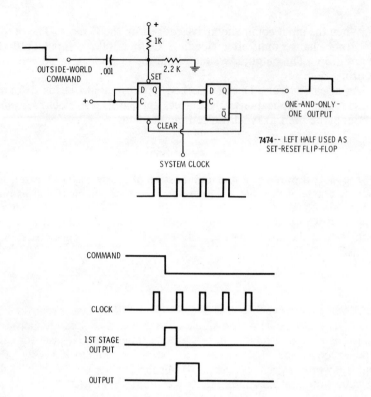

Fig. 5-17. The one-and-only-one synchronizer.

mediately, n clock cycles have to be output before the reset occurs. Again, an edge-clocked D flip-flop must be used.

Another way of looking at these last two circuits is that the first flip-flop absorbs the time difference between the random input and the system timing; the second stage then performs the actual synchronization.

THE RESYNCHRONIZER

There are several internal uses for synchronizers that can turn out to be rather handy. Resynchronizers are an easy way to eliminate propagation delays and glitches in gates and counters. They also let you convert a simple ripple counter with asynchronous logic and delays into a fully synchronous system with everything locked to the system clock pulses.

To use a resynchronizer, you perform all your logic *one clock cycle early* and then use the resynchronizer to pick the next clock cycle. For instance, suppose you had a long ripple counter and you wanted state

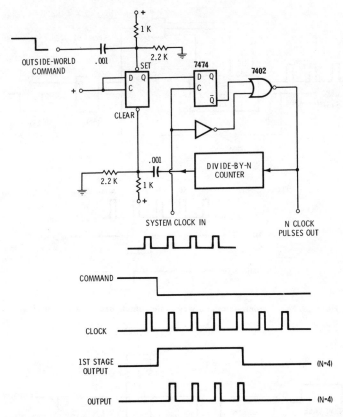

Fig. 5-18. The n-and-only-n synchronizer puts out n clock pulses in answer to a single outside-world command.

No. 38 synchronously decoded and locked to the system timing. You decode state No. 37 instead, using normal logic, and then use its output to drive a resynchronizer. The circuit is shown in Fig. 5-19. All the ripple delays, glitches, and gate propagation times vanish nicely, and the final output is once again synchronous with the system clock.

A resynchronizer then absorbs the remaining time left in slot No. 37. The only catch is that the total delays have to be less than one whole clock cycle, and that you can in fact do things one cycle early. This technique is a useful dodge that often can eliminate the need for a fully synchronous timing system. Ripple systems are inherently simpler, cheaper, and less power consuming.

THE AMBIGUITY RESOLVER: REMOVING BOBBLE

This is another specialized internal synchronizer. It is used to eliminate the 1-digit bobble that often appears in poorly designed elec-

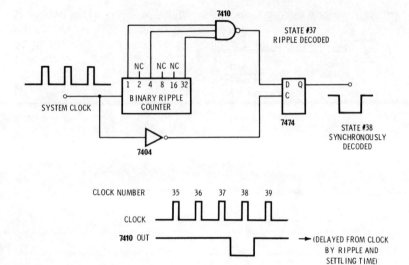

Fig. 5-19. Resynchronizers offer a way to tie outputs back to input clocking.

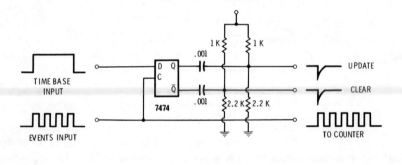

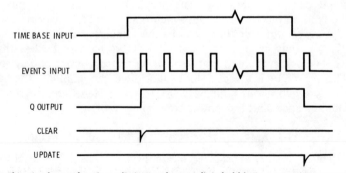

Fig. 5-20. This simple synchronizer eliminates the one-digit bobble in a counting system.

tronic-frequency counters and other digital displays. The bobble is caused by the input events being random in phase with respect to the On-Off gate that is providing a time interval. If an input event went by immediately before the time interval started, the output count will usually be one less than if the event happens immediately afterward.

To eliminate the problem, synchronize the time base to the events being counted with the simple gate synchronizer shown in Fig. 5-20. The output of this circuit does not open till the first event after the time gate arrives; the output continues till the first event after the gate goes away. This locks the measurement interval to the events being measured and eliminates the bobble. Incidentally, many times in print you will see statements about an inherent 1-count jitter in any digital instrument. There is nothing inherent about it at all—just add this simple circuit to eliminate the problem.

Besides using edge-clocked D flip-flops as synchronizers, there are one or two TTL synchronizer packages available that do the same job. These vary in availability and cost and are usually too specialized to stock for one or two circuit uses. The 74120 is typical.

THE BUCKET BRIGADE

The *bucket brigade* is an electronic stepper. It is made from JK flip-flops. It sequentially provides an output ground lasting one clock in-

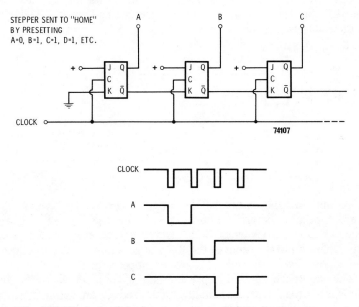

Fig. 5-21. The bucket brigade acts as a sequential synchronous stepper.

terval on successive stages, just like an electromechanical stepper. Fig. 5-21 shows the details.

To "home" the stepper, the first stage is cleared to 0 (Q grounded) and all remaining stages are set to 1 (Q positive). This puts all ouputs high except for the first. Stage 1 is enabled to go back positive on the first clock pulse. Stage 1 also enables stage 2 to go to ground on the first pulse. So, when the clock pulse arrives, stage 1 goes back positive and stage 2 synchronously drops to ground. (Note that a J = 1 and a K = 1 tells the stage to change its output, e.g., go from a 1 to a 0.)

At the next clock pulse, stage 2 goes back positive and stage 3 drops, and so on down the line. Output states last for one, and only one, sequential clock interval. The outputs follow each other in order.

The circuit can be open-ended or can close on itself to give a continuous-rotation stepper. Output states do not overlap and they are synchronous with the clock.

It turns out there are more efficient ways to generate and decode all the states of a long-sequence counter (see Chapter 7). To prevent disallowed states (more than one output grounded at once), the circuit must be sent to "home" when power is first applied and, preferably, immediately before each cycle.

SEQUENTIAL PASS-ON

The *sequential pass-on* is a series of independently clocked, cascaded D flip-flops. It is useful for predetermining counters, locks, and burglar alarms. The circuit is shown in Fig. 5-22.

TO INITIALIZE, PRESET ALL STAGES TO 1

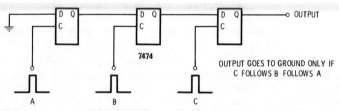

Fig. 5-22. The sequential pass-on.

To initialize the circuit, all flip-flops are preset positive. If clock event A occurs, the ground on the first D input gets passed on to the second stage. If clock event B occurs and follows event A, the ground gets passed on to the input of the third stage. Finally, if event C occurs and follows events B and A, a ground appears at the output.

The circuit can be used in predetermining counters where the thousands, hundreds, tens, and finally units produce an output when the right count is reached. In electronic combination locks, the proper sequence must be punched in. If the wrong sequence is used, external lock-out circuits can be added to sound an alarm or start a time delay.

A variant of this circuit is handy for burglar alarms. In normal tape-and-switch systems, either a complex time delay or an unprotected door or an outside switch is needed to let the last person leave the building at night without tripping the alarm. To get around these alternatives, a sequential pass-on is set up that stops one stage short of arming the alarm. The last person leaving is then free to leave via any protected door. Opening and closing the door advances the pass-on one stage and arms the system.

DIGITAL MIXER

A D-type flip-flop can be used as a digital mixer to produce the difference between two square waves of different frequencies. Fig. 5-23 shows the circuit.

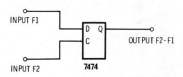

Fig. 5-23. A digital mixer using a single type-D flip-flop.

Assume initially that F1 and F2 are identical in phase and frequency. The D input will be 1 the instant clocking occurs, and the output will be a 1. Now, let the frequency of F1 very slowly "slip cycles" with respect to F2. The output will alternate at the difference frequency $F2 - F1$, and we have the equivalent of a digital mixer or down-converter.

There are several serious restrictions to using the circuit. First, both inputs must be fixed or slowly varying square waves; thus, you cannot mix several frequencies at once as you can with an analog circuit. Second, jitter in the output is inherent, for the Q output can drop only immediately after clocking, thus quantizing the output square wave. The worst-case jitter is one-half the clock frequency.

For instance, if both clock and D signals are near 1 kHz, the worst-case jitter can be around half a millisecond. If the frequency difference is less than 50 hertz or so, this jitter is tolerable, but as the difference gets larger, the jitter becomes intolerable. Thus, the circuit works best when it is taking a small difference between two nearly identical frequencies.

Another limitation (sometimes a handy feature) is that the mixer is harmonic sensitive. For instance, inputs of 10.000 and 10.030 kHz will give you a 30-hertz difference frequency. So will 10 kHz and 20.030 kHz or 30.030 kHz, or any other harmonic difference.

The circuit is very handy for signal generators that use frequency synthesis, particularly where a counter goes on the output to minimize the jitter. It also has applications in electronic music. It is a very useful circuit anywhere you can use a slightly noisy difference between two nearly identical frequencies or their harmonics.

.   .   .   .   .   .

While this chapter has emphasized using the JK and D flip-flops, any and all of these techniques are obviously extendable to the more complex MSI logic blocks that use flip-flops as their internal operands. The question of whether to use simple gates or large logic blocks is yours to answer. It depends on economics, system size, availability, and the practicality of ordering and stocking several ICs just to fill one or two oddball applications.

CHAPTER 6

Divide-by-N Counters

A divide-by-n counter is a logic block that produces one output pulse for n input pulses. It can also be used as a scaler in which an applied input frequency is reduced by a factor of n.

Counters form an extremely important group of TTL applications, particularly in the areas of timing systems and digital instruments. For instance, in a digital instrument called a *frequency counter,* we might have six decades of decimal counters and associated *decoder/drivers* powering a 6-digit display readout. The time base of the counter might consist of a 1.0-MHz crystal oscillator and up to seven cascaded decade dividers to get a precise measuring interval of 0.1, 1, or 10 seconds.

Digital clocks are basically counters. Some of these start with the 60-hertz power-line frequency and divide by 60 to get a 1-pulse-per-second output. This is in turn divided by 10, by 6, by 10, and by 6 again to get the minutes and hours information. If we like, we can continue to add counters for AM/PM, day, and year indication.

A television servicing dot-and-bar generator might start with a 189-kHz crystal oscillator, used for 12 vertical bars. This is divided by 6 to get a 31.500-kHz half-screen rate. Two divisions follow this—an *even* divide-by-2 for the horizontal rate at 15,750 and an *odd* divide-by-525 to get the *interlaced* vertical output of 60 hertz. By factoring the divide-by-525 into a divide-by-15 and a divide-by-35, we can obtain a 900-hertz intermediate frequency, useful to get 15 horizontal lines.

Traditional counter design methods required you to start with gates and JK flip-flops and work up to the desired count sequence. The design process was lengthy and introduced problems such as glitches and disallowed subroutines. With TTL, there are a wide variety of standard counter MSI blocks available which can be used directly or suitably modified to obtain other count lengths.

In this chapter, we will discuss desirable qualities in a divide-by-n counter and generally look at the various counter types. This will be followed by some simple low-modulo counters, in turn followed by a look at the standard MSI blocks and how to use them. High-modulo cascadable counters and decoding techniques are next in line. We will end with a counter for an electronic music synthesizer. A few specialized counters based on shift-register techniques have been saved for the next chapter.

COUNTER QUALITIES

There are many features that might be desirable in a counter. We might call these counter *qualities*. Let us see what some of these qualities are and how they can influence our choice of a counting system.

Modulo

The *modulo* of a counter is simply n, or how many states the counter goes through before repeating. A *decade* counter has a modulo of 10. In a divide-by-3 counter, n is obviously 3. In a *variable modulo* counter, n can be any of a range of selected values.

We can look at n as the number of clock cycles it takes a counter to return to a given state condition. Or, we can call n the number of input pulses needed to get a carry on the output, counted from the previous carry. Or n can be the ratio of *frequencies* between input and output, with the output frequency being $1/n$ times the input. TTL counters are independent of how fast or how often the input pulses arrive, up to the maximum permissible frequency limit. Counter operation is identical in static operation, random pulses, pulse bursts, or continuously applied frequency modes.

The maximum n of any counter is the binary number equal to the number of cascaded binary dividers in the chain. For instance, a counter consisting of four cascaded dividers can count to any n up to $2^4 = 16$. A 10-stage counter can count up to 1024 and so on. By suitably interfering with the count sequence, we can usually shorten the count to anything less than 2^n, but we can never lengthen it.

Weighting

Practically all the counters in this chapter are based on binary dividers that have their count sequence or starting point suitably interfered with to produce a desired count length. If we can assign a *count value* to each counter output, we have a *weighted* counter. For instance, in the 4-stage binary-ripple counter of Fig. 6-1, the first stage has a

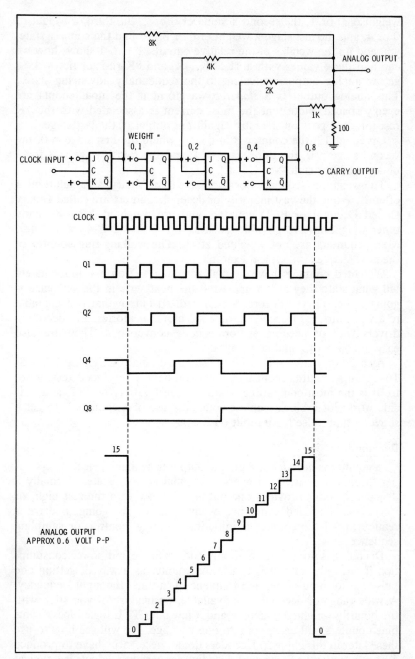

Fig. 6-1. Weighted counters such as this 4-stage, 1-2-4-8, binary ripple counter are easily converted to equivalent analog signal levels.

weight of 0 or 1, the second a value of 0 or 2, the third, a weight of 0 or 4, and the last stage a weight of 0 or 8. To find the counter state, you add up the weights of the relative outputs. Fig. 6-1 shows how we can add these values with a 1K, 2K, 4K, and 8K resistor network to get an analog output equivalent to the sequentially advancing states. This analog output is a *stairstep* waveform if the input counts are evenly spaced. Note that the most current is associated with the 1K resistor, so it goes on the most significant output of the last stage.

On count 12, the counter is in a state where the first stage = 0, the second stage = 0, the third stage = 4, and the fourth stage = 8 for a binary 1100 or state No. 12.

The weighting sequence does not have to be binary, although it most often is. While the vast majority of decimal counters are called Binary Coded Decimal or BCD counters and are weighted 1-2-4-8, many other weightings are possible, such as 1-1'-2-5, 1-2-2'-4, or 1-2-4-5. Many counters are not weighted at all. The walking-ring counter of the next chapter is a typical example.

Weighted counters have several advantages. You can immediately tell what state they are in and what the next state in the sequence is going to be. They also form a standardized output that is acceptable to a wide variety of decoders, data selectors, memories, and decoder/drivers without needing elaborate code conversions. They are also easy to convert to analog voltages.

As a general rule, stick with the standard binary weighting 1-2-4-8-16- . . . up-counting sequence unless you have a very good reason not to. It is the most compatible with the widest variety of TTL and outside-world logic blocks, unless your only use of a counter is to get a single output pulse for n input ones.

Decoding

A counter is *decoded* if a unique output is available, electronic-stepper fashion, for each and every individual counter state. Normally a decoded counter provides one output of n low with the rest high, or vice versa. Decoded states are essential if we are going to drive a readout, or if the counter is initiating a timing, control, or sampling sequence.

Decoding is not needed and only adds expense and power consumption if our only interest is to use the counter as a way of getting one pulse out for n pulses in, or a frequency 1/n times the input frequency. A wide range of decoders are available, particularly if you stick with the binarily weighted counters, and a few later TTL logic blocks combine counters and decoders into one package. We will see how to use these later in this chapter. Decoders do not necessarily have to produce 1-of-n outputs; the 7-segment decoding for certain readouts is a typical example.

Synchronism

In an *asynchronous* or *ripple* counter, a change in the output of one stage initiates a possible change on the next stage, which in turn can use its output to initiate a following stage, domino fashion. Substantial propagation delays can build up during the ripple-through time, and output stages will not be completely valid until the counter has completely settled. Fig. 6-2A shows a divide-by-8 ripple counter. The *ripple* or *settling* time may be a good fraction of a microsecond long on longer counters. During this time, any decoded intermediate states will be invalid, and decoding spikes, called *glitches,* may be present. These spikes must not be allowed to initiate any invalid sequences elsewhere in the circuit.

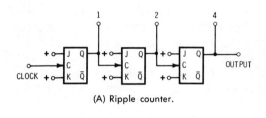

(A) Ripple counter.

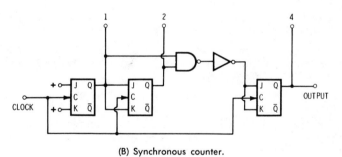

(B) Synchronous counter.

Fig. 6-2. Two types of divide-by-8 counters.

In a *synchronous* counter, the output changes immediately after the system clock arrives. All properly enabled stages change simultaneously, and propagation glitches are not normally produced. In general, synchronous counters are faster, more expensive, and use more supply power. At the same time, they are a better choice for high-frequency work or circuits where output glitches must be minimized. Note that you can sometimes have the best of both worlds if you only need one or two synchronous states—simply use the resynchronizer of Fig. 5-19 by decoding one count early and relocking outputs to the system clock. Fig. 6-2B shows a synchronous divide-by-8.

Presettability

Most TTL counters have a clear capability in which the count may be returned to 0. A few of the MSI logic blocks also have parallel inputs that let you *preset* a counter to any count you like. These are handy for shortening count sequences with feedback, for allowing you-set-it variable modulo counting, and for letting you enter parallel data as in the example of the digital clock shown in Fig. 7-4.

One handy use of the preset inputs is to provide a second clear input. This is done by presetting all 0's and is handy if the length of a counter is being shortened by a decode-and-reset scheme but still needs an external clear capability.

Count Direction

The majority of TTL counters are *up-only* counters—they count only in a direction of increasing states on a weighted basis. In an unmodified binary sequence, you can pick complementary outputs or add inverters to convert to a down-counter. You can *not* do this with non-binary lengths. A BCD counter normally counts from 0 through 9. Complement everything and it will count from 15 down to 6, not from 9 down to 0.

One series of *down-only* counters is available in the MC4016/4018 series. These are useful for backward-counting sequences and are particularly easy to unit-cascade for long sequences where you load in a number and count it down to 0.

True up/down counters are also available that will either add to, ignore, or subtract from the count at any time. The 74190 and 74192 are typical. While these are the most flexible and versatile of counter blocks, they also are usually more expensive, harder to get, and more power consuming than the regular up-only versions. If a full add/subtract capability is essential, these are the logical choice to use; otherwise, the simpler counter systems can be used.

Unit Cascadability

Counters may normally be connected together in sequence, so the output of the first is the input to the second, and so on to lengthen the count. In this case, n will be the *product* of the modulos of the two counters. Normally, ripple counters clock on the falling or negative edge of the clock, so that as the output of one counter drops, it triggers the next down the line. With some synchronous counters, the advance of the counter on the positive-going clock edge and logic from a previous group of stages enable the input to a following stage so it advances in synchronism with the clock edge.

Unit decade cascadable counters are another matter entirely. For many long programmable count sequences, it would be nice to have a series of thumbwheel switches. If we dial a 345 into these switches, we would like the counter to divide by three hundred forty-five. If we simply connected three ordinary divide-by-n counters so one output drives the next input, we would divide by $3 \times 4 \times 5$, or 60, instead, and things would get very confusing if one of the counters should happen to be set at 0.

What we really need is a counting system that allows 300 counts *plus* 40 counts *plus* 5 counts to get the total. Ordinary counters will not do this, and it takes a combination of look-ahead and feedback techniques to handle this problem. The 4016 and 4018 series are unit cascadable and work on a down-count basis. The 74160 through 74163 are also unit cascadable and work on an up-count basis. This type of counter is particularly useful in process controls and frequency synthesizers, or anywhere else we might like to set a division ratio in decade-coded switches.

Symmetry

The output of a counter is *symmetrical* if it is up for half the time and down for half the time when fed a constant-rate input. This is often desirable if we are going to convert the output to a sine wave or if we wish to obtain a time reference that is on for exactly half the interval. Any counter can be made to have a symmetrical output if we go to enough trouble. For instance, on an even-length counter, we can count to half the length we need and add a binary divider on the output. Odd-length symmetrical counters are theoretically possible by alternating the clocking edges. Symmetrical outputs are not usually available except in straight binary dividers, and you have to suitably provide for them where needed.

SOME PITFALLS

Let us also take a brief look at problems that arise in the designing of counter sequences of special length. In many cases, the use of TTL logic blocks greatly minimizes these problems, but they can still cause trouble if not allowed for.

Disallowed States

Any counter of less length than its unmodified binary length can get into one or more disallowed states or disallowed subroutines. Each and every state *outside* of the normal count sequence must be checked to prevent hangups or undesirable count sequences. With the majority of counter circuits designed around MSI counter devices, the sequences will self-clear after a few clock pulses. This is *not* true of the shift-register counters of the next chapter, where more details on this particular problem will be found.

Available Clearing

If a Clear input is available on a counter, it will set the counter to a 0000 . . . state. This state should be part of the count sequence desired if a clear is needed. If it is not, a few extra counts will be needed between the clear and a desired count sequence. By the same token, if the clear is used in a decode-and-reset count-shortening circuit, it cannot also be used to provide an external or system-level clear, unless gating is available. One way around this problem is to use a counter with both clear and parallel-load capabilities. A parallel load is identical to a clear if all 0's are loaded.

Self-Annihilating Coincidences

If the output of a circuit changes its own input, the resulting sequence can be very short—so short, in fact, that partial resets, erratic operation, or temperature-dependent operation will result. For instance, suppose that reaching 0 count drops the output line of a counter. If this line is used to load another number back into its own input the output once again goes high, very shortly after loading, giving a pulse that is only a few nanoseconds wide. The short pulse may be too short to properly activate other parallel inputs, and a partial load or a partial clear may result. The solution is to use either a monostable circuit that is irrevocably triggered for a fixed-width pulse, or to add enough delay with a capacitor or extra inverters to make sure the pulse is wide enough.

Many counters have a setup time less than the ripple delay time. If they do, this problem does not exist. Carefully reading the data sheet for the counter used and drawing out the timing sequence, including all propagation delays, will usually indicate whether a partial clear or preset is possible.

A Too-Short Reset Pulse

The same type of problem can crop up if a reset pulse is very short in a system. Conceivably an output carry can be produced and routed to the next stage after the clear or reset has gone away, again ending in an erratic count or partial reset. The widest possible reset pulses should always be used. If at all possible, a reset pulse having a minimum width of at least 10 microseconds is recommended to give all stages a chance to settle before the reset line is released.

Slow Reset Rise and Fall Times

Some of the older TTL counters were sensitive to the reset rise and fall time and would oscillate if the circuits remained in their active regions for more than a very few nanoseconds. The lowest impedance that is practical should always be used on a reset line. Reset lines should never be left floating or allowed to go off a pc board without buffering or isolation.

Multiple Decoding

An error was intentionally left in Fig. 5-19. The decoder shown will decode state No. 37 properly. The trouble is that it will also decode states 39, 45, 47, 53, 55, 61, and 63. In any decoding scheme, *all* inputs must be used and accounted for. To decode only state No. 37, we would have to include the complements of the 2, 8, and 16 outputs as well as the 32, 4, and 1 lines. One exception to this is when there is forced reset before count No. 39. Then the state No. 37 is the only one that can occur, and we can use the simplified decoding.

In general, beware of any simplified or partial decoding scheme that does not use all possible inputs, for multiple outputs are often possible.

Noise Precautions

The TTL counters are especially sensitive to supply-line noise. The usual well-regulated 5-volt supply with one $0.05\text{-}\mu\text{F}$ despiking capacitor for each two or three MSI counter packages is recommended. The high-speed counters must be used with printed-circuit boards having wide supply lines. The breadboard, perfboard, or handwired types of construction are almost certain to cause problems with these devices.

As with the JK and D flip-flops, clock and input lines should also be clean, with reasonably fast rise and fall times. Mechanical contacts must be suitably debounced with the circuits of Chapter 4.

SOME LOW-MODULO COUNTERS

There are a few counters that are simple enough that it pays to build them with flip-flops rather than use an MSI logic block. Let us take a quick look at these before going onto the available MSI counters.

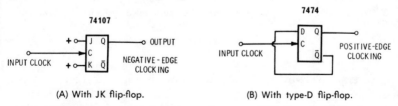

(A) With JK flip-flop.   (B) With type-D flip-flop.

Fig. 6-3. Divide-by-2 circuits. Both are synchronous, weighted, and self-decoding.

The divide-by-2 circuit is shown in Fig. 6-3. It is synchronous and self-decoding and may be built with either JK or D flip-flops.

Modulo-3 circuits appear in Fig. 6-4. The basic circuit is built from a dual JK flip-flop. It is synchronous, and two states are self-decoding;

the third state is decoded as shown. The other possibility, that of cross coupling in the other direction, results in a counter that has the 00 state outside of the count sequence. Hence, it is not normally used.

One possibility for a symmetrical divide-by-3 is shown in Fig. 6-4B. This circuit is useful in electronic music and anywhere else that a low-frequency, symmetrical output is needed. Its output will be symmetric only if the input clock is symmetric. The resistor and capacitor are needed to remove a glitch caused by propagation delays. The circuit shown should not be used above 100 kHz.

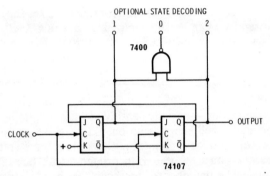

(A) Conventional divide-by-3 is synchronous, weighted, and self-decodes two of three states.

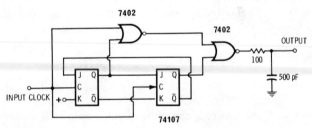

(B) Symmetrical divide-by-3 has a symmetrical output, provided the input is symmetrical to start with.

Fig. 6-4. Divide-by-3 circuits.

Several divide-by-4 schemes are shown in Fig. 6-5. Fig. 6-5A is a straight ripple counter, built with either JK or D flip-flops. Fig. 6-5B is a synchronous version, also weighted 1-2. Fig. 6-5C is a walking-ring counter (see next chapter) that is synchronous but unweighted. It is also decoded as shown.

Beyond modulo 4, it is most practical to look at the TTL MSI logic blocks already available and either use them directly or modify them with external feedback circuits.

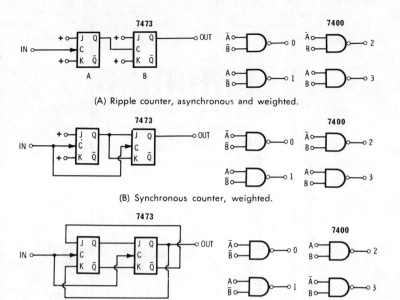

(A) Ripple counter, asynchronous and weighted.

(B) Synchronous counter, weighted.

(C) Walking-ring counter, synchronous and unweighted, with four output phases available (see Chapter 7).

Fig. 6-5. Divide-by-4 circuits.

SOME TTL MSI COUNTERS

Table 6-1 lists the main counters available. Most of these are decade (divide-by-10) counters or hexadecimal (divide-by-16) counters, although there are a few divide-by-12 counters listed as well. While all the units have equivalent "74" numbers, the 8280 series is better known by its Signetics generic device numbers, and the same thing is true of the Motorola MC4016 series.

By *organization,* we mean the arrangement of counters inside the package. For instance a 2×5 counter has two separate counters in one package. If you connect first to the binary divider and then connect its output to the divide-by-5, you will get a standard 1-2-4-8 weighted binary-coded decimal or BCD counter. On the other hand, if you connect to the divide-by-5 first and follow this with a divide-by-2, you get a counter weighted 1-2-4-5 with a symmetrical output useful for recovering sine waves, frequency synthesis, and other similar functions. It is also possible to use the two counter sections in totally different circuits, provided they can operate with a common clear.

By the term *unit cascadable,* we mean that a cascaded group of counters can be driven directly from a set of thumbwheel switches on a "by decades" basis. This will be explained in more detail in a later section.

227

Table 6-1. Some of the More Popular TTL MSI Counters (Undecoded Types)

Type	N	Direction	Type	Maximum Clock Frequency	Presets?	Unit Cascadable?	Organization	Clock
7490	10	up only	ripple	32 MHz	0, 9 only	no	2 × 5	neg edge
7492	12	up only	ripple	32 MHz	no	no	2 × 6	neg edge
7493	16	up only	ripple	32 MHz	no	no	2 × 8	neg edge
74160	10	up only	synchronous	32 MHz	yes	yes	1 × 10	pos edge
74161	16	up only	synchronous	32 MHz	yes	yes	1 × 16	pos edge
74190	10	up/down	synchronous	25 MHz	yes	yes	1 × 10	pos edge
74191	16	up/down	synchronous	25 MHz	yes	yes	1 × 16	pos edge
74192	10	up/down	synchronous	30 MHz	yes	yes	1 × 10	pos edge
8280	10	up only	ripple	35 MHz	yes	no	2 × 5	neg edge
8281	16	up only	ripple	35 MHz	yes	no	2 × 8	neg edge
8288	12	up only	ripple	35 MHz	yes	no	2 × 6	neg edge
MC4016	10	down only	ripple	8 MHz*	yes	yes	1 × 10	pos edge
MC4018	16	down only	ripple	8 MHz*	yes	yes	1 × 16	pos edge

*Minimum guaranteed values—the rest are typical.

Many faster counters are also available—up to 125 MHz, using Schottky devices. As a general rule, these devices cost more, are harder to get, and consume more supply power. Therefore, they should be avoided unless the speed is absolutely essential. Printed-circuit ground-plane construction is mandatory with these faster devices, and an oscilloscope at least as fast as the logic is also almost essential to design with them effectively.

MORE COUNTERS

Several modulo-5 counters are shown in Fig. 6-6. In Fig. 6-6A, the divide-by-5 portion of an 8280 is used. This is an up-only ripple

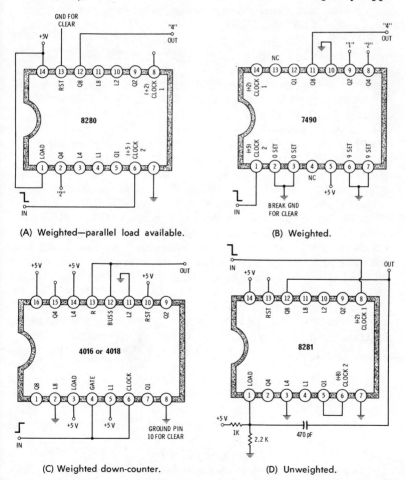

(A) Weighted—parallel load available.

(B) Weighted.

(C) Weighted down-counter.

(D) Unweighted.

Fig. 6-6. Divide-by-5 circuits.

counter. It is low in cost and has Preset inputs as well as a Clear available. You will find more operating details for these counters given in Chapter 2.

The 7490 can also be used as a divide-by-5, as shown in Fig. 6-6B. One disadvantage to its use is that you have to break the reset line from ground—i.e., ground is normal operation and reset is positive. There is also a 9-set pair of inputs that must also be held at ground. The four most common mistakes made with this particular circuit are: forgetting to ground the 9 sets, forgetting to ground the resets, forgetting to tie the two counter halves together when you are after a divide-by-10, and forgetting to condition and debounce mechanical or outside-world clock commands. Note also that the supply connections are a bit unusual. Better connections are available in a later series of devices, the 74290 and 74293.

In Fig. 6-6C, we use the 4018 as a weighted down-counter. This unit has a unique advantage. You can use the same circuit for any n you like up to 16 by applying in binary form the number you want to divide by to the preset inputs. This makes counter design very easy. For counts up to $n = 10$, you can use either the MC4016 or the 4018; above 10 you need the 4018. For instance, if you want to divide by 5, you will use a binary 0101. We apply a 1 (+5 volts) to the "1" input (pin 5) and to the "4" input (pin 14), while we ground (apply 0's) to the "2" parallel input (pin 11) and the "8" parallel input (pin 2).

A similar technique works with the synchronous 74160 and 74161, except that the complement of the number you are dividing by has to be entered into the parallel inputs.

Finally, Fig. 6-6D shows another basic technique that works for any count. We use the falling edge of the most significant bit to indicate that count 0 has just come up. At that instant, we parallel-load the difference between the maximum count we want and n. For instance, the 8281 is a hexadecimal or divide-by-16. If we jump to state 11 immediately when 0 comes up, we will get a sequence 11, 12, 13, 14, 15, (briefly to 0—preset to 11) . . . 12, 13—this gives us a 5-state counter. Any count can be handled this way; a sort of universal fix for any count length. The circuit is unweighted, and the feedback circuitry on the load line is limited to 5 MHz or less unless we are very careful about the time constants and just how we parallel-load. If we wanted to, we could also use only the divide-by-8 portion of this counter and preload it to 3. If we did this, the count sequence would run 3, 4, 5, 6, 7 . . . 3, 4, 5, 6, 7.

These counters appear in Fig. 6-7. Figs 6-7A and B are similar to the ones we used for modulo 5, only this time we use the 6 part of a 2×6 counter, instead of the 5 part of a 2×5.

We can use a 7490 for a divide-by-6 in the "trick" circuit of Fig. 6-7C, but we lose the Clear capability unless we add an external gate.

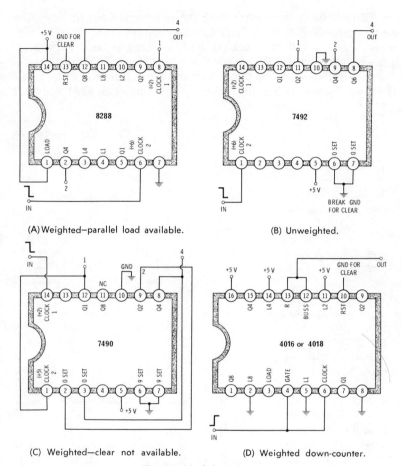

(A) Weighted—parallel load available.

(B) Unweighted.

(C) Weighted—clear not available.

(D) Weighted down-counter.

Fig. 6-7. Divide-by-6 circuits.

It is a weighted output. In Fig. 6-7D, we use a 4016 or 4018 by parallel loading a 6 on its inputs.

A synchronous divide-by-6 and divide-by-5 appear in the next chapter. Six is obviously factorable into 2×3, so we can also do a divide-by-6 by cascading a divide-by-2 and a divide-by-3, in either sequence. Putting the binary divider on the output gives a symmetrical square-wave output. A unique pair of divide-by-6 counters with special decoding appears in the electronic dice circuit of Fig. 7-14.

DIVIDE-BY-SEVEN

Several of the modulo 7 circuits appear in Fig. 6-8. Fig. 6-8 is the now familiar encode-and-count-down, using the 4018. A 7 is parallel-loaded into the counter every time the counter reaches 0. Thus, the count proceeds 7, 6, 5, 4, 3, 2, 1, (0—jump to 7), 6, 5, ... Fig. 6-8B is a 7490 with feedback on the 9 set lines to get a 7-count sequence. It is unweighted.

A new technique called the *decode and reset* is shown in Fig. 6-8C. Here, we detect state 7 of the divide-by-8 portion of an 8281 and reset

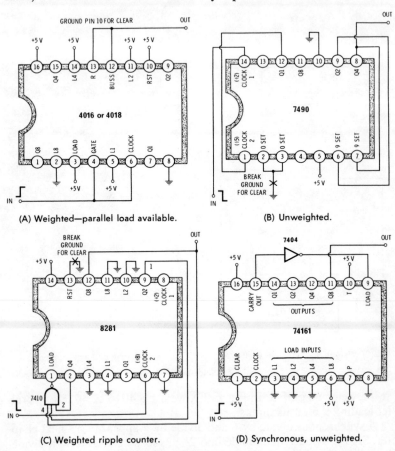

(A) Weighted—parallel load available.

(B) Unweighted.

(C) Weighted ripple counter.

(D) Synchronous, unweighted.

Fig. 6-8. Divide-by-7 circuits.

to 0, giving us a weighted ripple counter. By presetting a 0, we "save" the main Clear line (pin 13) for external clearing. You have to be certain the ripple propagation delay time and the time through the 3-input gate is longer than the required setup time, or a circuit like this can produce a self-annihilating coincidence. This is not a problem with the 8281; it can be with other counters. Ideally, extra delay or a monostable circuit is called for when this technique is used.

Another new approach is shown in Fig. 6-8D. Here, we use the 74161, detect state 15, and load an 8 into the Preset inputs. The count sequence goes 8, 9, 10, 11, 12, 13, 14, (15—jump to 8), ... It is synchronous, but is unweighted and cannot be cleared since 0 is outside the count sequence. It is also possible to combine the decode-and-reset technique of Fig. 6-8C with the 74161 and get a fully synchronous, weighted, clearable counter. Once again, an external gate is required.

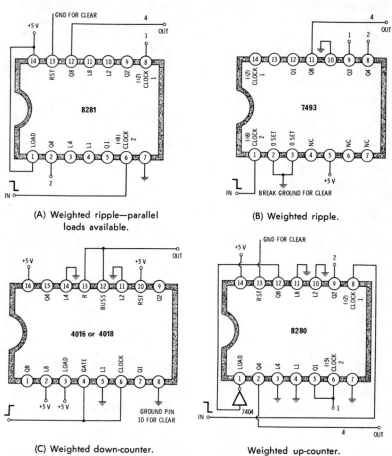

(A) Weighted ripple—parallel loads available.

(B) Weighted ripple.

(C) Weighted down-counter.

Weighted up-counter.

Fig. 6-9. Divide-by-8 circuits.

Another synchronous divide-by-7 appears in Fig. 7-13. A circuit similar to Fig. 6-6D can also be used by using the transition to count 0 to jump to state 9. The count proceeds 9, 10, 11, 12, 13, 14, 15, (jump to 9), 10, 11, ...

DIVIDE-BY-8

Eight is easy since it is a binary number. It can obviously be built with either of the circuits of Fig. 6-2, and a fully synchronous, decodable, 8-stage walking ring appears in Fig. 7-9. It also has eight different output phases available.

Fig. 6-9 shows some more possibilities. Figs. 6-9A and B use the divide-by-8 sections of the 8281 and 7493 directly. Fig. 6-9C parallel-loads an 8 into a 4018 and down-counts it to 0. Fig. 6-9D uses the 1000 state of an 8280 to clear itself. It is weighted, and the count proceeds 0, 1, 2, 3, 4, 5, 6, 7, (8—jump to 0), 1, etc. A Clear is available. The same thing may be done with a 7490, using one of the Clear lines for count shortening and the other for an external clear-to-0. The inverter is not needed with the 7490.

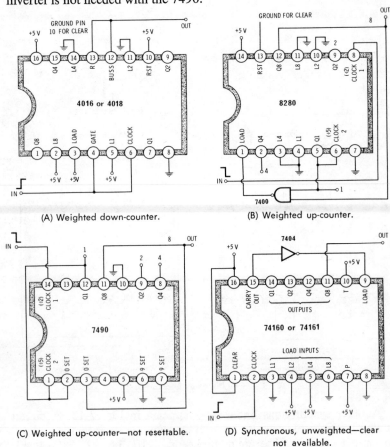

(A) Weighted down-counter.

(B) Weighted up-counter.

(C) Weighted up-counter—not resettable.

(D) Synchronous, unweighted—clear not available.

Fig. 6-10. Divide-by-9 circuits.

234

DIVIDE-BY-9

Two cascaded divide-by-3 counters can be used for a divide-by-9. Fig. 6-10A loads to 9 and down-counts. It may also be cleared as shown. Fig. 6-10B uses a decode-and-reset for a weighted ripple counter. Fig. 6-10C is a 7490 with internal feedback, and Fig. 6-10D is a synchronous, unweighted counter that detects state 15 and jumps to 6. A Clear is not available. Alternately, state 9 can be detected and used to clear for a resettable, divide-by-9, weighted, synchronous up-counter at the price of an external 2-input NAND gate.

DIVIDE-BY-10

All of the decade counters can be used without modification to realize the divide-by-10 functions. For those counters composed of a 2×5 organization, we can place the binary counter first and end up with a 1-2-4-8 weighting. Alternately, we can place the binary counter second and end up with a symmetrical output and a 1-2-4-5 weighting. Typical circuits appear in Fig. 6-11. Concepts for decoding these counters so that they can drive readouts and interface circuits will appear later in the chapter.

DIVIDE-BY-11

Decade counters cannot be used by themselves beyond $n = 10$, so we must turn to the modulo-12 and modulo-16 counters for a base-11 count.

In Fig. 6-12A, we load an 11 into a 4018 and down-count it to 0. In Fig. 6-12B, we use feedback decode and reset on a 8288 to shorten the count by one, giving us a weighted, clearable ripple counter. In Fig. 6-12C, we use the state 0 dropping of an 8281 to preload a 5 into the counter. The count proceeds 5, 6, 7, 8, 9, 10, 11, 12, 13, 14, 15, (0 —jump to 5), 6, 7, ... Fig. 6-12D is a synchronous but unweighted version using the 74161.

DIVIDE-BY-12

This count may be obtained by cascading $2 \times 2 \times 3$, 4×3, or 6×2 counters; we can also use the 7492 and 8288 directly. Base-16 counters may also be shortened as shown in Fig. 6-13.

THIRTEEN THROUGH SIXTEEN

These counts can only be handled by the hexadecimal or base-16 counters. Fig. 6-14 shows how we can shorten the count sequence in

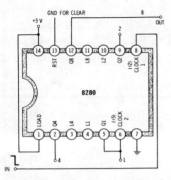

(A) Ripple up-counter, weighted 1-2-4-8.

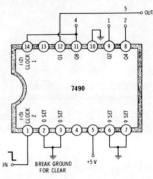

(B) Ripple up-counter, weighted 1-2-4-5.

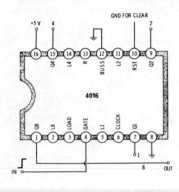

(C) Ripple down-counter, weighted 1-2-4-8.

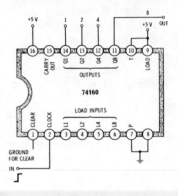

(D) Synchronous up-counter, weighted 1-2-4-8.

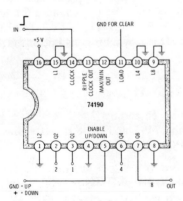

(E) Synchronous up/down counter, weighted 1-2-4-8.

Fig. 6-11. Divide-by-10 circuits.

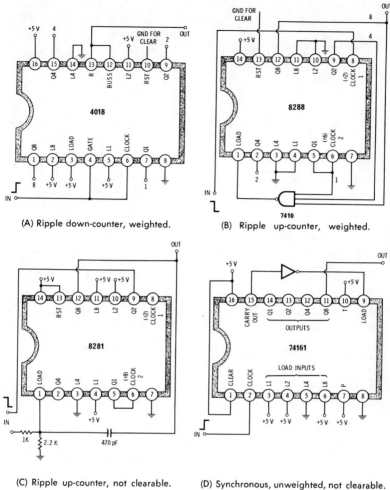

(A) Ripple down-counter, weighted.

(B) Ripple up-counter, weighted.

(C) Ripple up-counter, not clearable.

(D) Synchronous, unweighted, not clearable.

Fig. 6-12. Divide-by-11 circuits.

various ways, while Fig. 6-15 shows the connections for the unshortened base-16 counters.

UNIVERSAL COUNT SEQUENCERS

Beyond base 16, we usually have to use two or more ICs for the count sequence. By suitably cascading binary counters and shortening the count sequence any count length we like can be formed.

Fig. 6-16 shows how we can use a pair of MC4018s to divide by any number from 1 to 256. In this system, the number you want to divide

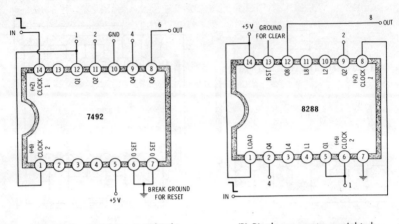

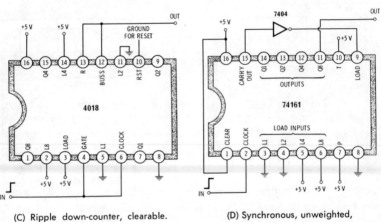

(A) Ripple up-counter, weighted 1-2-4-6, clearable.

(B) Ripple up-counter, weighted 1-2-4-8, clearable.

(C) Ripple down-counter, clearable.

(D) Synchronous, unweighted, not clearable.

Fig. 6-13. Divide-by-12 circuits.

by goes into the parallel inputs; the counter loads that number and counts it down to 0. We can also reset to 0.

To program the counter, enter the binary equivalent of the number you wish to divide by on the program inputs. For example, for a divide-by-51, $51 = 32 + 16 + 2 + 1$. Put 0's (ground) on lines 4, 8, 64, and 128. Put 1's (+5 volts) on lines 1, 2, 16, and 32.

The output will be one input clock pulse out of 51. Weighted down-count outputs are available on unused pins.

In Fig. 6-17, we cascade two 8281s and load a new parallel number on dropping to count 0. The number we load is 256 *minus* the count we want to divide by. If we only use one stage, the number is 16 *minus* the count we want to divide by, and three stages would be 4096 *minus* the count we wish to divide by, and so on. For example, for a divide-by-191, first find 256 minus 191 = 65. Convert 65 to binary = 64 + 1. Put 0's on the 2, 4, 8, 16, 32, and 128 lines by grounding them. Put 1's on the 64 and 1 lines by connecting them to 5 volts. The count is unweighted and cannot be reset to 0 because 00000000 is not part of the count sequence.

In Fig. 6-18, we gain synchronous operation with the 74161. This time, the number we load is 255 *minus* the count we want to divide by, and once again, we do not have a Clear capability as 0 is outside the count sequence.

Again, to give an example, for a divide-by-132, first find 255 minus 132 = 123. Convert 123 to binary = 64 + 32 + 16 + 8 + 2 + 1. Put 1's (+5 volts) on lines 1, 2, 8, 16, 32, and 64. Put 0's (ground) on lines 4 and 128.

There are several other possible approaches to high-modulo divide-by-n circuits, but few are as flexible or as easily done as the circuits of Figs. 6-16 through 6-18. Sometimes we can factor the number into component parts and simply connect two or more counters together to get the desired result. For instance, a divide-by-35 is a modulo 7 connected to a modulo 5, and so on. This has the advantage of bringing out an intermediate frequency, but it almost always takes more counter stages and is harder to decode.

The more or less obvious decode-and-reset technique can be done, but it always takes more gates and is very hard to change counts since the gate connections must also change. This method does have the advantage of being weighted, retaining 00000 in the count sequence, and can be made synchronous. Pitfalls to watch out for are decoding glitches and reset pulses that are so short the stages do not have time to clear properly. One method of avoiding some glitch situations is to NAND the decodings with the complement of the input clock line. A too-short pulse can be eliminated with a monostable circuit or a set-reset flip-flop that is set with the decoding and reset with the next clock edge.

Note that the down-count sequence of the MC4018 becomes an up-count sequence if we do a complete decoding and simply interchange the output lines suitably.

Note also that the three circuits of Figs. 6-16 through 6-18 will *not* work with decade counters, as certain division ratios will not be possible. To avoid this problem, a unit-cascaded system must be used.

UNIT-CASCADED COUNTERS

A few counting systems let us separate the decade units into individual groups. Each group can be in turn controlled by an individual thumbwheel switch. Fig. 6-19 shows how we can use the MC4016 for decade unit cascading. In this manner, if the decade selectors are set to 345, the counter counts to 300 *plus* 40 *plus* 5 for the total and then repeats. Note that a non-unit-cascadable counter would divide by 60 in the same case.

The circuit works on a *look-ahead decoding* scheme. Each successive stage detects count 0, and an output pulse 0 is then produced only if *all* the stages are simultaneously 0. This detected 0 is then used to reload the number to be divided back into the counter for the next round.

For instance, suppose our counter is set to 345 and a 0 comes up in the count sequence. This 0 reaches around and parallel loads a 5 into the units counter, a 4 into the tens counter, and a 3 into the hundreds counter. The counter is allowed to run. In 5 counts, the unit counter produces a carry, but it does *not* reload a 5 since the other counters are not yet to 0. Thus, the unit counter counts to 5 once and goes on as a decade or divide-by-10 counter for the next 340 counts.

Similarly, the tens decade takes 45 counts to produce a carry—5 from the initial clocking after count 0, and 40 more for it to advance 4 counts. At this time, a loading command *still* is not produced, for the hundreds counter is not in state 0. The tens counter goes around 4 counts the first time, and 10 counts for the next 30 times.

Each carry from the tens decade subtracts one count from the hundreds decade. The first of these arrives 45 counts after 0; successive ones arrive every 100 counts. When the hundreds counter gets to 0 simultaneously with the decade counter and the units counter, 345

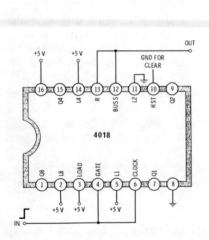

(A) Divide-by-13 ripple down-counter.

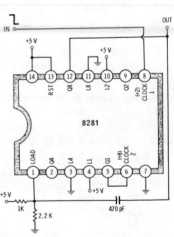

(B) Divide-by-13 ripple up-counter.

Fig. 6-14. Divide-by-13,

counts will have occurred, and the counter reaches around and loads a new 345 to start a new sequence.

We can cascade as many stages as we like to pick up a thousands or a ten-thousands capability. Important uses of a circuit like this are in frequency synthesizers and predetermining process-control counters. If we prefer to work in binary, octal and hexadecimal loading schemes can be used with the MC4018 as well.

Similar unit cascading can be obtained with the 74160 and the 74190. The 74160 is synchronous and faster, while the 74190 offers up/down capability. One disadvantage to either of these systems is

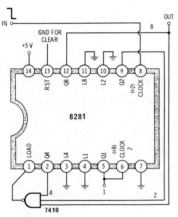

(C) Divide-by-14 weighted up-counter.

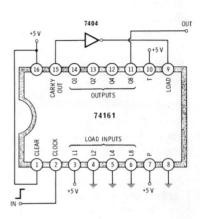

(D) Divide-by-14, synchronous, unweighted.

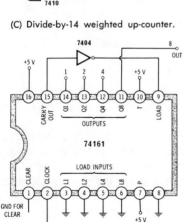

(E) Divide-by-15, synchronous, weighted.

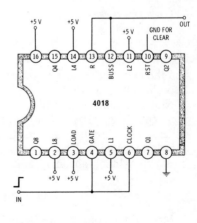

(F) Divide-by-15, ripple down-counter.

-14, and -15.

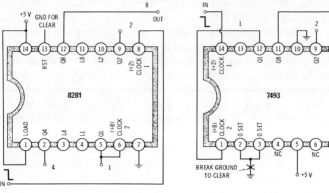

(A) Ripple up-counter, weighted 1-2-4-8.   (B) Ripple up-counter, weighted 1-2-4-8.

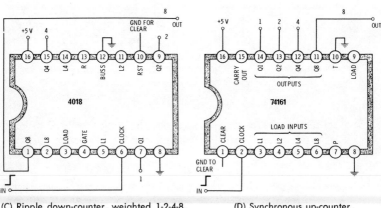

(C) Ripple down-counter, weighted 1-2-4-8.   (D) Synchronous up-counter, weighted 1-2-4-8.

Fig. 6-15. Divide-by-16 circuits.

that the number you load is the *difference* between a maximum count and the one you want, and thus takes a special switch code. They are also difficult to set to 0.

Note that unit cascadability is a unique quality. You can only obtain it in counting systems that have a look-ahead means of detecting either a 00000 count or a maximum count in a sequence. Ordinary decade counters will not operate in this manner unless you add your own external look-ahead capability.

DECODING STATES

Most of the counters we have discussed so far only produce a carry output or a frequency 1/n that of the input. When we want a separate, unique output for each state of a counter, we have to go through a

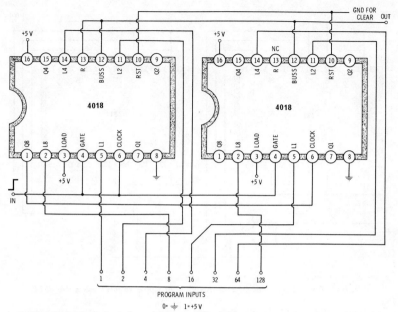

Fig. 6-16. Divide-by-1 through 256, weighted down-counter using the MC4018.

decoding process. Some simple examples of decoding appeared in Fig. 6-5 where all four possible states of the divide-by-4 counters are extracted with NAND gates.

Any state of any counter sequence can be decoded with a NAND gate that has enough inputs. These inputs are connected to the Q output of those flip-flops that are positive during the proper state and to the $\overline{Q}$ output of those flip-flops that are grounded during the state to be decoded. If complementary outputs are not available, inverters may be used instead.

While this is an obvious route when only a few states need decoding, a wide variety of MSI decoders are available that will convert the individual states of any counter into a 1-of-n or a unique digit pattern. If these systems provide only a TTL type of output, they are usually called *decoders*. If they also provide enough current or have a high enough voltage capability to drive a readout, they are called *decoder/drivers*. Sometimes a storage device is placed between the counter and the decoder/driver. This allows the count to continue while an old answer is being displayed, and the circuit is called a *latch*. Fig. 5-8 is a typical latch circuit.

Decoder Pitfalls

In general, there are three pitfalls to watch for when using MSI decoders: glitches, overlapping decodings, and mismatch between the

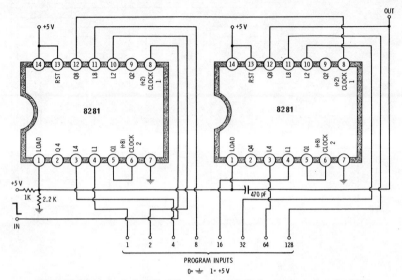

Fig. 6-17. Divide-by-1 through 256, unweighted ripple counter using the 8281.

decoder and its load. These may or may not be important in a particular application.

In general, the MSI decoding process is not synchronous, and unwanted brief output states, called glitches, may be produced during

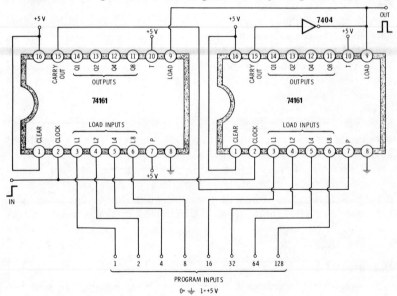

Fig. 6-18. Divide-by-1 through 256, unweighted counter using the 74161.

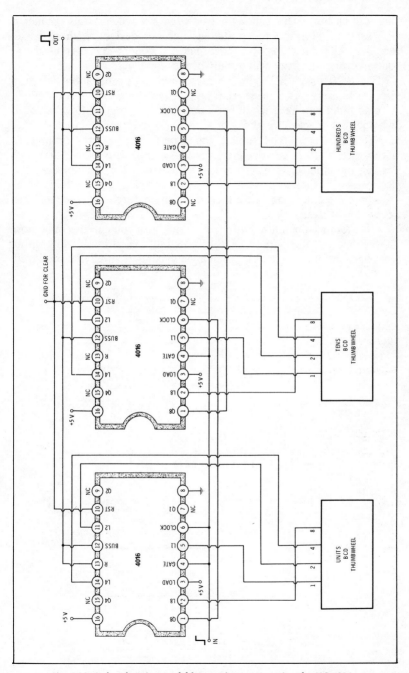

Fig. 6-19. A decade-unit-cascadable counting system using the MC 4016.

the settling time. This usually is true even if a synchronous counter is in use, depending on the particular decoder design. With negative-level-clocking flip-flops and NAND gates, decoders that involve the $\overline{Q}$ output of the first stage will usually produce glitches.

Fig. 6-20 shows how glitches are caused by propagation delays in ripple counters. As a basic rule, half of the states will decode glitch-free and half will have glitch potential. The key to glitch production is whether the propagation delay produces an overlap or an "underlap" of the decoder logic. The total glitch time is very short—around 15 nanoseconds. If we are driving a readout or a resistive load, the glitch will go by undetected. The problem comes up if the decoder output is to be used further to drive a JK flip-flop or other clocked logic block —where the glitch can cause a clocking prematurely or twice as often as we might like.

Glitches are difficult to eliminate. Sometimes you can use only those states that are glitch-free. Another possibility is to inhibit the output of a decoder during the time when a glitch can potentially be produced.

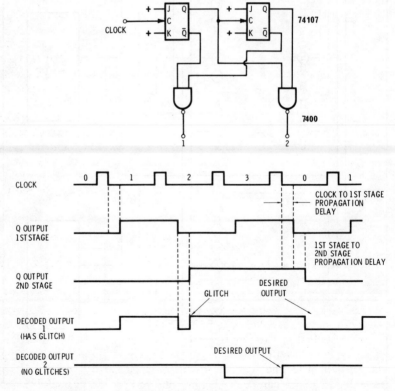

Fig. 6-20. A divide-by-4 decoder with one glitch-free stage.

One possibility is to use the complement of the system clock. By picking the clock duty cycle properly, the outputs are inhibited from an instant before a glitch is possible to a reasonable time afterward. One brute-force approach is to simply add RC filters to the output—perhaps a 100-ohm series resistor and an 0.01-μF capacitor; this reduces system speed and adds parts. The walking-ring counters of the next chapter avoid the problem entirely; they synchronously decode glitch-free, but they become inefficient for long counts. One final deglitching possibility is to decode one count state early and resynchronize on the next system clock pulse; this is shown in Fig. 5-19.

If the decoded outputs are not going to be used for clocked logic, chances are the glitches will not be a problem in your system. Fortunately, this is the case in the majority of decoded counter applications. Note that even fully synchronous counter/decoders can glitch slightly if the propagation time from a 1 to 0 transition is different than from a 0 to a 1. These glitches are much briefer than ripple glitches and are often "swallowed" by normal circuit strays, although they can be a problem in very high speed systems. Fig. 5-9 shows one solution.

Decoder overlap is a second pitfall. Sometimes the previous state will remain on for a brief instant after the next one turns on. Normally, this will present no problems as the time is very brief, but if a definite break-before-make action is essential in the circuit, both outputs must somehow be inhibited during the transitions. Once again, the clock or its complement may be used, with the clock duty cycle arranged to provide a proper amount of "daylight" between the two states.

The final major pitfall concerns using decoders with outside-world circuits. To drive a Nixie® tube or neon display device, you need high-voltage outputs. To drive a LED display, you need high-current outputs, current-limiting resistors, and a decoder/driver matched to the common-anode or common-cathode characteristics of the readout. A careful cross-check of the LED and TTL data sheets is essential to prevent mismatches.

SOME DECODER CIRCUITS

Fig. 6-21A shows how we can use a 7442 to decode a 1-2-4-8 BCD decimal counter to ten output lines. The selected line goes low on a given state; all others remain high. Fig. 6-21B shows the same chip can be used as an *octal* or base-8 decoder, or to decode any count sequence of eight states or less. This is done by applying a permanent 0 onto the 8 line. Note that as a decimal decoder, this must use the 1-2-4-8 code. As an octal or lower decoder, it can use any code, simply by relabeling the output lines. The numbering will only be correct for the 1-2-4 code, but any code can be used. Thus, the 7442 is a universal decoder for all counters of eight or less states.

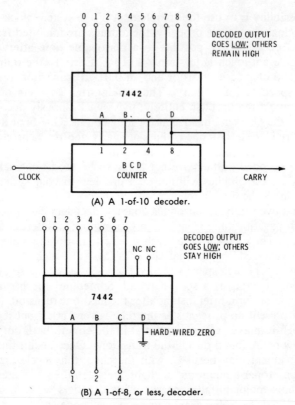

(A) A 1-of-10 decoder.

(B) A 1-of-8, or less, decoder.

Fig. 6-21. Decoding states with the 7442.

Two other specialized base-10 decoders are the 7443 and 7444. These work with specialized nonweighted codes called the *excess 3* and *excess 3 gray codes*. If we are going to decode only a short count sequence, the 74155 and 74156 are dual 2-line to 4-line decoders; this lets you decode two modulo-4 counters in one package. The 74156 is an open-collector version.

Fig. 6-22 shows the 74154 and 74159 (open-collector) 4-line to 16-line universal decoders. These are 24-pin package devices that convert any 4-bit count sequence into 16 states. The count outputs are only numbered correctly for the 1-2-4-8 code, but since each and every possible state is decoded, one output has to correspond to some state in a sequence, and relabeling will handle any code. The selected output goes low. All others remain high. There are also two Enable inputs. If either or both are high, all outputs go and remain high.

We can also use the Enable inputs to expand the decoding as far as we like. Figs. 6-23 and 6-24 show 32-state and 64-state decoders. These circuits also serve as *data distributors* by removing one of the

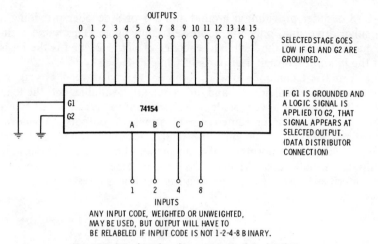

Fig. 6-22. A 1-of-16 decoder or 16-point data distributor.

Enable inputs from ground and using it as an input. Data entered here is sent to the selected output.

MATRIX DECODING

Whenever a very large number of decoded outputs seem to be called for, a *matrix* or X-Y technique can sometimes be used instead. For instance, suppose we were trying to light 1-of-64 light emitting diodes. Instead of decoding 1-of-64, we could use an 8×8 matrix with a

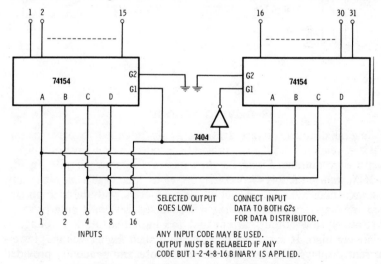

SELECTED OUTPUT
GOES LOW.

CONNECT INPUT
DATA TO BOTH G2s
FOR DATA DISTRIBUTOR.

INPUTS

ANY INPUT CODE MAY BE USED.
OUTPUT MUST BE RELABELED IF ANY
CODE BUT 1-2-4-8-16 BINARY IS APPLIED.

Fig. 6-23. A 1-of-32 decoder or 32-point data distributor.

1-of-8 decoder providing a ground and a 1-of-8 decoder providing a positive drive line; only the addressed lamp lights. This same technique was used on the keyboard encoder of Fig. 3-21 and is the basis of the *multiplexed* digital displays of Chapter 8.

For matrix techniques to work, both ends of whatever it is you are driving must be individually and independently available, and the load must be a diode or have a diode in series with it to prevent *sneak paths* backwards through unwanted combinations of outputs. Whenever these restrictions can be met, the matrix technique offers a drastic simplification from normal 1-of-n linear decoding. Note that positive outputs normally take driving transistors or other non-TTL devices; the interface is usually a matter of a transistor and a resistor.

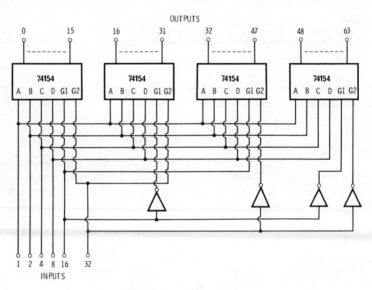

Fig. 6-24. A 1-of-64 decoder.

DRIVING READOUTS

Several decoder/drivers are specifically intended to drive certain types of readouts, unlike the previous decoders which have only TTL-compatible outputs. Fig. 6-25 shows several readout circuits. In Fig. 6-25A, we use the 74141 decoder/driver to directly drive a Nixie tube display. It has a 60-volt output that is compatible with the high-voltage neon display devices. Since it is a specialized device, it only provides a relatively low-output current and the output saturation voltage is relatively high. It may also be used with such higher-voltage, lower-current displays as liquid crystals and fluorescent readouts, provided the readout needs a 1-of-10 code.

Note that this IC works with a 5-volt supply, and if any of the output voltage reaches one of the inputs, permanent damage can result. For instance, if you are probing the circuit and accidentally short pin 2 (output 9) to pin 3 (input 1), the IC will almost certainly be destroyed.

If we are interested in driving lamps or printer solenoids, the 7445 is a better choice. Each output has a maximum voltage of only 5 volts, but up to 80 mA can be driven. The selected output goes low. This is shown in Fig. 6-25B.

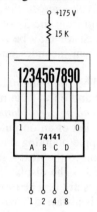

(A) Driving a Nixie tube display.

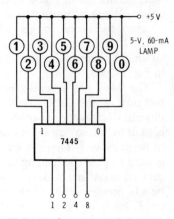

(B) Driving lamps or a printing hammer interface.

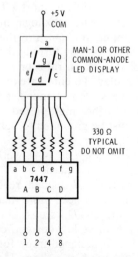

(C) Driving a 7-segment common-anode LED display.

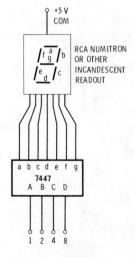

(D) Driving a 7-segment incandescent display.

Fig. 6-25. Decoder/drivers must be matched to their displays.

The 7447 (Fig. 6-25C) is a BCD-to-7-segment decoder that provides a grounded output on a segment that is to be lit and a positive output on a segment that is to remain unlit. It is shown with the MAN-1 style LED readout, a common-anode type of device. LEDs are basically diodes. In the on condition, their forward voltage drop is around 1.7 volts. As with a neon lamp, these are current-operated devices, and some form of *series current limiting* is absolutely essential to keep from destroying the device. This is what the current-limiting resistors are for in Fig. 6-25C. The value of the resistor is easy to calculate. When an output is on, there is 3.3 volts across the resistor, obtained by subtracting the 1.7-volt LED drop from the 5-volt supply. For a 10-mA segment current, a 330-ohm resistor may be used, and so on. The same IC is used to drive a 7-segment incandescent display in Fig. 6-25D.

The 7447 has several *blanking* options. The *ripple-blanking* input will turn off the display only if it is to be a 0 and only if the more significant decades are also 0's. This is called *leading zero blanking* and is used to "erase" all the unwanted 0's on the left of an output number to be displayed. There is a corresponding ripple-blanking output that is used to pass the leading zero information on to the next less significant stage. A low state on this input extinguishes the display if it is to be a 0, provided that all more significant stages are 0. The input to the ripple blanking on the most significant stage is always a hard-wired 0.

Because of a pin multiplexing trick, you can also use the ripple-blanking output as an ordinary blanking input, simply by shorting it. This is one of the few cases where it is permissible to short a TTL output externally. This is made possible by a wire-AND logic inside the chip. With this pin used as a blanking input, you can turn the display on or off at will. Ground turns the display off. By turning the display on and off very rapidly with a controllable off-on ratio or *duty cycle,* you can control the brightness of the display. To eliminate any flicker, a blanking frequency of at least 100 Hz is recommended, and much more than this if the displays are also further multiplexed. There is also a lamp test input to the 7447. It must be grounded to light all the segments.

There are several other decoder possibilties. The 7448 works backward from the 7447; its output is a logic that needs to be inverted with driver transistors before a common-anode 7-segment readout can be driven. This is useful for circuits where you need more than the 40 mAs of output current per segment of the 7447. Its own output current is only 6.4 mA. While it can directly drive low-current, common-cathode readouts such as the MAN-4, it is designed more for driving a driver transistor of some sort. The 7446 is a high voltage 7447, good to 30 volts, and useful with liquid crystal and fluorescent displays, while the 7449 is an open-collector version of the 7448, good to 10 mA and useful for driving medium-power common-cathode readouts by shunting supply power around the segments.

ONE-PACKAGE COUNTER/DECODERS

All of these decoder/driver systems we have discussed so far take two or three integrated circuits per decade, besides possibly requiring seven current-limiting resistors as well. By going to newer TTL devices, several single-package solutions to the same problem can be obtained.

Note that some LED displays contain their own latch and decoder/ driver. If this type of display is used, all we need to operate it is a BCD counter. Hewlett Packard makes several displays of this type; the 5082-7300 series is typical and eliminates the need for the latch, decoder/driver, and resistors.

Several TTL devices are also available that combine a counter, latch, and decoder/driver. The Motorola MC4050 and 4051 are typical and provide 7-segment outputs. The 4050 grounds an output to light it; the 4051 makes an output positive to light it. Both of these devices still need current-limiting resistors when driving a LED display. They will directly drive such displays as the RCA Numitron and other incandescent displays.

The 74143 and 74144 also combine a BCD counter, a storage latch, ripple zero and blanking logic, a decoder/driver with 7-segment outputs, and decimal-point logic. They are provided in a 24-pin package and are synchronous. The 143 includes the equivalent of internal LED current-limiting resistors by providing an output current rather than a voltage; the 74144 is intended to drive incandescent or other voltage-operated displays. A somewhat similar device intended for Nixie tube service and housed in a 16-pin package is the 74142.

A SYNCHRONOUS UP/DOWN COUNTING SYSTEM

Fig. 6-26 shows a cascadable, parallel loadable, synchronous up/ down counting system useful in registers, arithmetic calculations, and calculators. Only one package per stage is needed. As with many of the more complex MSI logic blocks, their use should be avoided unless the specific up/down function is needed, since the system costs more, requires more supply power, and may be harder to obtain or second source. The 74192 is a variation of the 74190 that allows the easy cascading of decades shown. One requirement is that you provide two clock lines—one for up-counting, and one for down-counting. This is easy to do, and the two clock lines let you *inhibit* or ignore count pulses easily.

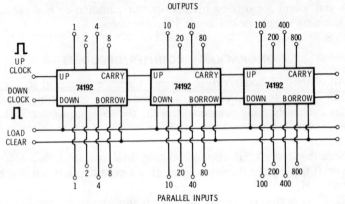

Fig. 6-26. Fully synchronous, up/down, parallel or serial access, weighted counter system.

AN EXAMPLE—ELECTRONIC MUSIC

Let us turn to a somewhat unusual application of counters and show how many of the counting principles we have talked about may be applied. Suppose that you wanted to generate all the notes of the musical scale on a one-at-a-time basis from a single frequency reference. How would you go about it?

The musical scale is divided into octaves. Going up one octave precisely doubles frequency; going down one octave precisely halves frequency. In each octave are 12 notes labeled C, C♯, D, D♯, E, F, F♯, G, G♯, A, A♯, and B in ascending order. In the normally used equally tempered scale, each note is $\sqrt[12]{2}$ higher than its immediate neighbor, or a frequency ratio of 1.05946:1. Thus, each note is roughly 6% higher in sequence, so that the thirteenth note ends up precisely twice the first. This 6% interval is normally called a *semitone*. One-hundredth of a semitone is called a *cent,* corresponding to a frequency increment of $\sqrt[1200]{2}$, or approximately 0.06%. For the scale to be pleasant and in tune, the notes must be generated to a 3-cent accuracy or better. A 1-cent worst case accuracy is more desirable, but cannot quite be obtained with the circuit we will show you.

All the frequencies of all the notes are listed in Table 6-2. We can work only on the top octave and can let all the other notes be derived from binary dividers. Thus, the frequency synthesis problem consists of generating 12 notes from 4186.0 Hz to 7902.1 Hz in a stable and accurate manner.

Since the twelfth root of two is an irrational number, there is no reasonable way to generate it exactly. Instead we must seek an approximation that is accurate, yet simple enough to realize. Some further properties of the equally tempered 12-note scale appear in Table

Table 6-2. Standard Frequencies for the 12-Note Equally Tempered Musical Scale

Octave Number	Note					
	C	C♯	D	D♯	E	F
0*	16.352	17.324	18.354	19.445	20.602	21.827
1	32.703	34.648	36.708	38.891	41.203	43.654
2	65.406	69.296	73.416	77.782	82.407	87.307
3	130.81	138.59	146.83	155.56	164.81	174.61
4	261.63	277.18	293.66	311.13	329.63	349.23
5	523.25	554.37	587.33	622.25	659.26	698.46
6	1046.5	1108.7	1174.7	1244.5	1318.5	1396.9
7	2093.0	2217.5	2349.3	2489.0	2637.0	2793.8
8	4186.0	4434.9	4698.6	4978.0	5274.0	5587.7

Octave Number	Note					
	F♯	G	G♯	A	A♯	B
0*	23.125	24.500	25.957	27.500	29.135	30.868
1	46.249	48.999	51.913	55.000	58.270	61.735
2	92.499	97.999	103.83	110.00	116.54	123.47
3	185.00	196.00	207.65	220.00	233.08	246.94
4	369.99	392.00	415.30	440.00	466.16	493.88
5	739.99	783.99	830.61	880.00	932.33	987.77
6	1480.0	1568.0	1661.2	1760.0	1864.7	1975.5
7	2960.0	3136.0	3322.4	3520.0	3729.3	3951.1
8	5919.9	6271.9	6644.9	7040.0	7458.6	7902.1

*Octave zero is very seldom used. Frequencies shown are in hertz and are valid for any electronic musical instrument, organs, and any conventional instrument except the piano.
"Middle C" is C4 at 261.63 Hz. Standard pitch is A4 = 440.

6-3. The series shown as "series A" is a train of numbers that accurately approximates the inverse of the needed twelfth-root-of-two ratio. It turns out that this particular choice of numbers is the best you can possibly use and still keep the largest number under 256 so that a 2-package, 8-bit binary counter can be used. Other number sequences will have at least one note off in frequency more than this particular sequence, even if certain others do have more accuracy.

So, to build a note generator, we use the A of 7040.0 as a reference to start the design. One hundred thirty-eight times this frequency is 971.520 kHz. Since this is an "expensive" crystal frequency, we can double it to 1,943.040 kHz and use a more available crystal, then divide-by-2. Better yet, we put the ÷2 at the output of the ÷n to get a symmetrical output. All we need now is a way to program a counter to

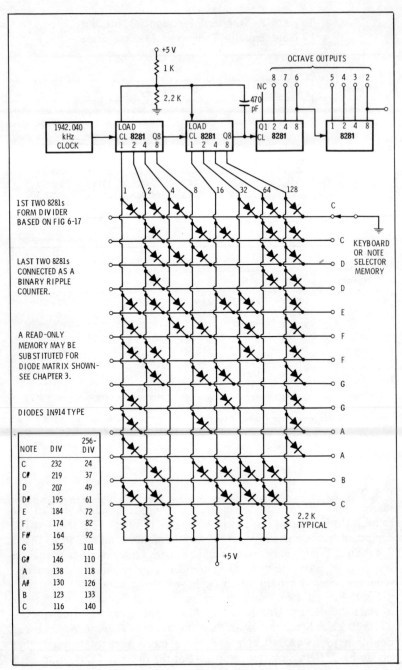

Fig. 6-27. Equal-tempered tone generator for electronic music.

Table 6-3. Some Properties of the Equally Tempered 12-Note Scale

Note	Ratio	Series "A"	Series "B"
C	1.0000	232	478
C♯	1.0595	219	451
D	1.1225	207	426
D♯	1.1892	195	402
E	1.2599	184	379
F	1.3348	174	358
F♯	1.4142	164	338
G	1.4983	155	319
G♯	1.5874	146	301
A	1.6818	138	284
A♯	1.7818	130	268
B	1.8877	123	253
C	2.0000	116	239

Series "A" is the most accurate approximation you can make and still stay within two 4-bit binary counters. It is the division ratio you use. Starting with a reference of 971.520 kHz and dividing down by 138 gives A8 at 7040.0, etc.

Series "B" is more accurate but takes nine bits. Normal reference frequency is 2.000240 MHz.

divide by 116-123-130, etc., which is easily done with the circuit of Fig. 6-17.

If we like, we could phase-lock an oscillator to the crystal reference. This would allow it to be permanently in tune, yet still moveable for vibrato and steel-guitar effects, etc. We could also generate all the notes at once by adding dividers, one for each of the 12 top-octave notes. Systems of this type are also available using MOS integrated circuits such as the Mostek MK5024P; they are simpler than a TTL generator would be, but cost more than the 1-note circuit of Fig. 6-27. The lower-frequency notes are easily converted to linear sawteeth with all lower-order harmonics present simply by adding 10K, 20K, 40K, and 80K resistors and summing to the sequential stages of the binary-divider chain, obtaining a stairstep waveform. With four resistors, all harmonics up to the sixteenth will be present. The next missing harmonic will be the thirty-second, and so on. Sawtooth outputs of this type are easily formant filtered to get any desirable musical voice. If the note must continue for an interval after key release, the circuit of Fig. 5-13 should be added.

CHAPTER 7

Shift Registers,
Noise Generators, and
Rate Multipliers

A *shift register* is a group of cascaded JK or D flip-flops set up so that on each clocking the contents of all the stages are moved or *shifted* one stage in a desired direction. Important uses of shift registers are to store data as a simple serial memory, to convert data from serial to parallel formats or vice versa, to provide a *buffer* between systems with different clock rates, and to form *counters* and *sequencers*.

Many different shift registers are available. Each circuit problem must be matched to the particular devices that can do the job in the cheapest way with the fewest packages.

In this chapter, we will first look at the different qualities that are desirable in shift registers. Then we will find out what the device-to-device tradeoffs are in terms of what is available. Three applications follow this: teletype transmissions, always-accurate clocks, and video display generators.

Following this, we will examine the shift register as a counter, starting with a simple stepper and then going to the even- and odd-length walking-ring counters. A very unusual and useful application of shift registers then follows—generating pseudo-random noise and maximal-length sequences, which are useful in electronic music, audio testing, cryptography, and computer security.

The chapter will end with a brief look at *rate multipliers,* little-known and little-used TTL devices that, while unsuited for many of the things designers try to do with them, provide a simple and interesting way to perform multiplication and division, squares and square root, logs and exponents, trig functions, and so on.

SHIFT-REGISTER CONNECTIONS

There are dozens of different TTL shift registers available. Due to pin limitations and chip geometry restrictions, you cannot expect to put every desirable feature into a shift register and still have a reasonable number of stages per package. Fig. 7-1 shows some common shift-register applications.

The most basic register form is the serial-in/serial-out or SISO register, a simple sequential memory that accepts one bit of information per stage. If there are eight stages, eight bits of information can be sequentially stored. Since the bits are passed on in order, the first bit in is the first bit out. Another use of the SISO register is to provide delay. Data at the input is delayed for n clock pulses where n is the register length. An 8-stage register delays input data for eight clock pulses. Clocking on a shift register is almost always on the positive clock edge or level.

A serial-in/parallel-out shift register or SIPO is shown in Fig. 7-1B. Here, an output is available at each register stage. This obviously takes more pins, but it lets us view the entire contents of the register at once or in *parallel-word* form. One use for a SIPO register is to convert a serial string of data into a parallel word. As an example, 8 sequential data bits can be marched into an 8-bit register, and if we sample at the right time, an 8-bit parallel word will be obtained.

Many registers have a Clear capability in which the entire contents can be made 0's. If there is also a way to put 1's into selected intermediate stages, a *parallel-load* or parallel-input register can be obtained. Fig. 7-1C shows a parallel-input/serial-output (PISO).

The fine print on parallel-load registers should be read very carefully. There are two loading schemes. Sometimes the parallel-load inputs are presets only. This means you can *not* selectively change a 1 back to a 0 on any selected stage. To properly use the parallel preset inputs on a register of this type, *you first must clear the registers to all 0's*. Then you are free to use the presets to convert those stages from 0 to 1 that you want. You cannot go backward and erase a 1 already in a register stage. The 7496 is one register of this type with a 5-bit capability.

A true parallel-load register lets you add 1's or 0's anywhere you want, anytime you want, without first clearing. The 74165 is typical of this type and is usually much easier to use.

Parallel-in/parallel-out (PIPO) registers take a number of pins since two pins are usually needed per stage. PIPO registers are generally limited to four or five stages per package as shown in Fig. 7-1D.

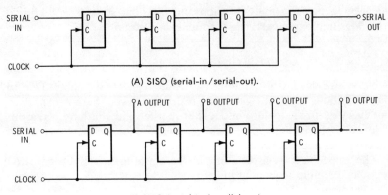

(A) SISO (serial-in/serial-out).

(B) SIPO (serial-in/parallel-out).

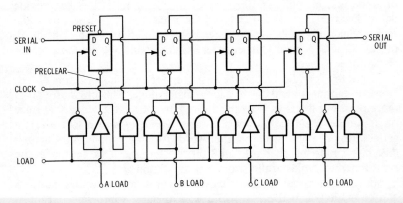

(C) PISO (parallel-in/serial-out).

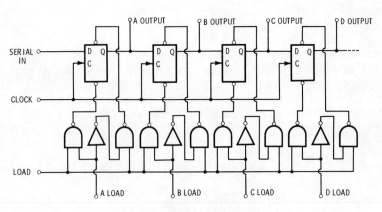

(D) PIPO (parallel-in/parallel-out).

Fig. 7-1. Four basic shift-register configurations.

Practically all registers have a serial input to the first stage, even if they are only intended for parallel use. Parallel inputs are either clocked or asynchronous, so that parallel loading takes place either immediately on or after the next system clock pulse, depending on the register selected. Other pins are often available to shift from clocking to loading and back again, and to inhibit the clock when clocking is not wanted.

Most shift registers shift only to the right. That is, they pass information one stage from input toward the output at every clock command. A few registers can shift in either direction on command. These are called right-shift/left-shift registers. Normally there are separate clock and shift-left and shift-right busses; the IC can be made to shift right or left or to ignore clock pulses as desired.

There are also several possibilities for "build-your-own" shift-register combinations, particularly using the 74174 Hex D flip-flop and the 74L98. Here, you can use external connections to shift in any desired sequence.

Table 7-1. Several Popular TTL Shift Registers

Type	Length	Parallel Out?	Parallel Load?	Direction	Clear
7491	8 Bits	No	No	Right	No
7494	4 Bits	No	Pre-set only	Right	Yes
7495	4 Bits	Yes	Synchronous	Right/left	No
7496	5 Bits	Yes	Preset only	Right	Yes
74164	8 Bits	Yes	No	Right	Yes
74165	8 Bits	No	Yes	Right	Yes
74166	8 Bits	No	Synchronous	Right	Yes
74194	4 Bits	Yes	Synchronous	Right/left	Yes
74195	4 Bits	Yes	Synchronous	Right	Yes

As with the clocked flip-flops, it is necessary to watch the kind of clocking and the kind of input to the registers. Most registers clock on the positive edge, and the input data can be changed at any time, but there are usually restrictions on the state of the clock when right-shift or left-shift commands are changed. As a general rule, the older registers are more restrictive of when and how often you can change the inputs. The newer ones are all edge-clocked D systems that let you change serial input or load at anytime. Be sure to consult the data sheet if you experience any difficulties.

If the output of a shift register is tied around to its own input, the data is made to recirculate. On an 8-stage register, 8 clock pulses in sequence are needed to get the data back into the original format. We will show that arithmetic or logic can be performed on the recirculation to derive a number of useful counters and sequencers.

WHICH REGISTER?

Some of the more popular TTL registers are listed in Table 7-1. Here you can compare the number of stages, the type of access, the shift pattern, and the general organization. Normal speeds of operation range up to 20 MHz with ordinary TTL. There is no lower limit, but as with flip-flops and counters, a good sharp rise time on the debounced and noise-free clock will prevent many noise problems. All the usual clocked-logic precautions apply—use a tightly regulated supply with good high-frequency bypassing and terminate all input leads, either to +5 volts, a logic source, or ground, as called for by the truth table and the application.

The 74164 8-bit, serial-in/parallel-out register and the 74165 8-bit, parallel-in/serial-out represent good choices for many applications. Either can be used as a serial-in/serial-out device as well.

If you need very long serial-in/serial-out registers, particularly at low speed, consider some other logic family. MOS SISO registers are available to 4096 bits in a single package at far lower cost per bit and with less power consumption than TTL. The tradeoff point is somewhere above 16 bits; beyond this, consider MOS. Below it or where elaborate data formats or high speed are needed, use TTL.

A TELETYPE TRANSMITTER

Let us take a look at some data format applications of shift registers. Suppose we want to transmit the ASCII output of the keyboard encoder of Chapter 3 down a single wire, or perhaps over a telephone line by way of a tone-generating *modem*. We would have to convert the eight ASCII bits into a serial sequence of bits. Further, we would have to arrange the sequence so the circuitry at the other end could tell when the sequence started and when it ended.

In general, there are two ways of sending data in serial form: *synchronously* and *asynchronously*. In asynchronous data transmission, all the words are sent at a constant rate, but the spacing between successive words can be any arbitrary length above a certain minimum.

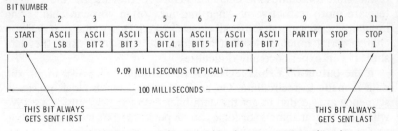

Fig. 7-2. The 100-wpm asynchronous 8-bit teletype or "150 Baud" code.

In synchronous systems, the data are always locked into a time frame, and "do nothing" words called *nulls* are placed between the real words to keep the spacing synchronous. Synchronous systems are almost always faster and more complex than asynchronous systems.

One standard asynchronous system is the "150-Baud" or "100-Word-Per-Minute" teletype system, used industry-wide for slow data transmission over ordinary phone lines. Its standards are shown in Fig. 7-2. Between transmissions, a string of 1's, called *marks,* equal to a shorted line, is transmitted. Each character or command to be sent consists of 11 bits and takes 0.1 second to transmit. The per-bit time is then 9.09 milliseconds, corresponding to a 110.0-Hz clocking rate.

The first bit is called a *start* bit. It is always a 0, called a *space* or an *open* line. This way, if the line breaks, a string of 0's sounds an alarm of some sort.

The start bit is followed by the 8-bit ASCII word, least significant bit first. The string ends with the parity or error-correcting bit in the last slot (the eighth bit of the word or the ninth bit transmitted). At least two more 1's in slots 10 and 11 must be present before a new character is transmitted, but any number of marks or 1's exceeding two can be transmitted.

The start bit tells the circuit on the other end that a new character is to be sent and that the next eight bits are important. Note that if the character has one or two leading 0's, there would be no way to tell what it was without the start bit. The stop bits give the receiving circuit time to reset itself and await a new character.

The series line between input and output is often called the *loop,* and loop currents are typically 20 or 60 mA. They are easily handled by any medium-sized transistor that is properly diode-protected against inductive transients.

It takes 100 milliseconds to transmit the character, which is equal to 11 cycles of a system clock of 110 Hz. This frequency has to be fairly accurate. If the frequency is off by one part in eleven, the receiving circuitry will be one bit ahead or behind by the end of the word. We have to do much better than this for reliable, accurate communications. An accuracy of 0.5% is recommended, although within 2% is usually tolerable in most systems.

Fig. 7-3 shows the circuitry involved. It starts with a 110-Hz astable oscillator, following the techniques of Chapter 4. This is used to clock a 10-stage register made of a 7474 dual D flip-flop and a 74165 PISO register. The last stage (the first to deliver output) is hard-wire programmed to parallel-load a 1. The next stage is programmed to parallel-load a 0, using the Preset and Preclear inputs. The next eight stages are programmed with the ASCII character, with the least significant bit nearest the output and the parity bit at the input. On a load command, the register is filled with a 1, a 0, and the ASCII command.

The serial input has a hard-wired 1 permanently applied to it. If enough clock pulses go by without a new character arriving, continuous 1's are put out.

Let us assume that a new ASCII character has just arrived, properly debounced and conditioned, perhaps with the circuit of Fig. 5-10. The instant a new character arrives, it is loaded into the shift register with the leading edge of a delayed "key-pressed data-valid" command, converted to a narrow pulse.

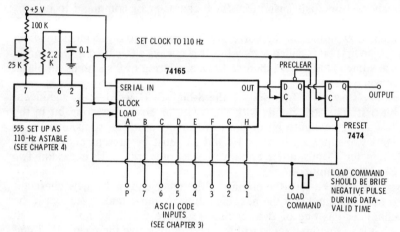

Fig. 7-3. Shift register used to convert parallel ASCII code to serial 100-wpm teletype code.

Up to this time, the register output has been the 1's it received from the serial input. Immediately after loading, the next clock pulse will be a 1 as well, obtained from the parallel load on the output stage. Note that this 1 can be any time width at all, from nothing to slightly less than one clock width, since the "new character" command could have arrived at any phase with respect to the clock. Thus, this output 1 is probably a bit short and is used to absorb the difference between clock timing and the instant the load command arrived. Since we had a string of 1's anyway, a short zero tacked on the end is ignored by the other end.

The next clock pulse, a *space* or full-width 0 is transmitted, telling the receiving circuitry to start. Note that this 0 will last an entire interval between clock pulses, thanks to the synchronizing performed by the previous 1.

The rest of the code follows in sequential order. At least two 1's at the end of the word must be provided by the serial input. Either we have to guarantee that a new character will not arrive within 100 milliseconds, or we have to lock out the new character to assure that at least two stop bits are transmitted following the parity bit. This can be done by sending back a "busy" signal upstream to the keyboard or encoder. From this point, the circuit continuously clocks out 1's, marking time until a new character is entered.

SELF-RESETTING ALWAYS-ACCURATE DIGITAL CLOCK

A digital clock can be made self-resetting and always accurate by occasionally tying it into a time service such as NBS stations WWV or WWVB or a television timing system. This will nullify the effects of a power failure, and the clock will always read the correct time. A serial-in/parallel-out shift register can be used to format the data from the serial form in which it is usually received to the parallel form normally needed for hours and minutes updating of the clock.

As an example, WWVB continuously transmits a time code on a 60-KHz carrier at a one-bit-per-second rate. At the beginning of each minute, a code starts spelling out 60 bits of BCD data that give the minute and hour in 2400-hour time, some time corrections, the day of the year, and some framing information. The first third of the code sequence is shown in Chart 7-1. Only this portion of the code is needed if we are not interested in also displaying the date.

Chart 7-1. First Third of WWVB Standard Time Code

Start of minute	framing pulse
1st second	framing pulse (minute detector)
2nd second	40-minutes bit
3rd second	20-minutes bit
4th second	10-minutes bit
5th second	logical 0
6th second	8-minutes bit
7th second	4-minutes bit
8th second	2-minutes bit
9th second	1-minute bit
10th second	framing pulse
11th second	logical 0
12th second	logical 0
13th second	20-hours bit
14th second	10-hours bit
15th second	logical 0
16th second	8-hours bit
17th second	4-hours bit
18th second	2-hours bit
19th second	1-hour bit
20th second	framing pulse

A receiver for WWVB has to receive the signal and extract the code, as well as provide proper synchronization for updating the clock. One circuit is outlined in Fig. 7-4. An obvious way to do the job would be to use a 20-bit serial-in/parallel-out register and provide an updating at 20 seconds past the minute. At that time, the correct minutes-and-hours information is loaded into a digital clock circuit that has its own time base *and* a parallel-load capability. A 20 is also loaded into the seconds counter at the same time to update the accuracy of everything at once.

Fig. 7-4 uses a slightly different approach. An 8-bit shift register and a 1-bit D flip-flop are used instead. At ten seconds past the minute, the hours information *only* is updated. At 20 seconds past the minute, the minute, the minutes-and-seconds information is updated. This gives the same result with a much shorter register.

More information on available time codes appears in NBS Special Publication No. 236. More information on receivers and clocks is contained in the July 1972 and July 1973 issues of *Radio Electronics*. Shift registers with slightly different formats may be used for the WWV and television time-updating systems.

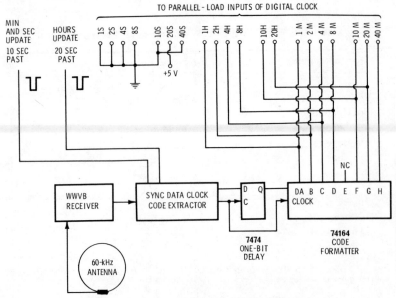

Fig. 7-4. Block diagram of self-correcting digital clock.

CHARACTER GENERATOR

Fig. 7-5 shows a high-speed application of a PISO shift register, once again using the 74165. MOS character generators are normally used to present the dot-matrix characters used in CRT-type computer-terminal displays and in tv typewriters and message systems. A group of five dots corresponding to one row of a 5 × 7 matrix is produced at once as output. These are parallel-loaded into the 74165 which is then clocked at a video rate. The output appears as serial video, with the extra input 0's providing for one, two, or three dot blanks between characters. The register is loaded at a word-rate that is within the speed capabilities of the slower MOS circuitry; it delivers output at a high-speed video rate that TTL is better suited to handle. Since we only briefly sample the MOS generator when we load, the majority of the time can be spent settling data, and we sample valid data at the fastest possible speed.

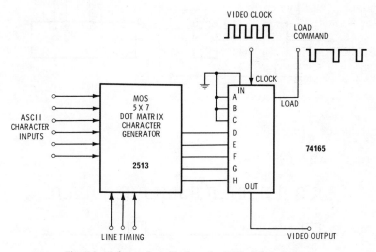

Fig. 7-5. High-speed application of a PISO shift register.

There are two very good reasons why a shift register, rather than a data selector, should be used in this application. The first is that the output data must be valid for the entire sampling time with a selector; thus it will be much slower. The second is that as the selector goes from point to point, brief disallowed states will raise havoc with the video circuitry later on. More details on this and several other register circuits appear in the September 1973 *Radio Electronics*. These three examples show you how shift registers can be used to format data into serial or parallel form in practical systems.

ANOTHER ELECTRONIC STEPPER

If feedback from register stages is allowed to determine the next bit to be entered in a serial register, we can use shift registers as *counters* or *sequencers*. One obvious possibility is shown in Fig. 7-6, where another stepper similar to the bucket brigade of Chapter 5 has been built.

To begin, we clear the register, clear the second D stage, and place a 1 in the first D stage of the 7474. This puts the counter in state 1000000000. Clock it once for 0100000000, again for 0010000000, and so on. Each time, the 1 moves over one stage. This gives a synchronous electronic stepper that has one output up and all the rest

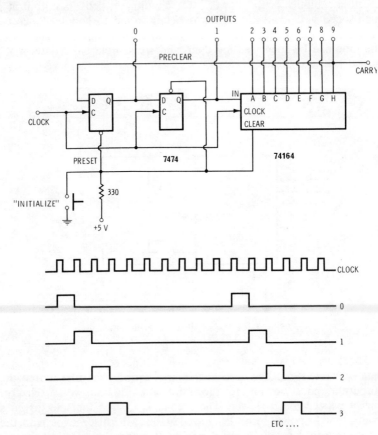

Fig. 7-6. Synchronous, self-decoding, ten-point electronic stepper.

down. After ten counts, the positive state is back at the beginning, and the rotation is continuous. As with the bucket brigade, the circuit is synchronous, decoding is inherent, and decoded-state overlap is very small. The circuit is also obviously inefficient for long lengths since ten stages of binary dividers could count to 1024; here the same stages can only count to 10.

This brings us to another general system problem called the *disallowed-state problem*. In *any* counting or sequencing system made up of n binary storage stages, there are apparently 2^n different possible conditions the circuit can get into. What happens if we start off in the wrong state or if we inadvertently acquire a noise pulse or make some other temporary error? Some systems are self-clearing, and the wrong state sequence will eventually lead back onto the right track. Others, such as the stepper, will go either into a *latch up* or *disallowed subroutine*. In the case of the stepper, if the counter is put into state 0001010000, we would have two outputs positive at once. Clocking would move the two outputs around together, but in no way will the circuit ever clear itself and get back on the right track without outside help.

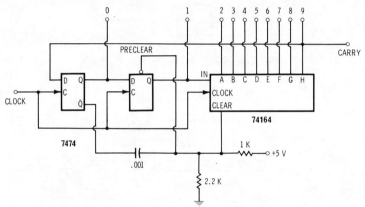

Fig. 7-7. Simple circuit for eliminating disallowed states.

With the stepper, there are 1024 possible states and only 10 good ones, which leaves 1014 disallowed states. We can use a reset button to get back in the 1000000000 state. Operation can be more automatic if as the first stage becomes 1, that action is used to reset everything else. This is shown in Fig. 7-7 and is preferable where a clearing button is not feasible—as on a piece of medical electronics gear or a satellite.

Even the Autoclear in Fig. 7-7 cannot handle all the states, for it will ignore a 1111111111 or a 0000000000 condition. 1022 out of 1024 are good odds though, but extra circuitry would be needed to get rid of these remaining two states. How would you do it?

THE WALKING-RING COUNTER

The stepper can be folded back on itself to produce an interesting shift-register sequencer called a *walking-ring counter,* also sometimes known as a *Johnson Counter* or a *switchtail ring*. Only half as many register stages are needed for a given count length, and the circuit turns out to be a good high-frequency one, as one, and only one, stage changes state at a time. Further, regardless of the length of the counter, all the states can be decoded with two input gates. Decoding and counting is synchronous, and overlap is minimal. Disallowed-state problems exist, but they are easy to fix. Let us take a closer look.

Fig. 7-8 shows a 3-stage shift register that has had its $\overline{Q}$, or the *complement* of its output, routed back to the input, so that with every

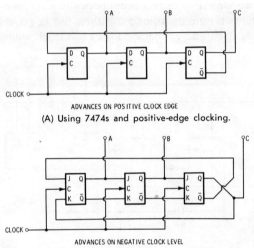

(A) Using 7474s and positive-edge clocking.

(B) Using 7473s and negative-edge clocking.

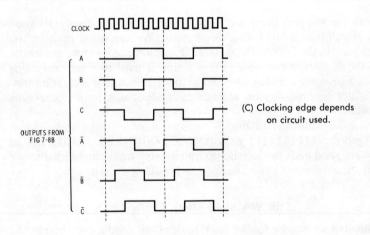

(C) Clocking edge depends on circuit used.

Fig. 7-8. Modulo-6 walking-ring counter.

clocking, the first stage turns to whatever the last stage *was not* on the previous clock.

Suppose we clear the register to 000. Since the Q output of the last stage is a 0, the $\overline{Q}$ output must be a 1. This 1 is presented to the input of the first stage, and on the next clocking we get a 100. We clock again for 110 and again for 111. This time the $\overline{Q}$ is a 0, so with the next clocking we get 011 followed by 001, and finally back to 000.

It takes six counts to get once around, so we apparently have a modulo-6 counter. Another interesting feature is that all outputs of all stages are at ⅙ the input frequency. Each output is a symmetrical square wave, and the square waves overlap to give a total of six available phases to the ring.

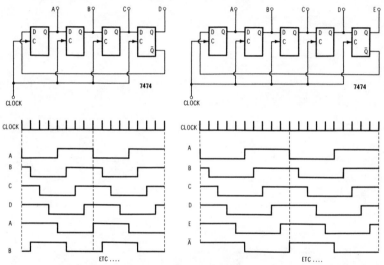

Fig. 7-9. Modulo-8 and modulo-10 walking-ring counters. JK flip-flops or shift registers may be used as well.

For a modulo-8 counter, we would need four stages, and five would be used for a modulo-10. We would have eight symmetrical square waves of different phases for the modulo-8 and ten for the modulo-10. Fig. 7-9 shows these counters.

Note that only one output changes for any clocking. This eliminates any race problems on decoding. We can decode all the individual states as shown in Fig. 7-10. Only two input gates are needed. Each output drives two gate inputs. Decoding is synchronous, and overlap is minimal. There are no glitches possible.

To find the decoder connections for longer sequences, write out the truth table. One unique state is decoded by NANDing the outside two Q outputs. A second that will be halfway around is obtained by NANDing the outside two $\overline{Q}$ outputs. Of the remaining states, every place in the truth table that you see a 1 followed by a 0, you hook up one gate input to the Q output of the 1 stage and the $\overline{Q}$ output of the following zero stage. Everywhere that you see a 0 followed by a 1, you do the opposite, and the decoding is complete.

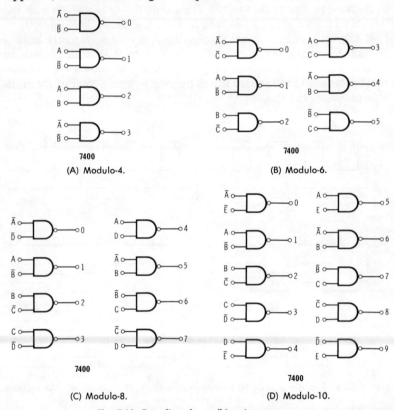

Fig. 7-10. Decoding the walking-ring counters.

The walking-ring counter is twice as efficient as the bucket brigade or the stepper of Fig. 7-8, but it is still inefficient compared to a straight binary counter. Three binary stages should have eight possible states, the six we talked about, plus 010 and 101. A 4-stage walking ring should have 16 states, the 0000, 1000, 1100, 1110, 1111, 0111, 0011, 0001, and back to 0000, and a disallowed group of 1010, 1101, 0110, 1011, 0101, 0010, 0100, and back to 1010. Five stages give 32 possibilities—10 good ones and 22 bad ones, and so on.

Once again, it is necessary to eliminate the undesired sequences. A simple CLEAR button works well. A universal way is to detect two outside 0's (first and last stage) and use this as a NAND gate to CLEAR to

0 all the inside packages. Any walking-ring disallowed sequence, regardless of its length, will eventually end up with two outside 0's. Note that this can be the same gate that is decoding state 0 in a decoded-counter sequence, so the autoclearing can sometimes be "free."

To build a walking-ring counter, either the $\overline{Q}$ output of the last stage must be available or an inverter must be added.

THE ODD-LENGTH WALKING-RING COUNTER

If we use a JK flip-flop for at least the first stage of the counter, and feed back one side *one stage early,* we get an odd-length count sequence. Divide-by-3, -5, and -7 circuits are shown in Figs. 7-11, 7-12,

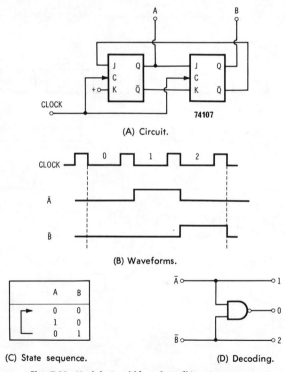

(A) Circuit.

(B) Waveforms.

(C) State sequence.

(D) Decoding.

Fig. 7-11. Modulo-3 odd-length walking-ring counter.

and 7-13. Sequence lengths up to 13 clear themselves, and there are no disallowed states as the count eventually works itself back to the proper sequence.

The one-stage-early feedback eliminates one count in one phase of the normal-length sequence, thus shortening the sequence by one. The divide-by-3 is particularly important as it is the standard 1-package way to divide by 3 synchronously. Two states are inherently decoded; a 2-input NAND gate is needed for the third.

As a class, walking-ring counters offer a novel approach to generating variable-phase or phase-shifted signals, or providing high-frequency operation with synchronous and safe decoding. They become

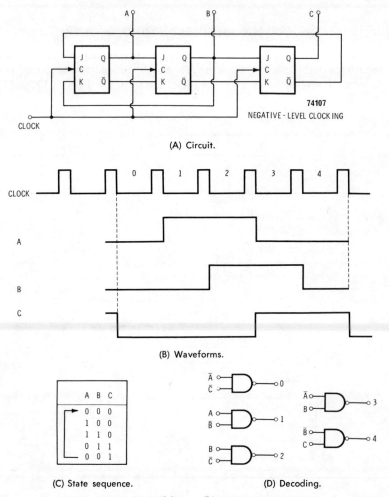

(A) Circuit.

(B) Waveforms.

(C) State sequence.

(D) Decoding.

Fig. 7-12. Modulo-5 walking-ring counter.

very inefficient for long count lengths, compared to binary dividers, but if high-speed, synchronous operation is needed with every state that is decoded and is not overlapped, they offer an attractive alternative to other systems.

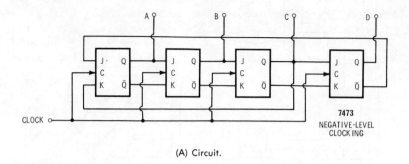

(A) Circuit.

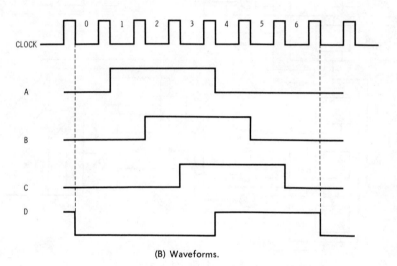

(B) Waveforms.

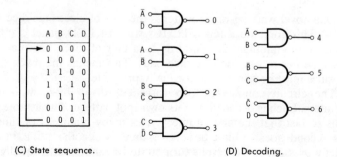

(C) State sequence.

(D) Decoding.

Fig. 7-13. Modulo-7 walking-ring counter.

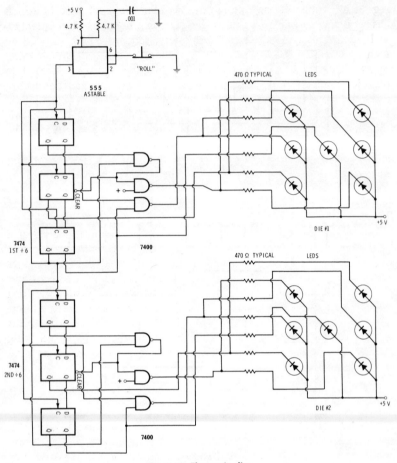

Fig. 7-14. Electronic dice.

ELECTRONIC DICE

One novel walking-ring counter is the pair of electronic dice in Fig. 7-14. This combine a few TTL ICs with 14 LED panel displays to produce the familiar spot patterns on a pair of dice. Any machine of this type has to provide true dice odds. This means the dwell time on all sides must be constant and equally probable.

The circuit consists of two cascaded, divide-by-6, walking-ring counters. Each is decoded into its own spot pattern. The astable circuit runs so fast that the first counter cycles many hundreds of times and the second goes around dozens of times while the ROLL button is briefly pressed, so the results turn out to be random and equally probable. Note that simultaneously rolling two 6-sided dice is the same with regard to probability as rolling one 36-sided die, each side of which has 1 of the possible 36 patterns that two dice together would display.

To decode the spots, we call the counter sequence 1-3-5-6-4-2. We then have even or odd and 4, 5, or 6 decoded free. The "even or odd" lights the center LED for 1, 3, and 5, while the 4, 5, or 6 lights two outside diagonal lamps for count 4, 5, or 6. Two other decodings are needed. "Not 1" is decoded to light the remaining two diagonal lamps, while 6 is decoded to light the center two lamps on either side. Although there are seven LEDs per die, only the proper number in the proper position can light for any die combination. The possible disallowed states are autocleared as part of the "not 1" decoding. Within 36 counts after the ROLL button is hit, the counters are correct.

OTHER SHIFT-REGISTER COUNTERS

Any combination of feedback which is from advanced stages of a shift register and which is routed back to its input will give us some sequence, even if it is only one bit long. If we start doing logical or arithmetic combinations in the feedback, the number of such possibilities is essentially infinite. To be efficient, the sequences must be long with respect to the 2^n possible states of an n-bit shift register. Otherwise, other counter techniques turn out to be more efficient in terms of packages or power. One exception to this is where the walking ring performs some useful functions that might be difficult or impractical to do otherwise.

THE PSEUDO-RANDOM SEQUENCER

One of the most interesting possible combinations of shift-register feedback is the *pseudo-random sequencer*. These sequencers have several nice features. First, they can be of *maximal length,* that is, they can be as long as a register sequence can possibly be. This turns out to be *one less than 2^n,* so the circuit is essentially as efficient as a binary counter. Second, the numbers appear in an *apparently random* order, although, of course, they repeat every time the sequence is clocked completely through $2^n - 1$ counts.

This gives you the equivalent of *noise that repeats.* This is handy for audio systems testing, computer security, cryptography, and electronic music. In fact, the pseudonoise turns out to be *better* than real noise. The randomness is constant over one total cycle, where real noise requires a very long (ideally infinite) time average to get true randomness.

Fig. 7-15 is a typical circuit. Here, we have taken a 6-stage shift register and EXCLUSIVE ORed the fifth and sixth bits, and then inverted them. If bits 5 and 6 are both a 0 or both a 1, then a 1 is sent to the

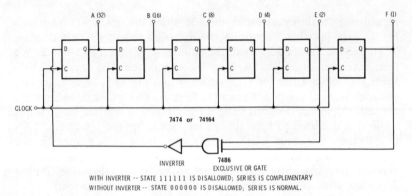

Fig. 7-15. A 63-state pseudo-random sequence generator.

first stage. If either, but not both, is a 0, then a 0 goes to the input of the first stage. The resulting truth table is shown in Chart 7-2.

Several things are obvious from the circuit. As you can tell from the state decoding, the numbers are well jumbled, and mathematically they turn out to be purely random if you select a short term group of them. There are 63 states in the sequence, or one less than $2^6 = 64$. The repeat time is $\frac{1}{63}$ the clock frequency. State 64 is a hangup—if you ever get all 1's, the circuit stays in that state till you do something about it. You can eliminate this state by presetting a 0 anywhere in the sequence. Clearing the register works as well.

LONGER SEQUENCES

Diagrams for sequences up to $2^{16} - 1 = 65,535$ are shown in Fig. 7-16, while Table 7-2 shows the connections for sequences up to length 31. A 31-stage pseudo-random register has 2,147,483,647 states. Thus, for a 1-MHz clock frequency, the sequence will repeat once each 2147.5 seconds or slightly over half an hour. At a 100-kHz clock rate, the repeat time would be slightly over five hours, and so on. Any short sample of these registers will look and behave like random noise, but will repeat once every $2^n - 1$ clock cycles. A few of the sequences that are above length 20 are not quite maximal length, but they are still long enough that you will not be able to tell the difference.

We can get at least four related maximal-length sequences per register length. If we add an inverter or use an EXCLUSIVE NOR for feedback, we get the complement of the original sequence, with all the 1's and 0's interchanged. If we look where the register has been instead of where it is going, we obtain a *backward* sequence. To do this, you look forward from the nth bit instead of backward. Instead of stages 5 and 6, on a 6-stage register you use 6 and 1, and so on. Finally, we can achieve a backward and complemented sequence by us-

Chart 7-2. Sequential States for the Circuit of Fig. 7-15.
Sequence Length is 63

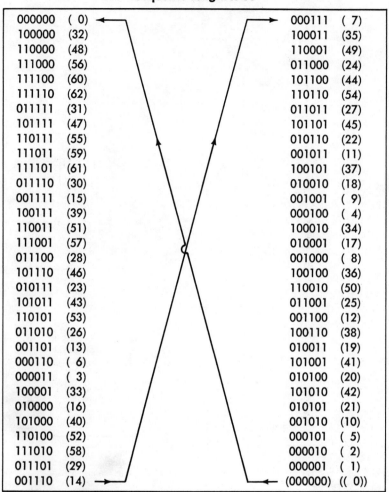

000000	(0)		000111	(7)
100000	(32)		100011	(35)
110000	(48)		110001	(49)
111000	(56)		011000	(24)
111100	(60)		101100	(44)
111110	(62)		110110	(54)
011111	(31)		011011	(27)
101111	(47)		101101	(45)
110111	(55)		010110	(22)
111011	(59)		001011	(11)
111101	(61)		100101	(37)
011110	(30)		010010	(18)
001111	(15)		001001	(9)
100111	(39)		000100	(4)
110011	(51)		100010	(34)
111001	(57)		010001	(17)
011100	(28)		001000	(8)
101110	(46)		100100	(36)
010111	(23)		110010	(50)
101011	(43)		011001	(25)
110101	(53)		001100	(12)
011010	(26)		100110	(38)
001101	(13)		010011	(19)
000110	(6)		101001	(41)
000011	(3)		010100	(20)
100001	(33)		101010	(42)
010000	(16)		010101	(21)
101000	(40)		001010	(10)
110100	(52)		000101	(5)
111010	(58)		000010	(2)
011101	(29)		000001	(1)
001110	(14)		(000000)	((0))

First (input) register stage is on the left.
Last (output) register stage is on the right.
Number in parentheses is decimal equivalent to binary word.

ing both techniques. With the complementary sequences, the 111 . . . .
11 condition is the stalemate. With normal sequences, the 0000 . . .
0000 hangs up. By presetting to some combination of 1's and 0's, you
can eliminate both possibilities. Note that Fig. 7-15 and Chart 7-2 are
for a complementary sequence that is resettable to 000000.

There are two general ways to use the sequences if you are going to
convert them to analog signals. These are shown in Fig. 7-17. In Fig.

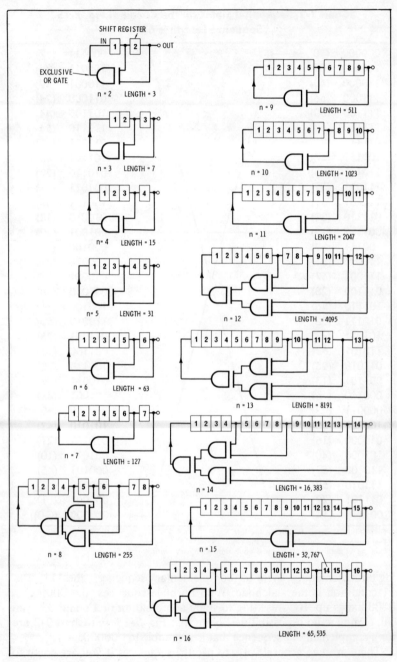

Fig. 7-16. Pseudo-random connections for 2 through 16 stages.

Table 7-2. Register Connections for Longer Sequences

Stages	Sequence Length	Feed EXCLUSIVE OR Gate From Outputs
17	131,071	14 and 17
18	262,143	11 and 18
20	1,048,575	17 and 20
21	2,097,151	19 and 21
22	4,194,303	21 and 22
23	8,388,607	18 and 23
24	16,766,977	19 and 24
25	33,554,431	22 and 25
26	67,074,001	21 and 26
27	133,693,177	19 and 27
28	268,435,455	25 and 28
29	536,870,911	27 and 29
30	1,073,215,489	23 and 30
31	2,147,483,647	28 and 31

7-17A, the noise is integrated with a time constant less than $\frac{1}{20}$ the clock frequency. The same noise pattern repeats every $n - 1$ clock cycles. If n is made large enough, the noise response becomes essentially dc to the cutoff frequency of the integrator, producing white noise. Filtering converts it into pink noise. A dc blocking capacitor is recommended to keep the integrator centered. Each sequence has an

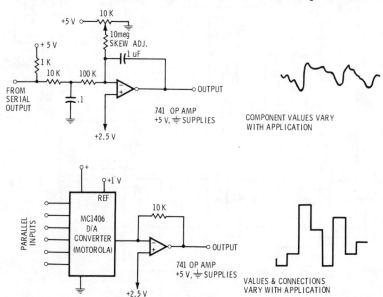

Fig. 7-17. Two ways of converting digital pseudo-random sequences to analog levels or noise.

excess of one 1 or 0 and would tend to eventually pin the integrator if the response extended down to dc. The output of this method is white noise, useful for audio testing.

In Fig. 7-17B, we directly convert the individual words in the sequence from digital to analog. This gives us a sequence of random analog levels useful in electronic music and similar applications where a series of uniformly timed steps of random analog values is desired.

One direct digital use of pseudo-random sequences was suggested in Fig. 3-10D. The sequence can be mixed with good computer data and the combined signal routed down a line as indiscernable scrambled noise. The data can be recovered by remixing with the identical sequence or a copy of it. Cryptography and computer security are two

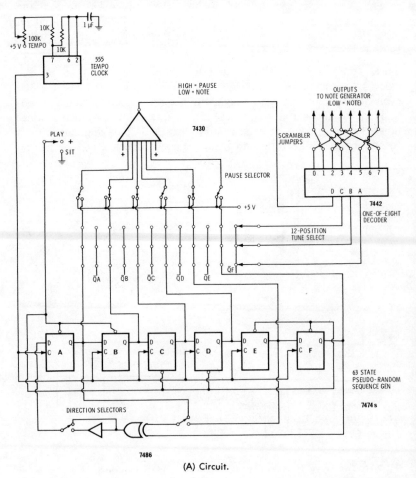

(A) Circuit.

Fig. 7-18. A music

applications. Similar techniques are used in some cable tv scrambling systems.

A MUSIC COMPOSER

A "composer" to generate random music tunes is shown in Fig. 7-18A. A pseudo-random sequencer of 63 bits is set up to run forward or backward. It always starts in a sequence with two 1's and the rest 0's, so that the disallowed-state problem cannot exist. Three of the outputs or their complements are chosen as a program, giving 1728 different sequences. These three lines are binarily decoded into eight lines. The eight lines are then used to control eight notes on a tone generator. The scrambler allows a further programming of the combinations. It is simply a panel with eight inputs and eight outputs that has any selected input connected to any selected output on a one-for-one basis.

To add variety, a pause circuit is added as shown. This eliminates $\frac{1}{2}$, $\frac{1}{4}$, $\frac{1}{8}$, $\frac{1}{16}$, or $\frac{1}{32}$ of the notes and replaces them with pauses in a

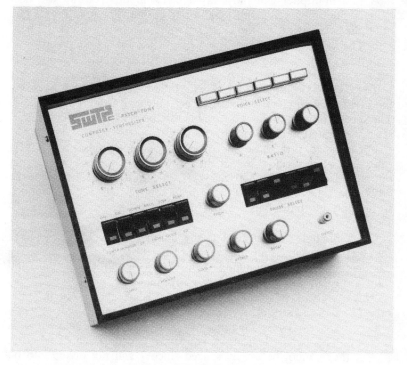

(B) Panel view.

composer-synthesizer.

wide variety of combinations. The ¼ positions usually give the most pleasing results. Many millions of combinations result. A commercial kit version of the composer-synthesizer is shown in Fig. 7-18B.

The circuitry is easily extended to longer lengths. By decoding 1 of 32 or 1 of 64 and recombining, note probabilities can be set up, and chording and multiple voicing becomes possible.

Another interesting musical use of pseudo-random sequences is instrument voicing, generating elaborate tonal structures unlike any known instrument.

THE RATE MULTIPLIER

Rate multipliers are very specialized TTL logic blocks. If you use them correctly, you can generate n pulse sequences, multiply, divide, square, exact square root, use logarithms and exponents, and do trig calculations with them. On the other hand, many people misapply them because they do not understand what the circuit really does. Let us take a closer look.

A rate multiplier generally has a clock input, a group of "how many?" rate-input commands, and a rate output. The first thing a rate multiplier does is divide the clock by some number n to get the base rate. The value of n is typically 64 or 10; the former for binary rate multipliers such as the 7497 and the latter for decimal rate multipliers such as the 74167.

There are two outputs. One provides the base rate, which is simply the divided-down clock decoded to get only one clock out of n out. The second output provides a variable rate of clock pulses. This rate is set by the rate-input commands.

For instance, if the base rate is putting out clock pulses at a 1-kHz rate, depending on how we set the "how many?" inputs, we can get output pulses at 1-kHz, 2-kHz, 3-kHz, . . . up to 63-kHz rate for the 7497. Thus the "how many?" rate-input controls tell us by how much to multiply the basic pulse rate. This is where the name "rate multiplier" comes from.

On command, we can get out any number of clock pulses (from 0 to 63) in the same time interval that we get one base-rate pulse. We can then multiply by any number from 0 to 63 with the basic unit, and units are easily cascaded for more performance.

This sounds like a great machine. And it is, except for one little detail. *The output rates are averages, and the rate pulses are normally unevenly spaced.* Thus, some pulse-to-pulse jitter on the rate output is inherent. This is only logical—if you try to decode 7 out of 64 clock pulses, they cannot be evenly spaced since 7 will not divide into 64 evenly. At least one of the interpulse intervals has to be longer than the rest.

Thus, jitter is *inherent* in a rate multiplier. The only time you can use a rate-multiplier system is when you are only interested in a final answer of "so many pulses over this time length," or where some pulse-to-pulse jitter is acceptable. It is a circuit for summations and averages, not absolute frequencies.

Fig. 7-19 shows the internal logic of the 7497. Suppose we apply a 64-Hz clock to it and properly enable everything. The Enable output will provide one clock pulse per second, and the base rate will be one pulse per second. We can get any number of pulses we want per second out of the Z output. To do this, we apply an input rate command onto lines A through F. For instance, if we put a 1 on the A line and a 1 on the B line, we obtain *three* pulses per second as the rate output at Z. Since A is weighted 1 and B is weighted 2, the sum appears at Z. Similarly, a 100110 command on the A through F lines applies a 2, a 4, and a 32 for a total of 38 rate pulses. We will get out 38 pulses during the interpulse period that delivers 1 hertz at the Enable output. The output pulses will be almost, but not quite, equally spaced, and we can get from 0 to 63 output pulses on command.

Some applications should strongly suggest themselves at this point. Here is a simple and effective way of generating n pulses on command, n being anything from 0 to 63. The only limitation is that the pulses will not be uniformly spaced. They will be of constant width set by the clock input, but they can only occur in time slots coincident with input clock pulses. To do this, we clear the multiplier and let it run for 64 counts. We use the output enable to shut down the clock. After every reset command, we get n pulses on the Z output. The frequency and width of the pulses are identical to the input clock, except that some will be missing in order to get out the proper number.

MULTIPLYING AND DIVIDING

The really interesting applications of rate multipliers involve computation. It is just as easy to multiply as it is to divide, just as easy to extract a square root as it is to square, and so on, up through making log and trig calculations. Rate multipliers are also ideally suited for this sort of application where you are only interested in a final answer and do not care if the pulses jitter a bit before getting there.

To build a multiplier or a divider, we add a down-counter, called the Y counter, and an up-counter with a digital readout, called the Z counter. The circuit for multiplication is shown in Fig. 7-20. Suppose we wanted to multiply 7 times 5. We load a 7 into the Y counter and set the X input to the rate multiplier to 5. We clear the multiplier and start the clock. On the first 64 clock pulses, 5 pulses go to the Z counter where the answer will pile up. On the 64th clock pulse, 1 is subtracted from the 7 in the Y counter (remember this is a down-

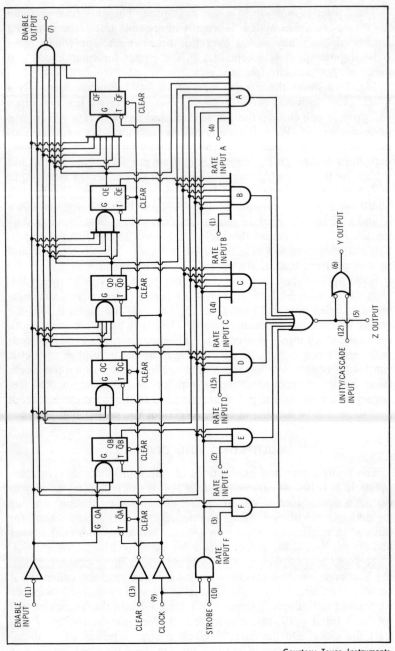

Courtesy Texas Instruments

Fig. 7-19. Internal logic of a 6-bit binary rate multiplier.

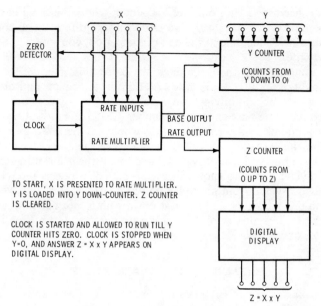

Fig. 7-20. Multiplying two numbers together with a rate multiplier.

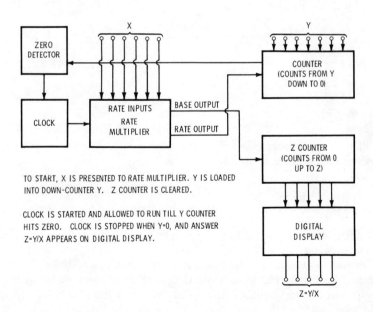

Fig. 7-21. Dividing two numbers with a rate multiplier. Note that the only difference between this circuit and the multiplier circuit of Fig. 7-20 is two interchanged leads.

counter), leaving us with 6 in the Y counter. The same thing happens with the next 64 clock pulses, five more pulses go into the Z counter which now holds ten, and at the end of the period, you subtract 1 from the Y counter.

This continues till the Y counter hits 0. At this time we stop the clock, and the answer, 35, is now stored in the Z counter and display. This is a way of multiplying two numbers together. We would have obtained the same answer for any number greater than 7 but less than 8, since all numbers are rounded off to whole numbers. To gain accuracy, you can cascade stages. If the contents of the Z register and display get too big, you can provide scaling to cut them down to size.

The divider circuit is shown in Fig. 7-21. All we do is interchange two leads to switch from multiplication to division! This time we load the 35 in the Y counter and count it down with 5 rate pulses at a time till we hit 0. The answer of 7 is racked up one count at a time in the Z register and display.

SQUARES AND SQUARE ROOTS

The squaring circuit is shown in Fig. 7-22. To generate a series of 1, 4, 9, 16, 25, 36, . . . pulses, we do the following:

Start with 1 pulse . . . . accumulate as 1
    add 2
Now generate 3 pulses . . . . accumulate as 4
    add 2
Now generate 5 pulses . . . . accumulate as 9
    add 2
Now generate 7 pulses . . . . accumulate as 16
    add 2
        etc.

This is sometimes called the method of *second differences*. An easy way to remember it is usually shown as:

1		4		9		16		25		36		49		. . .
	3		5		7		9		11		13		15		. . .
		2		2		2		2		2		2		2		. . .

The top line is the series of squares. The middle line is the first difference between the squares. The bottom line is the second difference. This method tells us to generate a rate and accumulate it, add 2 to the rate to be generated, accumulate that, and so on, and we will get an output in the accumulator that is the square of the number of cycles that were used in the operation.

The multiply and divide circuits applied a fixed number (the multiplier or divisor) as a rate input. Squares and square roots require that this number change by 2 each cycle. We need a new counter, called the X counter, as shown in Fig. 7-22. To square, simply set the X counter to 1 and turn on the clock. The first cycle, a 1, appears in the accumulator and whatever number we are squaring is subtracted by 1 in the Y register. The same 1 that does the subtracting in the Y register is doubled by detection of leading and trailing edges and is used to advance the X counter to 3. This time, 3 is added to the accumulator for a total of 4 (this is the second cycle $2^2 = 4$). One is sub-

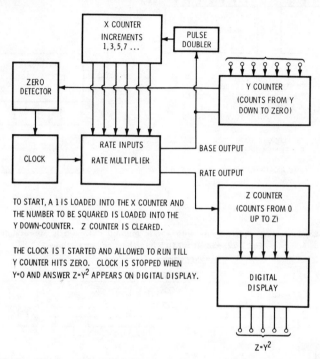

Fig. 7-22. Squaring a number with a rate multiplier. Pulse doubler increments the X counter by two counts for each base output pulse.

tracted from the Y register, and the 3 in the X register becomes a 5. The process continues till the Y register empties. At that time, we stop the clock and display the square of the original number that was in the Y register.

To extract the square root, we simply interchange the circuit of Fig. 7-22 to get the circuit of Fig. 7-23. This time, the number from which we want to extract the square root is loaded in the Y register, and it is counted down with the rate pulses. We accumulate and display the number of cycles it took to do this in the Z register and display, while 1-3-5-7- . . . . incrementing the X register every cycle.

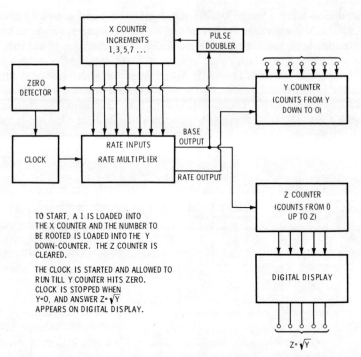

Fig. 7-23. Extracting square roots with a rate multiplier. Circuit is identical to that of Fig. 7-22, except for two interchanged connections.

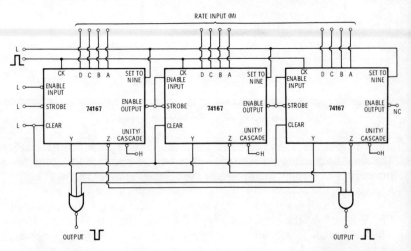

Courtesy Texas Instruments

Fig. 7-24. Rate multiplier ICs can be cascaded for more accuracy. Here are three cascaded decade multipliers, the 74167.

This may seem confusing, but some pen and pencil work or some breadboarding will make it clear. The rate multiplier is a powerful way of computing, although it is somewhat slow, being a serial type of device.

The same circuit also works nicely for logs and exponents with simple modifications, and extra parts can be added for sines and cosines. Complete details and a good bibliography appeared in the "Electronic Slide Rule" article in the *Electronic Engineer,* July 1968.

The only problem with the 7497 is that the input rate numbers have to be in binary form. For computers, this is more or less typical, and the circuit is easily expanded to any binary number. For smaller calculation problems, working with decimal decades is more desirable, and this is handled by the 74167. Fig. 7-24 shows how three decades can be combined for 0.1% accuracy and ordinary Binary-Coded-Decimal (BCD) input commands. Note that more packages are needed for a given amount of accuracy with the decimal devices, but that the binary devices may require some sort of conversion before they are readily used.

There are all sorts of opportunities for creative use of rate multipliers. They do not seem to be used much simply because designers are not familiar with them and the complex operations they are capable of. So long as only a final answer is required and a slight jitter in pulse positions is tolerable, the rate multiplier offers an interesting approach to a wide variety of practical problems.

CHAPTER 8

Getting It All Together

Now that we have all the basics needed to work with individual and grouped TTL circuits, the question is: What can we do with TTL?

How do you interconnect the basic circuits into working *systems*— systems that solve problems, entertain, or perform a useful outside-world task? If you go back over the previous chapters, you will find that we have already shown dozens of specific TTL applications.

In this chapter we will look at some more applications along with some whole-system concepts. First, we will examine digital counter and display systems, for they are the basis of many TTL digital measurement systems, including panel meters, digital voltmeters, counters, tachometers, thermometers, component testers, and many others.

After that, we will turn to some rather unique, medium-size, TTL system applications. These will include tv time displays, an alphanumeric computer terminal, a photographic printing computer, and an electronic music synthesizer. Finally, we will suggest a number of very simple 1- and 2-IC projects—low cost, easy-to-do TTL projects suitable as home test gear, training aids, or school or science-fair projects.

Throughout this chapter, our intent is more to give system-design concepts rather than specific how-it-works, every-part-listed details. We do this, first, to emphasize systems design; second, to present more ideas in less space; and third—above all—to encourage you to go back and fill in the missing details yourself.

Practically all you need to know is in the previous chapters. The rest you will have to learn for yourself.

DIGITAL COUNTER AND DISPLAY SYSTEMS

There are a number of advantages to the digital method of measurement as compared to traditional analog methods such as meters. First, digital techniques tentatively offer more accuracy. Analog systems that are more than 1% accurate are expensive, and if more than 0.1% accurate, they are very complex. Digital methods can expand to the limits of the number of decades you use, *provided your measurement time and reference accuracies are good enough.* Thus, .01%, .001% and even .0001% accuracy are rather easy to attain, and if you want, much more accuracy than this can be obtained.

Second, digital techniques are less likely to be misread. This is particularly true when a single number is displayed as compared to a cramped multiple-meter scale. Third, the digital route provides machine and computer output and computational advantages. And finally, with careful circuit design, digital circuits can often be cheaper and more reproducible than their analog equivalents. They often need fewer adjustments and less frequent calibration.

On the other hand, there are a few times when a "good old Simpson" (or Triplett, or whatever) meter-type display is better than using digits. This is particularly true if the relative *variations* in value and their rate of change are important. Digital techniques are best for most applications. The key test is—do you want accuracy or are you more interested in observing changes or variations?

Fig. 8-1 shows two digital-counter and display systems. In Fig. 8-1A, we have a continuous or instantaneous display system. Here, each decade counter has its own decoder/driver and readout. The input goes to the units counter. The output of the units counter drives the tens counter, the tens drives the hundreds, and so on, for the desired total number of digits. In Fig. 8-1B, we have added storage latches between counter and decoder/driver to give a strobed display. In this manner, the display provides a continuous old answer while letting the counter proceed to a new measurement.

Typically, you first clear the counter and then allow it to accumulate input counts till external circuitry tells you that an answer exists. You then *update* the display by strobing the memory. The memory accepts and holds the answer and continuously displays it, but the counter is free to continue.

Up-only ripple counters are usually adequate for digital display systems. The more expensive synchronous and up/down counters are used when you need high speeds or when you also need a computing capability.

In Fig. 8-1C, a binary divider has been added to the last stage, driving a readout that is simply a 1 when lit. This is called adding *half* a digit. A 3-decade counter counts to 999, while most 3½ decade counters count to 1999. This doubles the accuracy without greatly increasing the cost. Special readouts are available that include a 1 digit with polarity symbols. In Nixie systems a neon lamp serves as well.

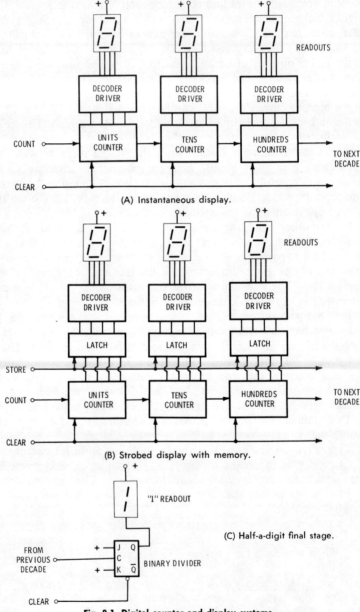

(A) Instantaneous display.

(B) Strobed display with memory.

(C) Half-a-digit final stage.

Fig. 8-1. Digital counter and display systems.

The choice of display is a problem in itself. The traditional readout device has been the Nixie tube for the past several years, but 7-segment and multiple-dot light emitting diodes predominate today. This is particularly true since the introduction of improved LED displays —low-cost, high-efficiency units that use sophisticated internal optics to give a very pleasing character shape with a minimum of material. The Fairchild FND70 is typical, although competitive units are offered by Hewlett Packard, Monsanto, Opcoa, Litronix, and others.

All LEDs are essentially diodes. They are *current*-operated devices, and, when on, they have a 1.7-volt forward drop. *External current limiting must be provided with all LED devices.* This can be done with one resistor per segment (often 330 ohms on a +5-volt system) or by using driver ICs whose outputs *specifically* include current limiting for LED use. Remember that any decoder/driver must match the display selected.

Some readouts include an internal latch and decoder/driver, while other combinations of counter/decoder/driver/latch exist as ready-to-go TTL packages. Typical are the 74142, 74143, 74144, and the Motorola MC4050 and MC4051.

Multiplexed Displays

Another approach to digital display systems that have lots of digits is the *multiplexed* system of Fig. 8-2. Multiplexing offers a way to *share* one decoder/driver among all of the display decades. To do

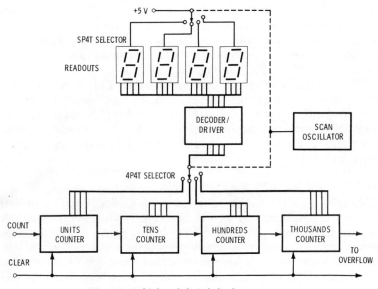

Fig. 8-2. Multiplexed digital display system.

this, the display is rapidly *scanned,* with selected elements lit to n times normal brightness for 1/n of a scan cycle. The scanning is fast enough that the eye averages everything out and sees the display as continuously lit. Scan rates typically range from 100 Hz upward.

Two selectors are used. One is a 1-of-n distributor that provides positive voltage to the individual decades. The segments of all the decades are connected in parallel and driven from a single decoder/driver. The input to the decoder/driver is connected to one decade at a time with a 4-pole data selector. At any given instant, only one decade receives supply power, and only the segments selected on that decade light.

In any multiplex system, it is essential that the display elements are nonlinear, have a threshold, or behave like diodes. Otherwise, *sneak paths* which run backward through the series connections of supposedly *off* elements, will result in ghosting. Fortunately, both Nixie tube and LED systems meet these requirements by themselves.

The "break-even" point on a multiplexed display is around four decades. Above that, you will save by multiplexing; the savings will increase as you add more decades. Multiplexed systems also can dramatically reduce the number of display-to-circuit interconnections, particularly when lots of digits are in use.

Counting Systems

Some 1-package MOS counting systems are now available that combine a full 4-decade counter, multiplexer, storage, decoder, driver, etc., into a single package. These are relatively slow (200 kHz) and need external driver transistors, but should be considered as an alternate to TTL for many routine display applications. The Mostek MK5005 and MK5017 are typical; the first is a 4-decade digital instrument system; the second is for digital alarm clocks.

Fig. 8-3 shows a commercial snap-together TTL counting system that consists of individual decade modules that mount on a main "mother board" type of system. The mother board is changed to provide different digital functions such as a 4-decade counter, a 6-decade counter, a clock, a tachometer, and so on. Both ripple and synchronous up/down snap-in modules are available.

Leading-Zero Blanking

Leading-zero blanking is a way of lopping off all the 0's to the left of the first significant digit in a display. Fig. 8-4 shows how much the appearance of a display is improved in this manner. The technique also minimizes errors, particularly when there are other 0's in a number, and saves on supply power. The 7447 decoder/driver provides for automatic leading-zero elimination, as do several other decoder systems. If the leading-edge blanking is not available, you can add it

Courtesy Southwest Technical Products Corp.

Fig. 8-3. Southwest Technical Products LED DCU assembly.

externally with a few gates. The top decade is arranged to unconditionally extinguish its own 0. The next decade down blanks its 0 only if the top decade also does so. The next stage blanks only if the first two do, and so on down the line.

Filters

Optical filters between viewer and display can dramatically improve the contrast and viewability. They should always be used. In the case of Nixie tubes, an orange filter is best, while deep red works best with

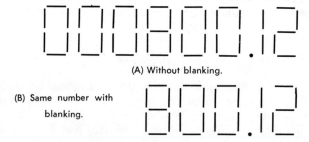

(A) Without blanking.

(B) Same number with
blanking.

Fig. 8-4. Leading-zero blanking improves display appearance, minimizes errors, and reduces standby power.

traditional red LEDs. One good deep-red filter is #2423 Plexiglas, which is readily obtained at a plastic supply house. Circularly polarized filters from Polaroid corporation offer even better contrast enhancement, as do several controlled-angle viewing filters offered by 3M and others. These latter filters are a clear sheet with an opaque honeycomb type of structure inside. From the intended angle you can see through the filter, but off to either side of the intended angle the screen turns all black. Incident light is similarly restricted.

If brightness control of a display is needed, it is usually best done with a duty-cycle modulation basis, such as the circuit of Fig. 4-22. The object is to rapidly turn the display off and on so that the eye sees the ratio of the on to off time as a relative brightness.

Overflow

Another important feature of a digital display is some means of overflow detection. An analog meter pins at full scale, but a digital display starts over again. A reading of 6539 could really be the four right-hand digits of a 976539 reading. Fig. 8-5 shows how overflow

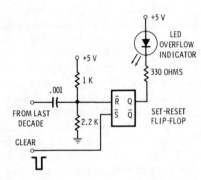

Fig. 8-5. Overflow detector and indicator should be included on all digital displays.

detection is added to a digital display. The carry of the most significant decade sets a flip-flop which drives an overflow indicator or blinker. It is reset by the same circuit that resets the counter for a new measurement.

THE SPEED-RESOLUTION PRODUCT

Just as there are well-defined limits to the accuracy of an analog circuit, there are restrictions to the accuracy and resolution of a digital display. One such limitation is called the *speed-resolution product*. It simply says that it takes longer to get more accuracy and that extreme resolution probably will take much too long.

For instance, with a 1-MHz clock rate, we can get 5-place accuracy in 0.1 second. Six-place accuracy takes a full second. If we try for 10-place accuracy, it will take up 2 hours, 36 minutes, and 40 seconds. The only way to "beat" this system is to use the fastest possible clock (usually limited by cycle times and external circuits to much less than the "wide open" counter speed) or go to a sophisticated and complex parallel computational system such as computers use.

ACCURACY

The following rule cannot be overemphasized: **The accuracy of any digital display system can be no greater than the accuracy of the information it is working with.** For instance, if you are using the power line as a time base, you could use 75 decades in your display and still be no more accurate than the 0.1% or so accuracy of the power line. If you have a voltage-to-digits converter that is only 1% accurate or whose linearity or temperature performance is only 1%, no amount of digits above 3 will improve the accuracy.

In general, the display resolution should be matched to and slightly exceed the accuracy of what is being measured. There is no point in adding extra digits beyond what the input circuitry can deliver in the way of accuracy. Besides costing money and using supply power, the extra digits probably will jitter or bobble, or otherwise behave erratically.

The resolution of a digital display defines its best possible accuracy. Note that this applies to the highest digit *lit* and not to the total number available. The usual accuracy is limited to plus or minus one count in terms of the displayed number. Thus, a 200 displayed on a 3-decade system could be a 199 or a 201 in reality—a 1% error.

The so-called inherent 1-count jitter in a digital display is easily eliminated by synchronizing the input time reference to the measurement cycle, as shown in Fig. 5-20. This generates a bobble-free display and brings the accuracy up to minus 0, plus one count.

Once again, use no more decades than you need to do the job, and be sure the input information has the needed accuracy before you attempt to display it.

EVENTS COUNTER

The simplest digital display is the events counter of Fig. 8-6. The counter is cleared and then it advances one count for each input event.

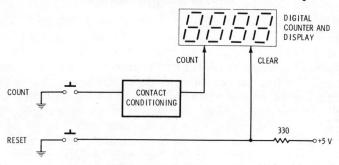

Fig. 8-6. Events counter.

This may be used to count production items or to accumulate the output of a rate multiplier or other calculation circuit. Usually the output is continuous instead of strobed.

Mechanical contacts at the count input must be properly conditioned to be bounceless and noiseless so that each actuation provides one, and only one, count. A push button on the Clear line need *not* be made bounceless, for resetting a counter to zero 137 times in a row does the same thing as resetting it once, so long as the bounce is gone before the next count event arrives. With most counting systems it is important to make sure that the reset line always presents a low impedance to the positive supply (to ground with some others) at all times to prevent noise and stray coupling from providing erratic clearing and semiclearing.

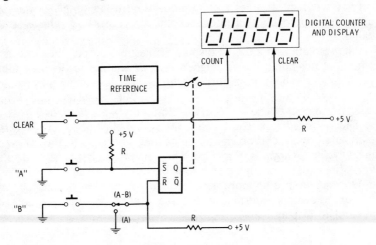

Fig. 8-7. Electronic stopwatch.

ELECTRONIC STOPWATCH

The electronic stopwatch of Fig. 8-7 is only a little more complex. A source of reference pulses of a known frequency or time spacing is needed. We reset a display counter and then start accumulating the reference frequency for only as long as the control switch is closed. At the end of a measurement interval, the display is updated, or the display can run continuously and will present a stationary answer at the end of the measuring time. The time reference is multiplied by the answer to get the elapsed time. For instance, with a 1-kHz reference, the pulses are spaced 1 millisecond apart. If we end up with a 6742 reading, the elapsed time is 6.742 seconds. A decimal point can be placed where it is wanted with external switching.

The circuit shown has two operating modes. In the A-B mode, event A starts the timing and event B stops it, thus measuring the time *between* events. In this mode, the contact circuit is self-conditioning, provided the contact on A has been released and has settled down before contact on B is made. Leading- or trailing-edge detection and conditioning can be added if the contacts are broken permanently in the timing application.

In the A-only mode, the flip-flop is disabled and internally arranged so that the control switch is closed for the *duration* of A. In this mode, contact A must be conditioned, for any bounce will end up as holes in the duration time, which will shorten the count. One interesting thing you can do if contact A is local is to run the ground lead from the A position of the mode selector through the normally closed contact of a spdt push button at A. This will locally self-condition for duration as well as interval measurement. Remote operation of the circuit of Fig. 8-8 is made possible by adding suitable cables to provide the grounds as needed.

This stopwatch can be used to measure anything from nanosecond intervals to hours of elapsed time if the proper reference and control signals are selected. Applications include radar distance measuring, physics experiments, biological and seismic monitoring, measurement of low-frequency signals by measuring the periods and calculating the inverse function, field and track events, sports car and automotive applications, photographic lab timing and shutter testing, etc.

Time and Frequency References

The stopwatch circuit and most of the other digital instruments need a time or frequency reference against which to compare input events. Whatever we are trying to measure is somehow converted into a time duration that is measured stopwatch-style, or a frequency duration that is accumulated events-counter style for a fixed time interval. Again, the digital instrument can be no more accurate than the time and frequency reference chosen.

Several possible references are shown in Fig. 8-8. In Fig. 8-8A, we use a high-frequency crystal oscillator (often 1.0 MHz) and a decade divider system to provide a chain of decade-related standard times and frequencies. In Fig. 8-8B, we use a single low-frequency crystal. This is done by using the crystal in a tuning-fork-resonance type of mode rather than the traditional vibratory modes. Low-frequency crystals used to be extremely expensive, but some are now cheaper and *smaller* than ordinary MHz region crystals, *Statek* units are typical.

Ordinary high-frequency crystals and these low-frequency ones may be used when the needed accuracy is less than five decades. For more than five decades, it is necessary to go to crystal-oven circuits with synchronous dividers.

A good frequency reference of 3- or possibly 4-place accuracy is the power line with its nominal 0.1 to 0.05% accuracy. A typical circuit appears in Fig. 8-8C. The power line is usually economical but limited to 3-place accuracy. A power-line 60Hz reference is obviously hard to obtain in a portable instrument.

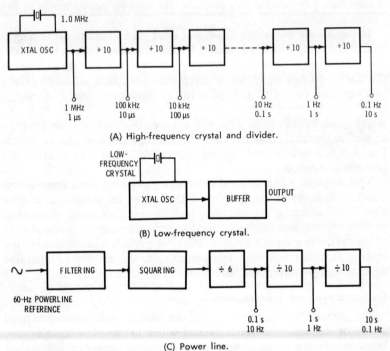

(A) High-frequency crystal and divider.

(B) Low-frequency crystal.

(C) Power line.

Fig. 8-8. Time and frequency references for digital instruments.

Several MOS integrated circuits are also available that ease the package count on some time-and frequency-reference circuits. For instance, the Mostek MK 5009 starts with a 1-MHz crystal oscillator and on command will give any reference frequency of 13, selectable from 1 MHz to 1 pulse per hour. TTL remains the best option for special timing sequences or higher frequencies, or for whenever only one or two reference frequencies are needed.

FREQUENCY COUNTER

A frequency counter (Fig. 8-9) is an "inside out" electronic stopwatch. It measures events per unit time. Usually a long time reference of 0.1, 1, or 10 seconds determines how long the input is to be counted. With a 1-second time reference, a reading of 6745 would be

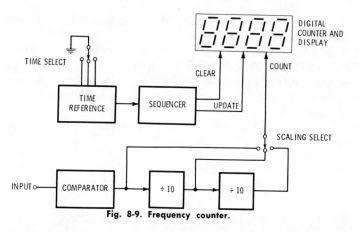

Fig. 8-9. Frequency counter.

6.745 kHz. With a 0.1-second reference, it would be 67.45 kHz. With a 10-second reference, it would be only 674.5 Hz.

Higher frequencies are handled with shorter time references, although these cannot usually be obtained from a line-operated time base. Another alternative is to add optional decade scalers of 10, 100, or even 1000. For instance, a 90-MHz input might be dropped to 9 MHz with a Schottky TTL decade counter. From there, it could be directly measured with a 1-millisecond gate, or it could be scaled further by 100 and measured with a 100-millisecond gate.

The input to a counter must be conditioned. The amount of conditioning depends on the application and the frequency range of interest. Usually a high input impedance is desirable for light loading on frequencies below 35 MHz or so; above that, a 50-, 70-, or 100-ohm input is needed to properly terminate cables and prevent reflections. Some input gain is almost always desirable, but not so much that at full gain input noise causes an erratic display on marginal signal levels. Snap action or hysteresis is desirable on low-frequency input signals, as is the optional ability to select a given trigger point to handle unusual waveshapes. From an operating standpoint, the fewer the input controls (ideally zero) the better, so circuits should have a very wide dynamic range.

A simple and cheap conditioner can be obtained by running a CMOS logic gate in its linear mode. More sophisticated circuits usually use integrated-circuit comparators, with the National LM311 being a good low-frequency choice. Premium units are available for higher-frequency operation.

The accuracy of the measurement depends first on the accuracy of the time base and secondly on the number of cycles counted. A 1-second time gate can give a one-part-per-million accuracy on a 1-MHz sine wave, but it will only have an accuracy of 3 to 5% on a low electronic organ note because it can only accumulate 20 or 30 events in a measurement.

One alternate way to measure low-frequency waveforms is to first filter them thoroughly so the fundamental is much stronger than any harmonic and then measure the time between positive zero crossings, stopwatch-fashion. The signal must also be noise free for this to work, and the inverse frequency has to be calculated.

The sequencer shown in Fig. 8-9 takes care of the housework—clearing the counter at the beginning of a time interval, updating the display at the end, optionally synchronizing, and then providing a short or adjustable time delay before the next measurement cycle is to begin. This is easily handled with a 555 timer or a gate or two.

BOBBLE AND UPDATE LIMITATIONS

If the time reference in any digital counter and display is not somehow synchronized to the input information, a 1-digit bobble will result. One way to synchronously eliminate bobble was shown in Fig. 5-20. In the case of a stopwatch, if the time reference can be held at reset before measurement so that the first cycle is of a constant and known length, any bobble will automatically be eliminated.

One other problem unique to some multiplexed displays is that there is sometimes an upper limit to the number of times you can update the display per second. If updating takes place faster than the scan rate, some numbers can remain blank, be missed or wrong, or show variable brightness. A good rule is to keep the update rate of any multiplexed display well below the scan rate.

On any digital display in which the input answer is changing a lot (because of keeping up with a fast variable, jitter, or noise), it is far better to throw out most of the measurements and only display one or two answers per second. This makes the display much easier to read.

CLOCKS

There is no point in building an *ordinary* digital clock with TTL because 1-chip multiplexed MOS integrated circuits are widely available that do the job far more simply and with much less power, besides being much cheaper. Typical units are the National MM5312 and the Mostek MK5017.

However, if you are building a timing system that is to be automatically self-resetting and always accurate, you need a parallel-load-capability system such as the TTL circuit shown in Fig. 8-10. A reference is divided down to 1 Hz. Progressive divisions of 10, 6, 10, 6, and then 12 or 24 provide the seconds, minutes, and hours information. An optional time-zone converter may be placed between the hours

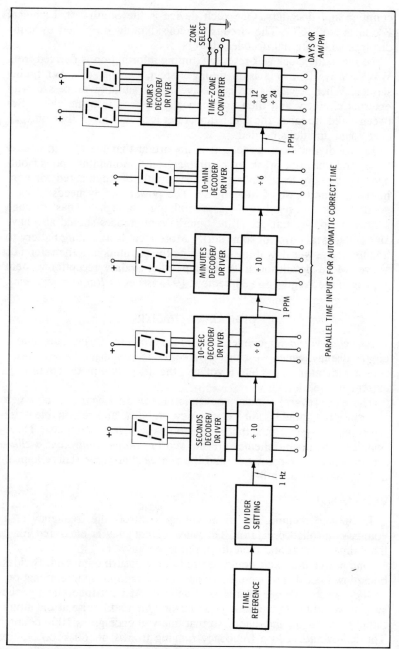

Fig. 8-10. Traditional unmultiplexed digital-clock circuit remains useful when automatic update of time or time-zone conversion is needed.

counters and decoders. One such device is the Southwest Technical Products No. 4671. The circuitry is considerably simplified by using displays with internal decoder/drivers.

To make the clock self-resetting, timing information is derived from WWV, WWVB, a television timing system, Omega, or other timing service. When a valid time is received, it is suitably processed with external circuitry and then automatically entered into the clock. Between valid updates, the local time reference fills in so that only an occasional update is needed.

In *any* digital clock system, it is important that the system is easy to set and does not break up completely on a momentary power outage. At the very least, setting circuitry should be engineered for non-interaction and ease of human use. The power supply needs to have good storage and regulation—as a minimum, enough to coast through a 1-second power outage. (Line time-base references should also have an oscillator takeover of some sort.) More ideal is a floating battery to handle any power downtime by keeping the counters and the reference active. More details on a WWVB parallel update reception system appear in the August and September 1973 issues of *Radio Electronics*.

DIGITAL VOLTMETER

A *digital voltmeter* converts a voltage we want to measure into a digital display. Since we can easily convert resistance, current, pressure, temperature, etc., into a voltage, the digital voltmeter circuitry is extremely useful.

There are several popular conversion methods. Regardless of which one is used, it should combine accuracy, stability, and reasonable noise rejection, all in a circuit that is not too expensive or complex. Three popular conversion schemes are the vco or *voltage-controlled oscillator,* the *dual-slope converter,* and the *charge subtractor.* These appear in Figs. 8-11 through 8-13.

VCO Method

In the vco method, the input voltage controls the frequency of a voltage-controlled oscillator. The output frequency is measured for a fixed time interval and then displayed as an answer.

One power-line cycle could be used as a measuring interval. Besides being low in cost, this would give us automatic input-hum elimination, as the 1-cycle average of a sine wave is 0. At least theoretically, the system would be transparent to power-line hum and noise at the input. Suppose we adjust the scaling so that one volt ends up as 1000 counts. The vco would need a frequency ranging from 0 to 60 kHz, or, we say that the vco has to have a 60-kilohertz-per-volt sensitivity. A 0.3-volt input gives us a frequency of 18 kilohertz. Each measurement picks up only $\frac{1}{60}$ of the 18,000 hertz, so we get a 300 display for a 0.3-volt input. The decimal point is set externally.

Traditionally, the vco systems have been limited in accuracy and temperature stability, but more recent circuits have vastly improved their potential. One suitable device is the Intersil 8038, which has a 0.1% linearity over a 1000:1 frequency range and extreme temperature stability. Cost is around $3, and very few add-ons are needed to get it to work.

One problem common to all vco systems is that they cannot give zero frequency for zero volts input. The net result is that either the start-up of the vco at low voltages is highly nonlinear, or else the vco is very linear down to zero volts but puts out a constant nonzero frequency at the minimum input voltage. If a linear system is desired, it is better to pick a vco that is linear down to zero input.

What do we do with the extra counts? We simply subtract them. One possibility is to start the counter by clearing it and then begin

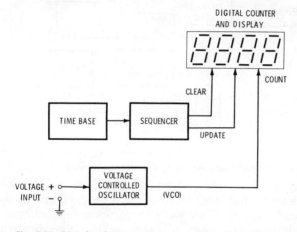

Fig. 8-11. Digital voltmeter using vco (voltage-controlled oscillator) method.

accumulating vco pulses. On count 1000 (or some other count $\frac{1}{10}$ full scale or so), we *reset* the counter back to 0, knocking off 1000 counts at the beginning of a measurement interval. Alternately, we could preset our counter to 1000 counts *less* than 0, e.g., within 1000 counts of full scale. Either way automatically subtracts enough from the answer to compensate for the 0-voltage frequency output. If the vco is off, a little input bias one way or the other will correct it.

Dual-Slope Method

The dual-slope system has been very popular for commercial digital voltmeters. It has a number of advantages, the biggest two of which are that the nonlinearities of the system tend to cancel themselves out, and that there is no accurate time or frequency reference needed. You do need a precise current reference.

The object of the dual-slope system (Fig. 8-12) is to measure an unknown input current for a fixed time. During this time, a capacitor is linearly charged. The capacitor is then discharged with a precise current reference equal to the full-scale input current. The time of discharge (i.e., how long it takes the capacitor to get back to its initial voltage) is linearly related to the input current. We measure this time and display it.

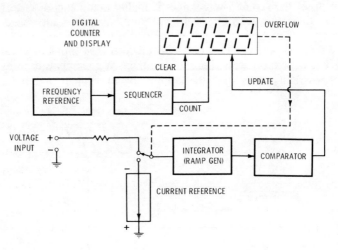

Fig. 8-12. Digital voltmeter using dual-slope conversion.

It does not matter what value the voltage on the capacitor reaches or how nonlinearly it is done, for we get a first-order cancellation of everything on the way back down. Likewise, we do not need extreme long-term stability of the time reference, so long as it is stable over the measuring interval. We do lose noise and hum rejection if the reference does not make the input time an even number of whole power-line cycles, but this is an option.

As Fig. 8-12 shows, we take a frequency reference that is often 100 kHz and route it to the counter. The sequencer can be a 555 astable that clears the counter once or twice a second to return the measurement sequence to the initial condition.

When the counter clears, the overflow switches the input selector so the ramp generator runs off the input current. The integrator or ramp generator then charges a capacitor to some value. The capacitor is allowed to charge till the counter overflows. Note that this will be precisely 10,000 times the reference frequency period in a 4-decade system, so we have an accurate and relatively long time. At that instant, the counter simply starts over, but the overflow flips the switch down so that the capacitor in the integrator is *discharged* with the current reference. When the capacitor gets back to a starting point (often zero volts), the comparator detects this and updates the display. The counter has gone completely around once, and the second time around it stops on a number proportional to the input current. The final number equals the input voltage when the constants are correctly chosen.

One design problem with dual slope is getting a comparator to work properly on very low level signals without having excessive noise problems. Ordinary op amps are usually far too slow for use as an output comparator, and getting operation started linearly is often a problem.

As a general rule, if you are *only* building a digital voltmeter circuit, the dual-slope system offers advantages in the 3- and 4-digit range; if you are building a system that already has a good time base in it for other uses, the other methods may be better.

Charge Subtraction

The *charge-subtraction* system used to be reserved for very accurate or wide-range temperature systems. With improved low-cost components, it is now a serious contender for almost any digital voltmeter system. The circuit needs two time-base references, a high-frequency one (often 1 to 10 μs) and a low-frequency one (often 0.1s). It also needs a current reference.

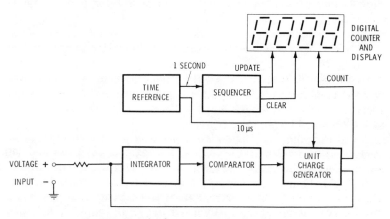

Fig. 8-13. Digital voltmeter using charge subtraction.

The circuit of Fig. 8-13 performs a balancing act. It is essentially a vco. The integrating capacitor is smoothly filled by the input and is emptied in discrete jumps that suddenly remove a precise amount of charge.

The input continuously charges a capacitor through an integrator circuit. Every time the voltage on the capacitor rises above 0, a comparator detects this, and a *unit-charge generator* routes a pulse of known current (perhaps 1 mA) for a known time (perhaps 1 or 10 μs) back to the input. Current multiplied by time is charge. This much charge is *removed* from the capacitor, and the capacitor voltage jumps back to the other side of 0. At the same time, one count is routed to the counter and display.

The lower the input voltage, the longer it takes for the capacitor to get back to 0 and the lower the frequency of the charge slugs that are removed.

The final result is a group of pulses whose frequency is linearly related to the input. The rest of the circuit is a frequency counter, often based on a 0.1-second time base. Since 0.1 second is 6 power-line cycles, we get hum cancellation as well. The comparator is not nearly the problem it was in the dual-slope method because immediately after switching, the input voltage is jumped well away from the trip point of the comparator.

Other Systems

These seem to be the three most popular volts-to-digits conversion systems in use today. By electronic standards, they are rather slow and are limited to a few conversion cycles per second. Faster converters are often called *Analog to Digital* or A/D converters. These are usually much faster, more complex, and quite often they are far less accurate.

One possibility is to run a digital counter into a *Digital to Analog* converter or D/A. This is compared to an input and the number that exists at the time the two are equal is displayed. This takes a counting system with all intermediate stages brought out and has no inherent hum or noise rejection, as it is an instantaneous system. It can be quite accurate since the main components of D/A systems are mostly precision resistors.

Other volts-to-digits methods are not overly practical for measurement systems, but they do see a lot of use in faster computer and data-acquisition systems. One method is the "brute force" method, with one comparator for each voltage level to be detected. This is the fastest possible method, but it is very complex and expensive. Another is the *successive approximation* method, where ½ the input is subtracted and compared, ¼ the input is subtracted and compared, ⅛ the input is subtracted and compared, and so on. This provides a system of intermediate speed with intermediate complexity. Most of these A/D techniques end up with a number, rather than a frequency or a time width; many are more difficult to do in a decimal BCD instead of a binary system.

DIGITAL TACHOMETER

Revolutions-per-minute is but another way of saying frequency, so any frequency counter system properly scaled should read rpm. The trouble comes when we try to get accuracy, for rpm figures, particularly at gasoline-engine idle speeds, are very low. For instance, a 4-cylinder engine running at 300 rpm is running at a frequency of 5 revolutions per second. If it is a 4-cycle engine, we get one pulse per cylinder per two revolutions, and a 10-Hz frequency is what we have to measure. For 0.1% accuracy, the measuring interval should be 100 seconds! Period-measuring schemes are possible, but some sort of 1/x calculation is needed and the noise susceptibility increases.

Fig. 8-14 shows how a phase-lock-loop frequency multiplier can be added to increase the accuracy of the system for a reasonable measurement time.

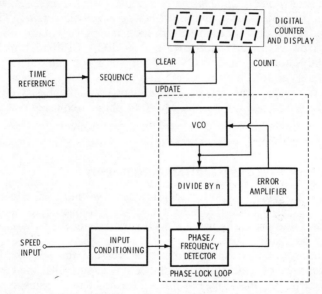

Fig. 8-14. Digital tachometer using phase-lock-loop frequency multiplier to increase accuracy.

Suppose the measurement interval is 0.5 second. Suppose further that we want 600 rpm to be 600 counts. We would need a *multiplied* frequency of 1200 Hz, or 120 times the input frequency rate.

So, we set up an oscillator that runs at 120 times the input frequency. We digitally divide it by 120 and compare this against the input. The output error from the phase/frequency comparison is amplified and used to correct itself and to follow the input frequency. The result is a speedup of 120 times, which we can measure 120 times more accurately in a given time interval. The system is called a phase-lock-loop system and is very popular for a number of applications.

Table 8-1. Selecting N for a Given Tachometer Range

Range	N for 0.5-Second Interval	N for 0.1-Second Interval
4 cylinder	60	300
6 cylinder	45	225
8 cylinder	30	150
Rpm	120	600
Rpm/10	12	60
Pps	2	10

There is only one catch. *This particular phase-lock loop has to have at least a 50:1 range or so and must not be harmonic sensitive.* This leaves out 99% of all the phase-lock-loop integrated circuits on the market. However, it does not leave out the RCA CD4046, which is ideal for this application. It is CMOS logic and has a controllable frequency range up to several thousand-to-one and directly drives a TTL or CMOS divide-by-n. An all-TTL system could be based on an Intersil 8038 vco and a Motorola MC4044 phase/frequency detector. Table 8-1 shows the values of n needed for various rpm ranges. A commercial tachometer kit appears in Fig. 8-15.

OTHER DIGITAL INSTRUMENTS

Most, if not all, of the other measurements we might like to take digitally are easily converted into a voltage, a frequency, or a time period, and thus are easily handled with variations of the basic instruments we have just talked about.

For instance, to measure current, we measure the voltage drop across a resistance, making the resistance low enough that the circuit is not disturbed by the drop. For linear measurement of ohms, a constant current source is used. For instance, a 1-milliampere current source will provide 1 volt with a 1K resistor, 2.2 volts with a 2.2K resistor, and so on. Ac operation is picked up by adding an operational amplifier connected as a full-wave rectifier. Such features as automatic dc polarity and autoranging are easily added.

A digital multimeter is simply a combination of these measuring instruments in a single package with the function selected through the use of one or two complex range switches. A digital panel meter does the opposite—it is designed and committed to a single measurement range.

Many specialized operations are easily monitored by voltage. For instance, pH measurement involves a dc-voltage measurement, but a very high input impedance is needed. Audio voltmeters can be based on an amplifier and a full-wave precision rectifier. Suitable distortion networks or log amplifiers can be added for log decibel indication. A single decade or two can be handled by a few diodes; multiple decades take a true log converter, often formed by placing two matched transistors in the feedback circuit of an operational amplifier.

Courtesy Southwest Technical Products Corp.

Fig. 8-15. Southwest Technical Products tachometer kit.

Pressure can be handled by using a transducer such as the National LX-1600 to generate an output voltage that is converted to a digital reading. You can use this for laboratory instrumentation, barometry, or altimetry. Resolution good enough for land survey or cave exploration work requires careful temperature compensation and calibration.

Temperature can be measured in several ways. One good method was shown in Fig. 4-28.

One interesting possibility is to combine a 4-decade counting unit and crystal time base into a single package and provide plug-ins for various measurement tasks. The commercial kit version of this is shown in Fig. 8-16. This unit is battery or ac operated and combines MOS, CMOS, and TTL circuitry.

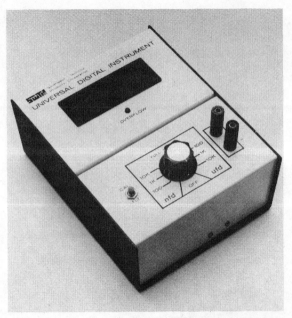

Fig. 8-16. Universal digital instrument accepts various plug-ins.

SOME SPECIALIZED TTL APPLICATIONS

Let us take a brief look at some very specialized TTL systems—circuits or systems that were difficult or economically impractical without the use of TTL. These include a television time display, a tv typewriter or computer terminal, a photographic printing computer, and an electronic music synthesizer. Complete details on these items would take a book in itself, so their description will be sketchy. As with the rest of this chapter, our aim is to show how to use TTL in whole systems.

A TELEVISION TIME DISPLAY

You can superimpose up to eight numbers or letters on an existing television display with the tv time display outlined in Fig. 8-17. The characters are 5×7 dot-matrix ASCII ones and can represent the time, the temperature, the weather, a paging call, a channel number, etc. The circuit assumes you have the information in a parallel and ready-to-display form that is ASCII- and TTL-compatible.

A character generator similar to Fig. 7-5 forms the heart of the unit. Eight-position data selectors pick the selected information for each of eight successive slots. Six selectors are needed for full alphanumeric capability, while only four are needed if we are only displaying numbers or colons.

Three connections are needed to interface with the television—a video input and horizontal and vertical sync outputs. The vertical sync starts a vertical delay that positions the display in the up and down direction. At the end of the delay, the next 16 horizontal lines are activated in pairs of 2. The horizontal delay sets the back-and-forth position and starts a gated oscillator that counts out 64 dot positions

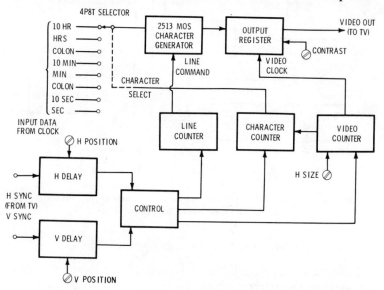

Fig. 8-17. Block diagram of TTL system for superimposing time display on an existing tv program

and then shuts down. These are arranged by eights to provide for each number or character. Every two horizontal lines, a new "what line is it" command is routed to the character generator to sequentially generate all the needed dots in the right places. At the end of the sixteenth line, the circuit shuts down and then repeats on both fields. By adjusting the delays and the video clocking rate, you can position and control the size of the numerals. Twelve TTL ICs do the job, helped out by a 2513 MOS character generator.

TV TYPEWRITER

The *tv typewriter* system shown in Figs. 8-18 and 8-19 is a much more complex version of the time-display circuit. It internally stores 1024 characters and can present an entire message or computer readout on the screen of an unmodified television set via antenna terminal

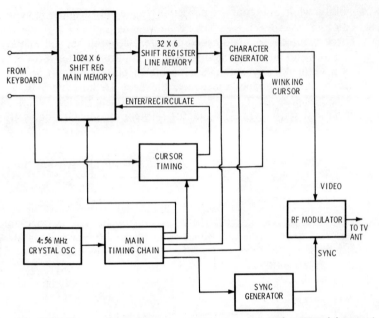

Fig. 8-18. Block diagram of tv typewriter system to store and display 1024 alphanumeric characters on an unmodified television set.

Fig. 8-19. Tv typewriter system.

input. It is used for computer readouts, news and weather displays, answer-back systems for cable tv, communications aids for the deaf, ham rtty, preschool teaching aides, inventory and personnel monitors, and many other applications. Cost in kit form is slightly over $100. Thirty-three integrated circuits are used. Seven are MOS LSI, one is a regulator, and the remainder are TTL.

The character generation scheme is essentially similar to the tv time display. Instead of data selectors, six 512-bit recirculating shift-register memories march the characters into place as needed. Since each character has to return for seven sequential lines, a second hex 32-bit register is used to "borrow" the characters from the main memory as needed.

The TTL timing chain starts with a 4.56-MHz crystal and provides all the needed intermediate frequencies down to the vertical 60-Hz sync rate and the 6-Hz cursor winking-and-repeat rate. A companion TTL cursor circuit provides the equivalent of up/down counting to determine the position of new characters; full editing capability is provided. More details on this system appear in the September 1973 *Radio Electronics* and the *TV Typewriter Cookbook* (Sams Cat. No. 21313).

A PRINTING COMPUTER

Ordinary digital clock and stopwatch circuits can be reworked for many photographic applications. The digital printing computer (Fig. 8-21) is different. It is a photographic printing timer that works directly in fractional f stops, rather than seconds. Just like the photo-

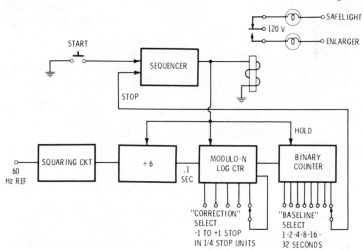

Fig. 8-20. Block diagram of TTL photographic printing computer that works directly in logarithmic fractional f-stop increments.

graphic process, it is a logarithmic, rather than a linear, device. In critical color work, the effective exposure can be made a quarter-stop denser or thinner without regard to the actual time exposure.

One stop is a doubling or a halving of an exposure. Half a stop can be approximated as 1.4 times or 0.7 times. A quarter stop can be approximated as 1.2 times or 0.8 times base-line exposure.

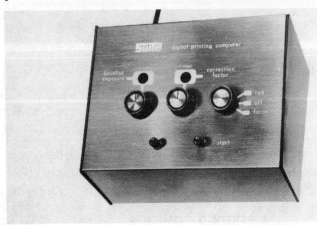

Fig. 8-21. Digital printing computer.

We start with a 0.1-hertz reference derived from the power, and route it to a variable-modulo counter programmed as a divide-by-5,-6,-7,-8,-10,-12,-14,-16, or -20 to accurately approximate a shift of −1, −¾, −½, −¼, 0, +¼, +½, +¾, and +1 stop from base-line exposure. A binary divider then sets the base line at 1,2,4,8,16, or 32 seconds, giving us a range of 0.5 to 64 seconds, more than enough for any possible printing task. The circuit is basically a "preset and run to overflow" type. More details are in the April 1972 *Radio Electronics*.

ELECTRONIC MUSIC SYNTHESIZER

An all-TTL monophonic music synthesizer can easily be built following Fig. 8-22 as a guide. You start with the equally tempered note generator of Fig. 6-27 and run it 16 times as fast as the note you want to produce.

To produce a note, connect the selected 16× tone reference to a divide-by-16 counter and 1-of-16 decoder (the 74154 with diodes or a 74159). Each output goes to a slide potentiometer arranged to bias an emitter follower. The slide potentiometers are scanned in sequence. You set the *waveshape,* otherwise known as the *timbre* or *harmonic*

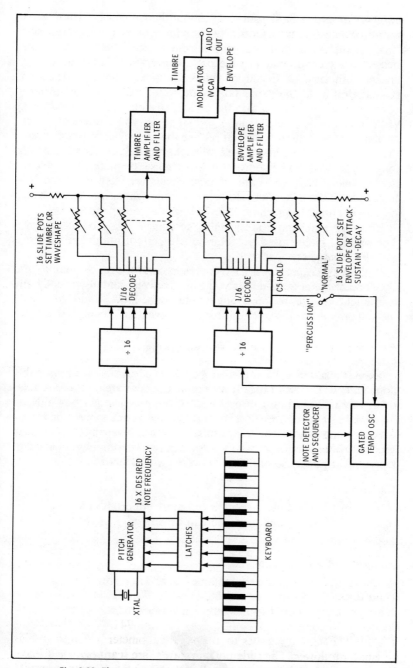

Fig. 8-22. Electronic music synthesizer can be built entirely with TTL.

content, by setting these slide pots so that their pointers "draw" a picture of the desired waveform. This provides the tone quality or color.

A second low-frequency oscillator runs a second divide-by-16 connected to a second array of slide pots. This counter is arranged to go around only once, and you set the *envelope* or attack-sustain-decay structure on it. In the *percussion* mode, you arrange the circuit to go once around and stop so that the attack, sustain, fallback, and decay of the note are completed. In the *normal* mode, you arrange the circuit to hang up in position 5 till you release the key. This way, depressing the key generates the attack and fallback, but the note is sustained as long as you hold the key down. On key release, the note completes the decay cycle. Echos and multiple-note effects are easy this way. You have to latch the note after release so the tone synthesizer knows which note to continue to produce. The 74174 is a good choice.

Envelope and timbre are suitably combined in a modulator stage. The original circuit used a Motorola MFC6040; multiplier ICs or a MOSFET stage serve as well.

With the slide pots, you have complete control over the timbre and envelope of the note, and thus you can effectively imitate virtually any instrument you desire, on a single note basis. How would you make the system *polyphonic* so that it handles more than one note at a time?

SOME TTL PROJECTS

Here is a selection of a number of project ideas that are reasonably done with TTL. They range from simple to elaborate, but all are relatively low in cost. You can use most of the projects as study aids, as home, lab, or school test instruments, for electronic games, or as science fair and school paper projects. They are given more or less in order of increasing complexity. Practically everything you need to know for any of these projects is covered in this book.

Logic Pen

A simple LED state checker is the most important and most basic piece of TTL test equipment you can own. Add a monostable multivibrator to detect pulses as well as 1's and 0's.

Bounceless Push Buttons

Put two or three in a self-contained box. They are essential for cycling digital logic and for troubleshooting. Two-input, gate-type debouncers are preferred to the simple inverter type.

Power Supply

Build up a good, high-current, regulated 5-volt supply for TTL. If you are using MOS circuits as well, better add a −12-volt capability.

Logic Demonstrator

Use a quad gate set up as a 2-input data selector. Then take a fancy switch, two push buttons, and a LED to show the 2-input AND, NAND, OR, NOR, EXCLUSIVE OR, and EXCLUSIVE NOR functions. Or if you want, do all sixteen 2-input functions.

Binary Counter

Combine a bounceless push button with four flip-flop stages or a single MSI circuit to illustrate binary counting up to 16, 64, or 256. Provide a count button and a Clear button. Add a switch to convert to a BCD base 10 counter.

Shift Register

You can take a bounceless push button and route it to four or more shift-register stages of flip-flops, or else use an MSI register. Provide a slide switch to enter 1's or 0's, and arrange things so you can recirculate the data from output to input, enter new data, or complement and recirculate. The last route shows walking-ring counters and disallowed sequences.

Flip-Flopper

Take a single JK flip-flop with preset and preclear, and arrange some switching to convert it into Set-Reset, Clocked Set-Reset, Toggle, Data (D), and JK flip-flops. This demonstrates the various types of flip-flops available and points out their advantages and limitations.

The New Logic—Data Selectors and Redundancy

Use an 8-position data selector and eight 4-position slide switches $(1, 0, D, \overline{D})$ to instantly design *any* logic function of four variables. Challenge the "old school" boys to a race. You should be able to do the design in $\frac{1}{100}$ the time!

The Pseudo-ROM

Build your own Read-Only memory out of a decoder, a diode array, and some switches or jumpers. A 16×4 arrangement would not be too unwieldy, but a 16×8 would be more useful. If you cannot find low-cost switches, use jumpers or 2-sided pc boards with diode interconnects. This system demonstrates what a Read-Only memory is, gives you instant solutions to complex logic problems, and lets you check a design before you program a real ROM. Be sure to buffer the output so it is TTL compatible.

Heads and Tails

Combine a power-line squaring circuit with a push-button and a binary divider to form a heads-and-tails coin-toss machine. Heads and tails will be equally probable if one LED is driven from the Q output and one from the $\overline{Q}$.

Pulse Generator

A 555 astable multivibrator can drive a 555 monostable circuit to give you a pulse generator with virtually any pulse width, duty cycle, and repetition rate you want.

Square-Wave Generator

Again, take a 555 and set it up as an astable multivibrator. Add a binary divider to the output to get a symmetrical square wave. Use it as a universal square-wave source (decade switch the capacitors, and adjust frequency 10:1 with a resistor). Hint: the dial will be cramped unless you use a log pot and put the dial markings on the *knob* and the index mark on the *panel*. As an alternate, use a reverse log taper pot, although it may be hard to find. Also watch for end effects on the potentiometer—the first 15% or so of rotation usually does not count.

Frequency Meter

Frequency counters are expensive—but a frequency meter is not, and it is more than useful if you only need a few percent accuracy. Set up a 555 as a monostable with 40% duty cycle at full scale, and integrate the answer with a meter and a capacitor. Add input gain and conditioning. Switch ranges with decade capacitors. Use the power line as a calibrator.

Analog Tachometer

This is nothing but a frequency meter recalibrated in rpm, with the scale adjusted to suit the number of cycles and number of cylinders in use. Be sure to provide input protection. In an automotive environment, you will also want supply regulation or a constant-current meter drive for accuracy.

Logic Laboratory

Work out a low-cost pin-connector and jumper system. Then put several gates and flip-flops in a box with some bounceless push buttons, a few state indicators (or one built-in indicator per logic block), and some sort of 555 astable/monostable circuit. This gives you a dig-ital-logic training aid, also good for simple logic breadboarding and teaching digital concepts. One commercial version of this is shown in Fig. 8-23. Use this book as a lab manual, or write your own experiments.

Time Base

Combine a 1-MHz crystal oscillator (trimmable to WWV) with several dividers to provide an accurate set of reference frequencies that

Fig. 8-23. Digital logic microlab kit.

can be used for calibration, accurate digital clocking signals, and time references.

RAM Demonstrator

A 7489 Random-Access Memory may be used as a 64-bit demonstrator of computer write-read operations. Add four switches for "1-0" input data, monitor the output with LEDs, and provide switching for write and read operation. Hint: do the writing with a push button to keep from changing addresses while you are entering data.

Metronome

Use a 555 astable and a suitably calibrated dial to build a metronome. The output will simply click a speaker. For a better tone, use the output to gate a second 555 tone oscillator. For downbeat effects, add a binary divider or two and gate an emphasis note by making the output louder or a different frequency once every two, three, four, or six counts.

Two-Tone Alarm

Use one 555 to change the frequency of a second to produce a commanding "twee-dell" alarm note. Add capacitors and charging voltages to get siren or wail.

Humidity Gauge

A commercial humidity sensor can be used to set the frequency of a 555 timer set up as a frequency meter. Recalibrate the meter dial in terms of percentage of relative humidity.

ALU or CPU Demonstrator

This is another IC-in-a-box type of project. Use the 74181 Arithmetic Logic Unit and suitable switching to demonstrate how central processing works in a computer. Combine several packages for 8, 12, or 16 bits.

Electronic Dice

This project was shown in Chapter 7. Use a high-frequency clock and two self-clearing modulo-6 walking rings. Decode directly into a LED die-spot matrix. This unit gives true dice odds—unless, of course, you use an aluminum or wooden case, add a few reed switches, and put a magnet under your ring!

Whole IC State Monitor

The commercial Digiviewer was shown in Chapter 1. You might like to use it or build up something similar, perhaps a smaller unit using LEDs and a series of snap-in masks. This type of system shows you at once everything that goes on in a digital IC, and the mask shows you what pin goes with which logic.

Home Alarm System

The conventional tape-and-switch protection system is hard to beat as a home or shop protection system. With TTL, you can add a flip-flop or sequential pass-on to let you leave any door without the need for an outside switch or an unprotected entryway.

Electrolock

A sequential pass-on circuit can be combined with a switch array to produce an electronic combination lock. Be sure to provide an alarm channel or a long time delay to operate if the wrong code is entered.

Logic Breadboard

Systemizing your breadboarding system can make work with TTL far easier. Take a breadboarding block and mount it on the front of a case. Place a power supply, some switches, a clock or two, and some state indicators in the box, along with good deglitching capacitors. This should greatly simplify TTL testing and circuit design. A logic breadboard system is available in kit or assembled form from EL Instruments, Incorporated, Derby, CT, among others. The assembled unit is shown in Fig. 8-24.

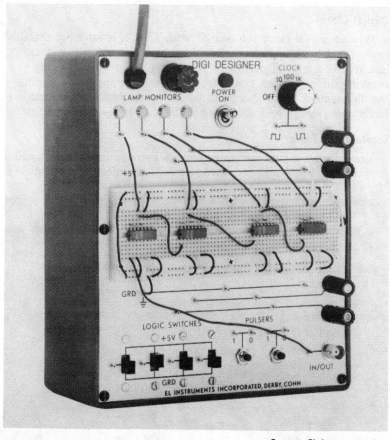

Fig. 8-24. Digital logic breadboarding system.

Pseudo-Random Generator

Build a long shift register and arrange some EXCLUSIVE-OR gates to provide pseudo-random maximal-length sequences of various lengths. Demonstrate forward, reverse, complementary, and complementary reversed sequences. Add an output integrator to provide audio noise for testing. Add a further output filter to change the white noise to pink noise.

Oscilloscope Time Base

Update a recurrent-sweep oscilloscope to triggered sweep by using an input-conditioning trigger circuit and a sweep generator. Various possibilities exist, depending on the make and model of the scope. Be sure to start with a scope whose horizontal circuits are dc coupled.

Digital Clock

While a digital clock can be built with TTL, it is far more practical to do the job with MOS—unless you are doing something complex, like receiving and displaying WWVB or Omega time. On any self-resetting timing system, concentrate on the reception and decoding—the digital-clock part is bound to work, but the input will almost certainly cause design and debugging problems. Hit the hard end first.

Digital-Logic Tester

You can test digital integrated circuits by providing a socket and a properly deglitched and regulated supply. Add a large matrix-selector

Courtesy MITS

Fig. 8-25. Digital IC tester.

switch so you can route logic signals to inputs and state monitors to outputs. In a more elaborate version, you can provide two sockets, one for a good IC and one for a questionable one. You then EXCLUSIVE NOR all inputs and outputs, and any output with a *difference* indicates a problem. Fig. 8-25 shows a digital IC test system manufactured by MITS, Albuquerque, NM.

Televison Convergence Generator

A dot-and-bar convergence generator is easy to do with TTL. Use the guidelines offered earlier in this chapter. For accurate color work, the system *must* have a horizontal frequency of precisely 15, 570 Hz and a vertical frequency of precisely 60 Hz. Do not attempt to cut corners by using free-running horizontal or vertical-sync generators.

Timbre and Envelope Generator for Electronic Music

Combine a random-access memory such as the 7489 with a digital-to-analog converter, and you have a controllable way to generate either the timbre or the envelope of a musical note. For initial experiments, you can hand-program the memory. Later on, work out a more automatic programming system, and, finally, for tones and shapes you are going to use often, switch to a read-only memory system.

Advanced Projects

Go back over the beginning of this chapter for some advanced project possibilities. One is a digital measurement system with a main frame containing a time base, counter, and readout, along with the plug-ins needed to measure time, frequency, voltage, current, speed, temperature, capacitance, pH, or whatever special functions you need. Both the composer music project of Chapter 7 and the full digital synthesizer of this chapter offer exciting and useful electronic music projects. More information on these and other electronic music appears in a continuing series starting with the October 1973 issue of *Popular Electronics*. A Tic-Tac-Toe TTL project can be worked up initially as a machine-plays-first and then improved upon by working up a machine-plays-second type of circuit, perhaps by using read-only memories. Finally, there are all sorts of applications for the tv typewriter system as is, or perhaps changed to pick up newer semiconductors as they become available. Can you do the same job cheaper with random-access memories? Can you make the machine accept Morse Code or teletype off the air and display it? How do you display news and weather? Finding a solution to these problems and others like them is what digital logic, and TTL in particular, is all about.

Manufacturers of TTL and Associated Products

Advanced Micro Devices
901 Thompson Place
Sunnyvale, CA 94086

API Super Strips
72 Corwin Drive
Painesville, OH 44077

Augat Inucorporated
33 Perry Ave.
Attleboro, MA 02703

CAE
1292 E. Colorado Blvd.
Pasadena, CA 91106

Cambion
445 Concord Ave.
Cambridge, MA 02138

Dynachem Corporation
13000 E. Firestone Blvd.
Santa Fe Springs, CA 90670

Fairchild Semiconductor
313 Fairchild Drive
Mountain View, CA 94040

Harris Semiconductor
Box 883
Melbourne, FL 32901

Intel Corporation
3065 Bowers Ave.
Santa Clara, CA 95051

Intersil, Inc.
10900 N. Tantau Ave.
Cupertino, CA 95014

ITT Semiconductors
3301 Electronics Way
West Palm Beach, FL 33407

Monolithic Memories, Inc.
1165 E. Arques Ave.
Sunnyvale, CA 94086

Molex, Inc.
2222 Wellington Ct.
Lisle, IL 60532

Motorola Semiconductor Products
Box 20912
Phoenix, AZ 85036

National Semiconductor Corporation
2900 Semiconductor Drive
Santa Clara, CA 95051

Raytheon Semiconductor
350 Ellis Street
Mountain View, CA 94040

Signetics
811 E. Arques Ave.
Sunnyvale, CA 94086

Solitron Devices
8808 Balboa Ave.
San Diego, CA 92123

Southwest Technical Products
219 W. Rhapsody
San Antonio, TX 78216

Spectrum Dynamics
2300 E. Oakland Park Blvd.
Ft. Lauderdale, FL 33306

Sprague Electric Co.
481 Marshall Street
North Adams, MA 01247

Stewart Warner Corporation
730 E. Evelyn Ave.
Sunnyvale, CA 94086

Texas Instruments
Box 5012
Dallas, TX 75222

Yellow Springs Instrument Co.
Yellow Springs, OH 45387

Index